RELUCTANT WITNESSES

Reluctant Witnesses

Jews and the Christian Imagination

Stephen R. Haynes

 Westminster John Knox Press
Louisville, Kentucky

First published 1995 by Macmillan Press Ltd, Houndmills,
Basingstoke, Hampshire RG21 2XS

First American Edition 1995

Published in the U.S.A. by Westminster John Knox Press,
100 Witherspoon Street, Louisville, Kentucky 40202–1396

PRINTED IN HONG KONG

95 96 97 98 99 00 01 02 03 04 — 10 9 8 7 6 5 4 3 2 1

Library of Congress Cataloging-in-Publication Data

Haynes, Stephen R., date.
    Reluctant witnesses : Jews and the Christian imagination /
Stephen R. Haynes. — 1st American ed.
        p.   cm.
    "First published 1995 by Macmillan Press Ltd, Houndmills,
Basingstoke, Hampshire"—T.p. verso.
    Includes bibliographical references and index.
    ISBN 0-664-25579-5
    1. Judaism (Christian theology)   2. Jews in literature.
I. Title.
BT93.H4   1995
231.7'6—dc20
                                        94–22554
                                           CIP

For Christiana

Contents

Acknowledgments

I wish to acknowledge gratefully the following publishers, who have granted their permission for the use of previously published material: Scholars Press, for permission to use excerpts from *Prospects for Post-Holocaust Theology: "Israel" in the Theologies of Karl Barth, Jürgen Moltmann and Paul van Buren (1991)*; Oxford University Press, for permission to use a revised portion of "Theology as Fiction and Fiction as Theology: Karl Barth and Walker Percy on the Jews," which appeared in *Journal of Literature and Theology* 5:4 (December, 1991), 388–407; and for permission to use a portion of "Thanatos and *Shoah*: Walker Percy's Parable of the Holocaust", which appeared in Volume 8 (1994) of *Holocaust and Genocide Studies*; and the *Journal of the American Academy of Religion*, for permission to use an excerpt from "Christian Holocaust Theology: A Critical Reassessment," published in the Summer 1994 issue of *JAAR*.

Several persons and organizations have contributed to this book. Research that eventually found its way into these pages was funded by the Rotary Foundation, the English-Speaking Union of Atlanta, the Memphis Jewish Federation, the Association for Religion and Intellectual Life, and the Rhodes College Faculty Development Endowment. The latter two made explicit contributions of time and money toward the completion of this project. Michael Leslie and James Clifton of Rhodes College read parts of the manuscript and offered insightful suggestions. David Jasper of the University of Glasgow read the entire manuscript. Professor Jasper's guidance and support have been crucial to my professional development since 1988, when I spent a year under his tutelage at the University of Durham. David has supported this work from the outset and has provided invaluable direction along the way.

Other persons to whom I am indebted include the members of the 1991 Coolidge Research Colloquium at The Episcopal Divinity School in Cambridge, Mass., especially Rabbi Richard Levy; the faculty members at Rhodes College who have shown interest in my research and have challenged me to think in new ways; my mother, Jean Haynes, who kept me up to date on the "prophecy books" discussed in Chapter 7; my students at Rhodes College; and my wife Natalie and daughter Christiana, whose willingness to allow me to spend many hours in front of a computer screen made the timely completion of this book possible. Christiana Hope, born on . Easter Day 1991, has, very simply, changed my life. This book is dedicated to her, in a spirit of thankfulness for such a tangible sign of divine favor.

Preface

Fifty years after the Holocaust in Europe we are only just beginning to come to terms with the problem of speaking about it. When I say "we", who do I mean? We as Christians? as Jews? as "post-moderns"? The language available to us depends very much upon our inheritance. Can any of us, for different reasons, speak properly of the Holocaust?

A visitor to the Holocaust Museum in Washington, DC, cannot fail to be struck by the narrative quality of the gruelling exhibition. The walk through the museum takes us through the experience of the Holocaust, interpreted of course, so that by the time we walk *through* the box-car we are sweating and almost stumbling with a mixture of fear, guilt, anxiety. As we walk, language becomes less and less adequate.

We need, urgently, a book like this, to begin to recall us to the responsibility of language in the face of an event which, more than any other in our time, has robbed us of speech and theology, language and narrative. Stephen Haynes knows his subject intimately, and writes with a sure hand of history, theology and literature. We require, in our time, voices which are prepared to speak clearly between the Jewish and Christian perspectives – across a divide which the Holocaust itself made so wide.

I recommend this book as a theological contribution where theology has either been rendered mute or so often has become an embarrassment. Deeply biblical, and at the same time lodged within a theological tradition which needs to find its voice again, this is a work which contributes significantly to that task, with elegance, literary insight and compassion.

David Jasper

[The Jews] could and can disappear just as little as God's faithfulness can come to an end ... This continued existence of the Jews which is so puzzling is a sign which cannot be ignored ... Yet they are no more than the shadow of a nation, the reluctant witnesses *of the Son of God and Son of Man ... whom they rejected, yet who has not ceased to call them....*

Karl Barth, "The Jewish Problem and the Christian Answer"

1

Introduction

[The Jews] are our supporters in their books, our enemies in their hearts, our witnesses in their scrolls.

Augustine, *On Faith in Things Unseen*

The history of the nation of Israel is indeed unlike that of any other nation throughout human history. No other nation has been so blessed by God and yet so hated by Satan. The factors of satanic persecution, divine judgment for sin, and divine blessing honoring the promises to Abraham are all evident throughout Jewish history.

John Ankerberg and John Weldon, *One World: Biblical Prophecy and the New World Order*

Why this extraordinarily neurotic way of reacting to anything to do with Israel – and to quite a lot of things to do with Jews elsewhere?

Norman Solomon, "The Context of the Jewish–Christian Dialogue"

"Jews are news." This phrase is sometimes offered as a facetious explanation for the international attention directed at events in and around the State of Israel. It is a half-joking justification for the incommensurate scrutiny Israel seems to receive in the news media. But though the words "Jews are news" have a modern ring, Jews actually have held a position of unique prominence in the collective imagination of the Christian West for centuries. In fact, even a cursory survey of texts that have influenced Western culture reveals that Jewish existence, Jewish exile and dispersion and Jewish stereotypes bear great symbolic weight in our collective traditions.

An illustration of the important but ambivalent position reserved for Jews in the Western mind is found in Dante's *Divine Comedy*. In Canto IV of *Inferno*, Dante's pilgrimage through the underworld takes him to limbo, where those who lived virtuous lives in the era before Christ spend eternity. These souls are cut off from the divine presence, but they are spared the suffering with which the other

1

denizens of hell are afflicted. Significantly, the favored souls of limbo are of two distinct classes: There are the virtuous pagans, a group that includes classical masters like Virgil (Dante's guide through hell); and the so-called saints of the Old Testament. This latter group of non-Christians enjoy particular privilege. For as Dante learns from Virgil, the Hebrew saints were granted paradise at the time of Christ's harrowing of hell. Virgil names Adam, Abel, Noah, Moses, Abraham, David, Jacob and Rachel among the former inhabitants of limbo who have achieved blessedness, despite lacking baptism.

"I would have thee know," Virgil informs the poet, "that before these no human souls were saved." Descending with Dante through the circles of hell, the reader realizes that these pre-Christian saints have fared much better than the baptized heretics and apostates who populate the lower levels of hell, and whose screams are an audible reminder of Christian truth. But if "Hebrews" such as Moses are objects of special blessing in Dante's *Inferno*, "Jews" like Judas are less fortunate. In the final canto, Dante and Virgil arrive at the ninth circle of hell. Here, in the dark realm inhabited by Satan himself, Dante is introduced to the most infamous of Jews:

> 'That soul up there which has the greatest punishment,' said the Master, 'is Judas Iscariot, who has his head inside [one of Satan's mouths] and plies his head without.' [1]

In Dante's memorable depiction, Judas the arch-traitor becomes literally and figuratively the devil's own.

Obviously, *Inferno* is about much more than treacherous Jews and worthy Hebrews. Speaking quantitatively, Romans are more prominent in *The Divine Comedy* than are Jews. Furthermore, scholars have noted that in relation to other texts from the Middle Ages Dante's masterpiece is conspicuous for its dearth of anti-Jewish polemic.[2] Nevertheless, all Jews – whether saints or sinners – are depicted by Dante as being quite different than the rest of us. As the only souls qualified to attain paradise without conscious faith in Christ, the patriarchs and matriarchs of the "Old Testament" are *sui generis*; while Jesus' unfaithful disciple personifies the unique perfidy of deicide. Thus, despite the absence of explicit anti-Judaism, the overall impression left by Dante's portrayal of Jews is of a people comprised exclusively of saints and traitors. Of course, every character in the *Divine Comedy* has been eternally assigned to salvation or damnation. But even in the company of souls whose destiny has been determined, Jews are special cases. To put this in spatial terms, there are no Jews in Dante's purgatory.

A thesis of this book is that Jews must always be special cases in products of the Christian imagination, because of the uniquely ambivalent place which the Jewish people inhabit there. Thus, what is really noteworthy about Dante's depiction of Jews is not the comparative sparsity of anti-Jewish polemic in the *Divine Comedy,* but the fact that neither Dante's honored Hebrews nor his despised Jews can be confused with what we might call average human beings. They are men and women of exemplary faith upon whom the divine favor eternally rests; or they are betrayers of friends, murderers of the innocent, killers of God. In Dante's calculus of transgression and punishment, God's chosen people are either supernaturally virtuous or utterly debased. Whatever else is said about the depiction of Jews in this masterpiece of Christian literature, it is clear that representatives of the Jewish people remain qualitatively "other."

Lest we be tempted, however, to consider such dichotomous renderings of Jews as "Catholic" or "medieval," it is useful to observe that an equally polarized apprehension of the Jewish people is manifest in the documents of a rationalized and iconoclastic Reformation culture. A few hundred years after Dante, in texts that are confessional rather than imaginative, blessed "Hebrews" and cursed "Jews" are relegated to the same disparate positions of honor and condemnation. The "Scots Confession" of 1560, for instance, offers a typological interpretation of the biblical patriarchs according to which all the faithful of the "Old Testament," including Adam, Noah and David, "did see the joyful day of Christ Jesus and did rejoice." The glory which adheres to the people and institutions of the Hebrew Bible is extoled as belonging to the "true Kirk," an entity preserved by God through all ages. The "Heidelberg Catechism" of 1563 again honors the Hebrew ancestors of Christ, whose gospel was "revealed in the beginning in the Garden of Eden, afterward proclaimed through the holy patriarchs and prophets and foreshadowed through the sacrifices and other rites of the Old Covenant, and finally fulfilled through [God's] own well-beloved Son." Yet in a nearly contemporaneous Reformed document, the "Second Helvetic Confession" of 1566, the appellation "Jew" is utilized exclusively in references to doctrinal error. The author(s) of this creed, determined to vilify what they perceived as the theological folly of Roman Catholicism, found it appropriate (and no doubt effective) to associate Catholics with those arch-heretics the Jews. Here, as in many Protestant creeds of the Reformation era, millenarianism is condemned as a "Jewish dream."

A century later, the authors of the "Westminster Confession" (1647) treat the relationship of Christian and pre-Christian humanity by introducing the distinction between a "covenant of works" and a "covenant of grace," a sophisticated Reformed version of the standard dichotomy between Christian freedom and "Jewish" legalism. With this bifurcated covenant, the Westminster divines imply that the church has superseded the synagogue, which depends on a covenant that is "incapable of life." Still, in order that the heroes of the "Old Testament" may be located on the salvific side of this divide, the two covenants do not strictly correspond to the eras before and after the advent of Christ. In fact, "under the law [the covenant of grace] was administered by promises, prophecies, sacrifices, circumcision, the paschal lamb and other types and ordinances delivered to the people of the Jews, all fore-signifying Christ to come." In general, Protestant confessions in the Reformed tradition assign high status to the Hebrew patriarchs and matriarchs, since they "did see the day of Christ Jesus and did rejoice." At the same time, they reiterate the classic anti-Jewish distinction between works and grace and dismiss some of their opponents' views as "Jewish" errors and fantasies.

I have chosen Dante and the Reformed confessions as textual windows on the Christian imagination because both are regarded as representing relatively positive apprehensions of the Jewish people. The author of a recent book on the character of Judas and the growth of anti-Semitism in Europe has singled out the author of the *Divine Comedy* for making a "conscious effort to avoid connecting the perfidy of Judas with the dishonour of the Jewish people as a whole."[3] And theology in the tradition of Calvin is frequently recognized for its philosemitic attributes, including a high level of respect for the "Old Testament" and for biblical Hebrews and their descendants. I refer to these texts, then, as a way of suggesting that even in Christian documents where anti-Jewishness is relatively inconspicuous one is likely to encounter deeply ambivalent and dichotomous portrayals of Jews.

Other examples of the virtual inability of Christians to conceive of Jews as typical human beings are found throughout the history of preaching. In fact, one particularly intriguing aspect of Christian homiletical discourse is the perennial failure of preachers to distinguish between biblical and contemporary Jews; between, that is, the heroes and antiheroes of the Bible and the persons who reside across town or down the street. Like the association of "Jewish perfidy" with the treachery of Judas, the linking of biblical Hebrews and every subsequent generation of Jews is still quite common, and sermons are a medium in which it has thrived. Historian Frank Felsenstein cites a sermon delivered in London in 1648 as a prime example of the Christian tendency to paint all Jews with broad and ancient stereotypes. Felsenstein notes carefully how the anonymous preacher inexplicably switches from past to present tense in the process of describing Jewish perversity. In an almost imperceptible transition, he proclaims that the Jews who killed Christ *are* hypocrites, a generation of vipers, etc.[4]

Felsenstein makes much of this abrupt shift, and it provides an illuminating glimpse of the Christian mind at work. But this tactic is more of a commonplace in Christian preaching than Felsenstein seems to be aware. Not long ago I was in attendance when a respected Protestant clergyman preached on the New Testament story of Jesus and Zaccheus. Toward the end of his sermon, the preacher made the impassioned observation that "the Jews did not understand what Jesus was doing [in associating with Zaccheus], and they still don't understand!" As one who had over time become sensitized to negative Christian portrayals of Jews, this sudden but significant shift in attention struck me as unwarranted and pernicious. Within one sentence, the minister had jumped several thousand years and as many miles. The same "they" which in the biblical text refers to Jesus' contemporaries in first-century Palestine was being employed to denote living Jews of the congregants' acquaintance. I am certain that anyone caring to know would find that such back and forth movements between real Jews and the "Jews" of sacred text is typical in Christian discourse of all kinds.

Further examples could be compounded, but I hope the point is clear: Persons raised in the Christian tradition have great difficulty viewing Jews as human beings like themselves. Walker Percy's claims to the contrary notwithstanding,[5] when Christians are confronted by the word-sign "Jew," they are more likely to conjure theological types and antitypes, not to mention cultural and literary stereotypes, than to think of real individuals with the same hopes, failures and foibles as non-Jews. Some have misunderstood this mythologizing tendency and claimed that for Christians the only good Jew is a dead Jew, or a [converted] Christian. But the Christian attitude toward the Jew has never consisted in a simple desire to bring an end to the Jewish people through persecution or conversion. Rather, the crux of the Christian outlook is that every Jew, whether they are cast in an angelic or demonic role, is part of a chosen race that in some mysterious way represents God.

Ultimately, it was this assumption which allowed Jews to persist in a relatively secure state within pre-modern Christendom. But it also determined that Jewish actions and beliefs would become objects of unnatural scrutiny and bizarre fantasy. Furthermore, most Christians through the ages have believed that they understood the Jews' history and destiny with greater probity than Jews themselves. For in the Christian imagination the existence and survival of the Jew have been invested with religious significance, even – and especially – when Jews refuse to recognize this significance. This book will argue that, whatever else may be said about the status of Jews in Christian and post-Christian Western societies, Jews continue to function in the Christian mind as fundamental symbols in the divine alphabet.

This is an exploration of the way representative Christian authors imagine Jews to be. Many recent works have addressed the history of Jewish–Christian relations, some tracking a local ebb and flow and some the broader tidal movements in that history. This work is neither an exhaustive historical survey nor a detailed description of conditions in a single region or historical epoch, but a wide-ranging analysis of a complex of ideas that is located across the chronological and ideological spectra of Christian thought. I realize that ideas, however compelling, cannot be divorced from the real and ongoing history which Christians and Jews share. Nevertheless, it is not my primary aim to evaluate the historical effects of mythical thinking; rather, I wish to document the variegated expressions of a deep and deeply ambivalent mythical construct.

Over the last thirty years, a variety of Christian and Jewish scholars have written convincingly of the role of Christian belief in preparing the European mind for the advent of racial anti-Semitism and the Holocaust. I offer this study of the witness-people myth as a complement to rather than a repudiation of their work. I am keenly aware, in fact, that if the religious dynamics of anti-Judaism and anti-Semitism had not been investigated so thoroughly by those whose work I cite, I would not be free to take a novel approach to this subject matter. Using a history of ideas methodology, I hope to demonstrate that animosity toward Jews, while fundamental to Christian theology and infecting the New Testament itself, does not represent the bedrock of the Christian imagination as it applies to the Jewish people. In the depths of the Christian mind is a mythical complex more ambivalent and more subtle in its pernicious influence than pure Jew-hatred.

I will use "witness-people myth" as a handy term for labeling a complex of beliefs and assumptions that has informed the Christian mind across the centuries. Where it is present in more subtle ways I will use the phrase "witness-people thinking." When it appears as a self-conscious articulation of Augustine's systematized version of the witness-people myth, I shall use the terms "witness-people doctrine," "witness-people theory," and "witness-people theology." But readers should bear in mind that at no time has any developed witness-people doctrine been articulated self-consciously by an official church body. Even in Augustine's case, elements of his witness-people doctrine are found scattered throughout his writings. In fact, the power of the witness-people myth is testified to by its longevity despite never being an element of church dogma or an unwritten test of faith.

I believe that the textual evidence cited in these chapters amounts to an implicit demonstration of my thesis that the witness-people myth is a deep structure in the Christian imagination. Perhaps Chapter 6 contains the strongest argument in this direction: If the witness-people myth is not deeply ingrained in the theological imaginations of Christians, then why is its presence routinely ignored by otherwise incisive Christian scholars who are seeking to reconstruct the church's theology of Israel? As I try to show in my analysis of Christian Holocaust theology,[6] scholars who are genuinely concerned with the effects of Christian ideology *vis-à-vis* Jews remain quite unaware of the myth's presence in their own discourse. In fact, it is precisely in their attempts to comprehend and repudiate historic Christian anti-Judaism that the Holocaust theologians inadvertently reaffirm the most fundamental Christian ideology about Jews – the conviction that the existence, fate, and redemption of the Jews are signs for God's church. Today, as in centuries past, well-meaning Christians have reverted to basic forms of cognition about Jewish existence and Jewish travail. Can Christians be liberated, then, from the hold of the witness-people myth? This question I will take up in the book's final chapter.

My overall aim is to comprehend in the most profound way possible my own religious tradition's ambivalence toward Jews – to comprehend both the "good" and the "bad" in the Jewish myth which is operative throughout Christian history, and to analyze the manifestations of the myth I have discovered in modern and contemporary Christian discourse. This ambitious aim has required me to formulate a wager. I am wagering that by assuming a broad perspective I will discover something deeper than persistent Jew-hatred, something in which all Christian notions about Jews, both "negative" and "positive," are rooted.[7]

I am very conscious of the fact that the term myth is employed in many ways by contemporary thinkers. For my purposes, the phrase "witness-people myth" refers to a complex of ideas and symbols that, often precritically and unconsciously, informs ideas about Jews among persons who share a cultural heritage or world view. I infer the existence of "the Christian mind" and "the Christian imagination" as sources and habitations for this myth. In this I have been influenced by two aspects of the structuralist conception of myth popularized by cultural anthropologists: that the nature of the mind reveals itself in the structure of myths as much as in the structure of language, and that the structure of myth is both formative and reflective of the human mind. To use Claude Lévi-Strauss's words, I want to understand "how myths think in men [sic], unbeknown to them."[8]

I believe that crucial for understanding the witness-people myth is the recognition that it is characterized by an inner tension produced by the coexistence of dual components that Lévi-Strauss calls "bundles." The bundles which distinguish the witness-people myth pertain to the reprobation and preservation/salvation of the Jewish people, and give rise to what I will refer to as the negative and positive dimensions of witness-people thinking. The ambivalence created by competing bundles is expressed in several pairs of notions which inform Christian discourse:

reprobation ("negative")	*preservation ("positive")*
the Jews:	but:
are killers of Christ	remain the people of God
are superseded	are not "cast off"

are dispersed	carry "books" that testify to Christ
are witnesses to judgment	disseminate the knowledge of God
must be preached to in love	will convert before the end of time
have lost their land	will be restored to their land.[9]

As will be demonstrated in the chapters that follow, these and similar ideas are found together in texts from every era of church history. Where Jews are concerned, we find simultaneous teachings of judgment and eventual redemption; policies of isolation/exclusion carried out amid protection from physical attack; affirmations of God-willed suffering along with warnings about Christian participation in Jewish persecution; and emphasis on the interplay of dispersion and preservation. Tension created by the often paradoxical convictions associated with the witness-people myth is finally resolved in the confidence that Jews are God's people and will return to God's favor.

As I am employing it, then, "myth" refers to a specific set of beliefs, assumptions and convictions about Jews that have been expressed consistently by Christians over centuries. But since I am concerned with charting the ways that mythical notions are transmitted in Christian texts, I have found it useful to combine this structuralist understanding of the term with a "semiotic" approach. As Roland Barthes elaborates it,[10] the semiotic or semiological understanding of myth begins in the observation that myth is a type of speech, a system of communication, a message. Myth functions as a semiotic system in that, like language, it is structured in terms of the relationship between a signifier, a signified and a third term – "the associative total of the first two terms"[11] – which is called the sign. According to Barthes, myth is a second-order semiotic system constructed on a previously existing linguistic semiotic chain:

language	1. *Signifier*	2. *Signified*
	3. *Sign*	
myth	I. SIGNIFIER	II. SIGNIFIED
		III. SIGN(ification)[12]

Barthes' diagram of interlocking semiotic chains suggests how **myth** gets hold of **language** in order to build its own system. **Myth** transforms a previously established *sign* into an empty *signifier* that has been "drained." Thus the *sign* in a language system becomes a SIGNIFIER in a myth system, a system with its own SIGNIFIED. In the myth I am analyzing in this book, the *sign* of a language system (actually the identity of the *signifier* "Jew" with a group of people believed to share common characteristics, history and origins) is taken over to form the empty SIGNIFIER that is the basis of the myth. In the metalanguage of myth, this *sign* which identifies "Jews" with real Jews and "Jewish history" with an accepted version of their story becomes the SIGNIFIER for a new SIGNIFIED (God, or God's designs). The association of "Jews"/real Jews with God becomes the SIGN (Barthes also calls it the SIGNIFICATION) by which the myth is recognized. While this mythical SIGN takes many forms – including associations of Jewish exile and divine punishment, Jewish preservation and divine providence, Jewish restoration and divine guidance, Jewish conversion and divine love – in each case the correlation of the Jew with God is central.

In claiming that the witness-people myth is both an ambivalent collection of assertions about Jews and a system of linguistic signs which Christian communities construct unconsciously, I intend no contradiction. The structuralist perspective on the witness-people myth elucidates how Christian notions about Jews are organized in the depths of the Christian imagination, while the semiotic perspective helps to explain how the imagination utilizes language to project these ideas upon real Jews. Each offers useful insight into the mysterious operation of the witness-people myth.

This book is a preliminary attempt to plot the parameters and depth of the witness-people myth in the Christian tradition. After describing the myth in more detail in the next chapter, in Chapter 3 I will chart the various forms which it assumes in Christian texts written between the fourth and eighteenth centuries. The focus for the remainder of the book is twentieth-century Christian discourse. After chapters devoted to identifying reflections of the witness-people myth in the writings of Karl Barth and Walker Percy, I will consider two diverse strains of contemporary theology – dispensational premillennialism and Holocaust theology. Having examined in detail these four twentieth-century manifestations of the witness-people myth, I will offer some conclusions in the final chapter.

Throughout the book I have emphasized figures and writings which tend to confirm my thesis about Jews and the Christian imagination. I believe the diversity in time, location and theological orientation represented by these select examples establishes beyond a reasonable doubt the perennial Christian proclivity to think of Jews as witness-people. If this tendency can be demonstrated to exist in the twentieth century in forms that are demonstrably continuous with those of the patristic era, *even in theologies that are self-consciously post-Holocaust,* then the bedrock of Christian myth relating to the Jewish people will have been struck. The implications of exposing this bedrock layer of the Christian imagination will be addressed briefly in the final chapter. I hope they will become the focus for further study.

2

The Witness-People Myth and Its Alternatives

The feelings of Gentiles toward Jews are marked by an absence of balance, impartiality and ease. They gravitate between opposite poles.

J. L. Talmon, "European History – Seedbed of the Holocaust"

In this chapter some leading features of Christian thinking influenced by the witness-people myth will be elaborated and some scholarly alternatives for understanding the Christian attitude toward Jews will be evaluated.

I. PRINCIPLES OF WITNESS-PEOPLE THINKING

Jews are an important sign. A useful index of the witness-people myth's influence among Christians is the degree to which Jews and their fate are profoundly significant for Christians. The special stature of the Jewish people was not lost in the angry disputes of the first century or the fateful parting of the ways in the second. Emerging "Christianity" of the first century CE defined itself primarily in relation to mainstream Judaism and its interpretation of Jewish Scripture.[1] From the second to the fifth centuries the Jewish communities scattered about the Roman Empire remained special objects of curiosity and derision for Christians, as a vast body of *adversos Judaeos* literature from the pens of the church fathers attests. Even as the authorities of Talmudic Judaism were almost completely ignoring Christianity, Jews and Judaism remained of crucial interest for Christians.[2] Since the time of Paul, in fact, the fate of "unbelieving" Jews following the appearance of Christ has been considered a divine mystery; and although this mystery is fully comprehended only by God, it is nonetheless significant for the church, since the ultimate salvation of Israel (Romans 11:26) is a sign of the consummation of God's plan for history. This notion that the past, present

12

and future of Israel cannot be unimportant for Christians has found expression in the writings of Christians in every generation since the first century.

The Jews are an ambivalent sign. Representations of the witness-people myth can be distinguished by their conflicted, ambivalent character. This ambivalence is deeply imbedded in Christian apprehensions of the nature and destiny of the Jewish people. It has been present from the beginning of the Jewish–Christian encounter, though it sometimes has been obscured by Christian anti-Jewish rhetoric. For instance, while early arguments for the superiority of Christianity over Judaism were anti-Jewish, they were ambivalently so, since these arguments concerned the identity of the rightful heirs to the Jewish inheritance.[3]

The witness-people myth gives rise to a diversity of thought-forms. The witness-people myth can be expressed in theological, legal, historical, or homiletical discourse, and has adapted itself to a multitude of cultural and historical situations into the twentieth century. The witness-people myth should not be confused with the irrational beliefs about Jews to which it has periodically become attached. Yet the two are related, since underlying such Judeo-phobic charges as blood libel, well-poisoning and the like is the assumption that Jews are prime movers in history and are likely to become arch-conspirators against Christendom. No doubt the witness-people myth predisposes the Christian toward scapegoating Jews and embracing superstitions, especially in periods of social crisis. But it is also the source of "positive" mythical conceptions of the Jewish people.

Witness-people thinking is insidiously dangerous. Though in itself more benign than some of the anti-Jewish ideologies to which it has given rise, the witness-people myth poses an insidious threat to Jewish life and integrity. Thus the problem with Christianity is both less and more serious than some chroniclers of Christian anti-Semitism have suggested. On one hand, the continuity between Christian anti-Judaism and modern anti-Semitism is not as unproblematic as some scholars, Christian and Jewish, have argued. On the other hand, the standard ways for perceiving Jews in the post-Holocaust environment are still animated by a myth which has contributed to Jewish suffering for nearly two millennia. While witness-people thinking is a *relatively* benign way of viewing Jews and assessing Jewish exist-ence, it may, unless it is acknowledged by Christians, continue to perpetuate mythical notions about Jews that are pernicious.

The witness-people myth and Christian anti-Judaism are inseparable, but not identical. Occasionally, well-meaning but over-zealous scholars ignore the paradoxical character of witness-people thinking and draw too close a connection between Christian anti-Judaism and modern anti-Semitism. Interestingly, it is often historians who must provide a corrective to such misleading notions. Examples include Yosef Yerushalmi's response to Rosemary Ruether's provocative work on the theological roots of anti-Semitism,[4] the responses of Eugene Fisher, Marc Tanenbaum and others to Hyam Maccoby's analysis of the Christian anti-Judaic myth,[5] and Marc Saperstein's response to a host of "continuity" thinkers.[6] A crucial historical fact to which all these critics point is the Jews' survival in European Christendom. This survival would have been inconceivable, the argument goes, without the desire of Christians at some level that it should have been so. To explain this, scholars like Yerushalmi, Saperstein, Tanenbaum, and Alan Davies emphasize the "affirma-tions"[7] *vis-à-vis* Jews that are part of the Christian tradition, and that correspond to the positive side of the witness-people myth. This argument receives an even sharper point when historians observe that in general Jews fared better than heretics in medieval Christen-dom. They point out that Jewish fate was qualitatively different from that of heretics like the Albigenses, whom were mercilessly persecuted and whose annihilation was perceived as desirable. These thinkers are not seeking to rescue Christianity from respons-ibility for its past. Rather, they are convinced that the future of Jewish–Christian relations is best served by historical accuracy and that scholarship which blurs important distinctions ultimately is less than helpful in the task of theological revision.[8]

The witness-people myth places a positive value on Jewish survival. Although witness-people thinking is "positive" only in a relative sense, it has functioned to insure Jewish survival in ages of Jewish powerlessness. In other words, it has emphasized the preservation of Jews, generally within Christian society, until the arrival of God's Kingdom. Yosef Yerushalmi has underscored the importance of the preservationist side of Christian teaching by observing that the church's treatment of the Jews could easily have been less favorable.

Yerushalmi asks: Why did the church not destroy the Jews? Why did Christians not treat Jews as they did the Samaritans or others they declared heretics? Why did Christian theology not lead to the actual enslavement of Jews? Why did the church not decree their forced conversion?[9]

An axiom of witness-people thinking that has underscored the preservationist impulse in Christian thought is the association of contemporary Jews with their supposed biblical ancestors. This association has contributed to a theological apprehension of contemporary Jews as descendents of Cain and members of a deicide race. But it also has guaranteed that the preservationist aspects of the myth remained in effect for successive generations of Jews. Ironically, the certainty that Jews are accursed children of their more faithful ancestors underlies the belief that they represent the "Israel" that Paul declared still has a role to play in salvation history.

II. JEWS AND THE CHRISTIAN IMAGINATION: ALTERNATIVE INTERPRETATIONS

A great deal of recent scholarly work has been devoted to unearthing the roots of anti-Semitism.[10] But there remains significant disagreement among historians, biblical scholars and theologians as to the role played by Christianity. Some scholars regard anti-Semitism as coeval with the emergence of Christianity and claim that previously Jews suffered only the prejudices typically directed at an unassimilated minority. Christian Jew-hatred is thus viewed as a unique ideology that is the ultimate source of anti-Semitism in the West. Other researchers, while acknowledging Christianity's contributions to anti-Semitic thinking, emphasize the modern dimensions of anti-Semitism or its pagan antecedents.

Even when questions concerning the relationship of religious ideas and ancient or modern anti-Semitism are bracketed, scholarly opinion remains seriously divided over the nature and extent of Christian anti-Judaism. Some perceive in the church's christological affirmations the origins of theological anti-Judaism. Some believe the problem originated in the complex of doctrine and myth which grew up around the passion of Jesus, others in what they refer to as the Christian "teaching of contempt" for Jews. Still others seek an explanation for Christian Jew-hatred in the fanaticism and intolerance that accompanies religious belief in periods of societal crisis.

What follows is a survey of prominent post-Holocaust interpretations of the Christian attitude toward Jews.

A.   The Teaching of Contempt

Among early post-Holocaust attempts to make sense of Christian
anti-Judaism and its influence in history was that of French scholar
Jules Isaac. Beginning in the late 1940s Isaac's research inaugurated
a new era in the study of the pagan and Christian roots of anti-
Semitism.[11] According to John Gager, the effect of Isaac's work was
twofold:

> 1) to lay the blame for anti-Semitism squarely at the door of Chris-
> tianity; and 2) to buttress the argument that anti-Semitism, while
> exclusively a Christian product, results from a misinterpretation
> by Christians of their own scriptures and founder, and stands in
> fundamental opposition to the historical origins and basic tenets
> of Christianity.[12]

At the end of his life Isaac defined the essential Christian contribution to anti-Semitism – which he termed the Christian "teaching of contempt" – as constructed from three beliefs: the dispersion
of the Jews as a providential punishment; the degenerate state of
Judaism at the time of Jesus; and the crime of deicide.[13]

Historically thorough and influential as was Isaac's contribution to
the discussion of Christianity and anti-Semitism, it failed in several
ways to penetrate to the heart of Christian apprehensions of the Jew.
First, the notion of exile as providential dispersion is really more basic
to the Christian imagination than either the belief in the degenerate
state of Judaism in the time of Jesus or the deicide charge. Second,
Isaac's understanding of the Christian mind is insufficiently dialectical,
since his "teaching of contempt" downplays the positive historical
effects of the providential exile theme. Third, Isaac appears to underestimate the depths from which Christian ideas about Jews arise. In
response to the Christian conviction that the Jews' dispersion followed
God's judgmental destruction of Jerusalem in the year 70 CE, Issac notes
that this conviction conflicts with "historical reality" since the dispersion actually began five hundred years before the Christian era. But,
of course, mythical notions are rarely susceptible to correction by a
rehearsal of historical facts.

B. Supersessionism and Triumphalism

More recent accounts of Christian anti-Judaism and its historical legacy have stressed the effects of standard theological schemes for interpreting Judaism *post Christum*. Focus has been on strategies of dispossession adopted by Christian writers beginning in the New Testament. Today the terms "supersessionism" and "triumphalism" are invoked routinely to suggest traditional Christian appraisals of the Jewish people's theological status. The appellation "supersessionist" is appended to any theology which implies that the Mosaic covenant was abrogated with the coming of Christ. Those who claim that in Christ the Jews' covenant with God was universalized – that is, opened to any Jew or Gentile who enters the new community of believers – are commonly branded "triumphalist." Use of both terms has become widespread, and it is not possible to credit one person with their origin. However, Franklin Littell, A. Roy Eckardt, and Douglas John Hall are among the Christian scholars who have lent them credence. In 1975 Littell wrote that "the cornerstone of Christian Antisemitism is the superseding or displacement myth ... [which] already rings with a genocidal note."[14] In 1979 Douglas John Hall declared in an influential article that "... anti-Judaism is a function of Christian triumphalism."[15]

C. Nonrationality and Irrationality

Another scholarly explanation for Christian Jew-hatred has underscored the irrational and "medieval" nature of anti-Jewish sentiment. A classic exemplar of this approach is Joshua Trachtenberg's *The Devil and the Jews* (1943), a book which emphasizes the uncritical character of popular thinking in medieval Christendom.[16] For Trachtenberg, anti-Semitism is rooted in superstition: "Hatred of the Jew is not the result of a rational process," but has its ultimate source "buried deep in the mass subconscious."[17] Throughout *The Devil and the Jews* are references to "the credulous medieval imagination," "perverted reasoning," "logical inconsistency," "superstitious attitudes," [the lack of a] "critical historical sense," and "the essential *non sequitur*" of official Christian attitudes.

Trachtenberg is successful in bringing into focus the "unreal," "theological" Jew of Christian legend and its effects on popular thinking in the Middle Ages. He also illuminates connections between the isolation and demonization of the Jew in the medieval era and the resulting popular credulity toward charges of ritual murder, host desecration, poisoning, and black magic. Furthermore, Trachtenberg's approach is important inasmuch as it undertakes to sketch the outlines of the Christian imagination's basic Jew-image by documenting its manifestations in medieval art and literature. Trachtenberg even reveals some awareness of the ambivalence that is a peculiarity of Christian perceptions of Jews.

Yet several considerations problematize Trachtenberg's reliance on irrationality as an explanation for Christian anti-Judaism. First, in the sense in which Trachtenberg uses the term "rationality" is a modern and not a medieval standard for judging religious beliefs. More importantly, explaining the medieval history of Jews in Christian lands requires more than an elaboration of the irrationality manifest in popular sentiment. It also requires close attention to the profound ambivalence that is evident in the writings and actions of medieval Christians. Finally, Trachtenberg's perspective on the relationship of Christianity and anti-Semitism fails to account for the persistence of irrational "medieval" Jew-hatred into the twentieth century. Ironically, Trachtenberg observes, "under our skeptical rationalism and scientific objectivity ... the conceptions of our forefathers are still potent motivating factors."[18] Trachtenberg extends the hope that when Enlightenment values have found a home among the masses, Jew-hatred, that lingering vestige of the medieval mind, will be displaced. It is possible that popular enlightenment may yet alleviate the scourge of anti-Semitism. But fifty years after the publication of *The Devil and the Jews*, such a hope seems naive at best.

A more recent and sophisticated attempt to employ irrationality in interpreting the relationship of Christianity and anti-Semitism is found in Gavin I. Langmuir's *History, Religion and Antisemitism* (1990). As a historian conversant with post-Holocaust scholarly discussions concerning the provenance of anti-Semitism, Langmuir seeks a neutral, non-religious and "objective" determination of the point in Western history at which anti-Semitism first loomed. Langmuir finds unsatisfactory the work of Christian scholars like James Parkes, Edward Flannery and Rosemary Ruether, all of whom he accuses of drawing a facile distinction between the authentic gospel of Jesus and the anti-Jewish Christianity which developed out of it. Langmuir alleges that each of these scholars has allowed religious commitments to control or distort their historical conclusions.

Langmuir's own analysis is based on his contention that religious beliefs are by nature "nonrational." While belief is not inherently irrational, religious "irrationality" is a dimension of "religiosity" that emerges as a reaction to rational doubt. According to Langmuir, the doubts that constantly must be suppressed by religious believers eventually spawn irrational fantasies. These fantasies in turn become "social irrationalities" that are transmitted by various societal media. Langmuir argues that by the eleventh century the nonrational medieval Catholic religion was well on its way to becoming irrational as well, partly because "religious authorities were willing to support irrational ideas that strengthened faith in their authority when evidence of the falsity of those ideas was not widely available."[19] If anti-Semitism is "the hostility aroused by irrational thinking about 'Jews'," then Christianity became a source of anti-Semitism beginning in the Late Middle Ages.

Langmuir recognizes that from the inception of the Christian movement believers troubled by religious doubts could hardly avoid thinking of Jews – and reacting with the nonrational ideas that comprise the core of anti-Judaism: a belief in the deficiency of Jewish understanding, the deicide charge, and the dispersion as punishment notion.[20] The verge of irrationality was reached, Langmuir believes, by violently anti-Judaic marauding peasants during the massacres associated with the First Crusade. Yet these crowds killed Jews for who they actually were (persons who adhered to Judaism and rejected Christian beliefs) and thus were acting on the basis of their nonrational beliefs. Even the legal degradation of Jews and the condemnation of the Talmud were nonrational reactions to real Christian-Jewish conflict.

Langmuir contends that the "chimerical beliefs" or fantasies about Jews which distinguish anti-Semitism first appeared in the twelfth century. The first such fantasy he dates to 1144 when the charge of "ritual murder" was brought against the Jews of Norwich. Subsequently, well-known fantasies of ritual cannibalism, host desecration, Jewish poisoning and "Jewish" physical characteristics were reported in various parts of Europe:

> Thus, by the late Middle Ages, in order to dispel doubts about their religion and themselves, many Christians were suppressing their capacity for rational empirical thought and irrationally attributing to the realities they denoted as "Jews" unobservable characteristics.
> ...
> The fantasies [from which they suffered] were given widespread social expression and incorporated in European historiography,

literature and art. They became deeply embedded in the mentality of millions of normally rational Christians.[21]

Langmuir maintains that the massacres at the end of the thirteenth century were the first killings of Jews motivated primarily by irrationality. Those who died were not victims of their beliefs – and thus should not be considered martyrs – but of their killers' delusions. These murders were the first historical anticipation of Hitler's Holocaust.

Defining anti-Semitism as the hostility aroused by irrational thinking about "Jews," Langmuir is able to challenge on historical grounds any meaningful distinction between Christian anti-Judaism and modern, racial anti-Semitism. He acknowledges that the rise of modernity brought profound changes to European civilization, but he argues that the modern "revolution in religiosity" failed to end religion's influence in Europe. New social and intellectual forces gave rise to xenophobia and an "agnostic anxiety" from which many sought refuge in "physiocentric" religions like Nazism. Because it was particularly susceptible to empirical disproof, Hitler's religion could be maintained only by massive irrationality. Langmuir delivers his *coup de grâce* against all endeavors to distinguish between religious and secular forms of Jew-hatred when he defines National Socialism in religious terms. Despite its modern dimensions, the Holocaust is interpreted as the most sweeping expression of religious irrationality ever witnessed.[22] Langmuir's two-pronged assault on accepted views of religion and anti-Semitism presents an implicit challenge to the assumption that religion was not a sufficient condition for the *Shoah*.

From the point of view of these scholars anti-Semitism is to be understood as an expression of irrational fears and fantasies. While Trachtenberg is unable to explain why irrationality has persisted among modern persons, Langmuir's method addresses precisely this question. His work reminds us that neither personal intelligence nor cultural enlightenment are effective barriers against prereflective and mythical notions about Jews.

D. Anti-Judaism and Christology

Another group of scholars regards the church's Christology as the ultimate source of theological anti-Judaism. Although Rosemary R. Ruether was not the first to view Christology as the basis for Christian anti-Semitism,[23] her book *Faith and Fratricide* has become almost synonymous with this approach. The crux of Ruether's argument takes the form of a question addressed to the church: "Is it possible to say 'Jesus is Messiah' without, implicitly or explicitly, saying at the same time 'and the Jews be damned?'"[24] The evidence brought to bear by Ruether in her analysis of anti-Jewish discourse from the formation of the New Testament to the Nazi era suggests the answer to her troubling question is "no." In alleging that anti-Judaism is "an intrinsic need of Christian self-affirmation," Ruether seems to assert the inseparability of anti-Semitism and Christianity, an inseparability scholars before her had qualified in some way.[25]

Ruether's arguments have convinced many, and have inspired a fruitful debate among those who remain unconvinced.[26] But Ruether has received criticism for seeming to imply a simple causal connection between Christian belief and Jewish suffering. This criticism was first articulated by historian Yosef Yerushalmi, who chided Ruether for what her work left unsaid:

> Throughout her summary of Christian theological anti-Semitism I could not help but ask: If such was the teaching, why did they not destroy the Jews?
> ...
> [Ruether] dwells exclusively on "reprobation." Of "preservation," ... we hear next to nothing. Yet both were present, and one can hardly understand the survival of the Jews in the midst of Christendom without taking both elements into serious account.
> ...
> The problem is not why the Jews were derogated, but rather – why were they not wiped out? ... That the church chose to take its stand on an *eschatological* rather than immediate conversion of the Jews was yet another factor of inestimable importance for the survival of Jewry.[27]

Yerushalmi also disputes Ruether's assumption of an essential continuity between "modern anti-Semitism" and the "theological and economic scapegoating of Jews" in the Middle Ages. Yerushalmi infers from Ruether's work that "genocide against the Jews was an inexorable consequence of Christian theological teaching." He denies this is the case, however, and argues instead that a quantum leap is required to explain the change from anti-Judaism to annihilation. Throughout his response to Ruether, in fact,

Yerushalmi elucidates the positive aspect of traditional Christian thinking about Jews, and the effects of its suspension in the modern period:

> The crucial problem in the shift from medieval to modern anti-Semitism is that while the Christian tradition of "reprobation" continued into the modern era, the Christian tradition of "preservation" fell by the wayside and was no longer operative.
>
> ...
>
> The slaughter of Jews by the state was not part of the medieval Christian world-order. It became possible with the breakdown of that order.[28]

Ruether occasionally alludes to the "paradoxical" nature of Christian thinking about Jews, in which reprobation and preservation are simultaneously affirmed. But Yerushalmi's response to her work entails a necessary reassertion of Christian ambivalence toward the Jew, which he rightly observes is required to explain Jewish survival in medieval Europe.

E.   The Deicide Myth

Another provocative attempt to comprehend Christian Jew-hatred has come from the pen of British scholar Hyam Maccoby.[29] Maccoby builds upon the research of Jules Isaac and others who have explored the Christian conception of the Jews as Christ-killers, but he dissents from this tradition in arguing that the deicide charge is rooted in a mythic structure that is the very basis of Christian faith.

Maccoby acknowledges some ambivalence in the Christian perception of Jews.[30] But he alleges that Christianity's defining characteristic is a "diabolization" of the Jewish people stemming from their mythic role as murderers of a deified Jesus. Maccoby identifies three sources for the Christian construct he calls the Sacred Executioner myth: pre-Christian gnosticism and its anti-Semitic mythology, the historical theme in which the church replaces Israel as the vehicle of God's promises, and the ancient mystery-cult myth of a god murdered by an evil force or rival god. Judas Iscariot is the chief point of contact with the mystery-cult tradition. Maccoby notes that analogues to the figure of Judas are always found in religious myths in which a god who offers salvation through death is opposed by an evil power who brings this death about. The crucial difference between the Christian drama of salvation and other ancient myths – the fact that Judas functions as an eponymous representative of all Jews – is also the characteristic which lends the Christian myth its deadly potency.[31]

Maccoby regards this anti-Judaic construct as the centerpiece of Christian doctrine. Christianity's uniqueness, in fact, lies "precisely in this amalgamation of gnosticism with mystery religion to form an anti-Semitic myth of unprecedented potency."[32] Over against Ruether and other Christian radicals, Maccoby maintains that anti-Semitism is embedded in Christian faith at the deepest level: "... Christian anti-Semitism derives not from some accidental and inessential layer of Christianity, but from its central doctrine and myth, the crucifixion itself."[33] Furthermore, post-Christian secular versions of anti-Semitism should be treated as "rationalizations" of the Christian myth in which it receives a scientific rationale.[34] This sad state of affairs was initiated by the Apostle Paul, who gave rise to the Christian anti-Semitic myth when he deified and de-historicized Jesus and cast his death as a cosmic sacrifice in which the Jews were unwitting agents of salvation. Paul's myth, forged in an apologetic attempt to present a depoliticized gospel to Rome, ultimately found "full imaginative life" in the New Testament gospels.[35]

One flaw in Maccoby's thinking is that his focus on the doctrine of the crucifixion as the essence of Christianity constrains him to understate the ambivalence in Christian thought regarding Jews. The experience of Jews in Christian lands can be summed up as follows, according to Maccoby:

> By being always present as the suffering culprits, paying endlessly for their murder of Jesus, [the Jews] lifted the guilt of that murder from Christians, who by venting their moral indignation on the Jews, could feel themselves to be accepted by Christ.[36]

This view of Jewish history proceeds tautologically from Maccoby's conviction that "it is endemic in Christendom that the Jews, the murderers of God, deserve all possible sufferings."[37] Such an unnuanced expression of the matter from the pen of a historian is striking. While Maccoby does achieve greater balance, the effect of much of his work is to leave misleading impressions of the historical record. In fact, he dismisses the effects of the preservationist side of the witness-people myth with the comment that the process of demonizing Jews as mythological murderers of the incarnate God "took several centuries to accomplish fully, for ordinary Christians tended at first to treat Jews as ordinary human beings..."[38] Maccoby does acknowledge that the Pauline hope in the Jews' salvation rescued them from annihilation on many occasions, but adds that this cut in two directions since millenarian sects believed that at the Second Coming of Jesus Jews would disappear through annihilation.[39] We may observe such a belief in action, Maccoby suggests, in the pogroms of anti-Jewish mobs during the Crusades. Although Maccoby admits that post-Christian anti-Semitism lacks the "moral restraints" inherent in the Christian variety, he implies that whatever actual protection Jews received in Christian Europe was accidental.

As his critics have noted, however, Maccoby's version of Christian faith is one constructed for easy denunciation.[40] Eugene J. Fisher, one of Maccoby's staunchest critics, points to the unsatisfactory nature of his "'straight line method' of historical accounting," noting that "it simply does not account for the positive side of the ambivalent New Testament and Patristic attitude toward Jews and Judaism ... Nor does it account for the actual Christian behavior toward Jews over the centuries."[41] Fisher offers a corrective to Maccoby's historical picture by arguing that Christian demonization of the Jews did not occur until the Crusade period.[42]

Maccoby's application of depth psychology and "history of religions" research to the search for the origins of anti-Semitism lends his work a novel and stimulating character. His charge that the sole remedy for anti-Semitism is a radical critique of Christianity's central myth of salvation gives Christians and Jews much to consider. But, like the other scholars whose work has been evaluated in this chapter, Maccoby is unable to explain the profound ambivalence toward Jews which has marked Christian discourse over the centuries. In the next chapter we will examine the historical and theological dimensions of the witness-people myth and in the process attempt to demonstrate its necessity for comprehending the Christian imagination.

3

The Witness-People Myth in History

The idea of the Jew as a killer of God and in punishment thereof a member of a race forever on the run is so deeply engrained in the minds of persons raised in the Christian faith that even a man like Pascal, the French Catholic theologian and scientist, considered their miserable fate a just punishment.

Dagobert Runes, *The Jew and the Cross*

I. THE WITNESS-PEOPLE MYTH AND CHRISTIAN HISTORY: AN OVERVIEW

A. The New Testament

The starting-point for any study of Christian texts must be the New Testament. As many have noted, the New Testament contains much to support the belief that the Jews have been rejected by God following their own rejection of Jesus. Indeed, the gospels of Matthew and John and the Epistle to the Hebrews contain many of the charges that ultimately made up the Christian teaching of contempt. Demonization of the Jews is anticipated in the statement attributed to Jesus in John 8:44 ("You are from your father the devil, and you choose to do your father's desires"),[1] an apparent admission of deicide is found in Matthew 27:25 ("His blood be on us and our children!") and supersessionist theology is a leitmotif in Hebrews.

All this becomes comprehensible, if not excusable, when the New Testament is read as an account of a parting of the ways between Jews who remained faithful to the way of Torah and "Christians – Jewish and non-Jewish – who chose the path of eschatological messianism."[2] Many New Testament polemical passages are intended to demonstrate the folly of Jews who have stubbornly clung to the old covenant, as well as the disapproval of God that is symbolized in the destruction of Jerusalem by the Romans. The important function of the fall of Jerusalem in early Christian polemic against "the Jews" is especially discernible when one compares Matthew's version of Jesus' parable of the Wedding Feast – with its references to a king who "sent his troops, destroyed those murderers, and burned their city" (Matt. 22:7) – with the Lucan Jesus' more benign rendition of the same parable (Luke 14:16–24).

What is easy to overlook on a superficial reading of the New Testament, however, is that this early parting of the ways did not lead Christians to repudiate their Hebrew roots. In fact, much of the early conflict between "Jews" and "Christians" was essentially a debate about which group was faithfully interpreting the Hebrew Scriptures. From the first century Christians were troubled by Jews' "misreading" of the Scriptures, and especially by the exegesis of Jewish leaders who Christians believed kept the people ignorant of the Bible's real meaning. Nevertheless, the Hebrew Bible or "Old Testament" has remained for Christians an inspired revelation from God. Despite occasional calls for a de-Judaization of Christian faith which would drop the "Old Testament" from the canon, orthodox Christianity officially has resisted the Marcionite impulse.

The ambivalence toward Christianity's Jewish heritage that results from the odd circumstances of its birth also finds expression in a paradoxical theme running through the New Testament: The Jews somehow remain chosen despite their decisive and inexplicable rejection of Christ. Has the failure of most Jews to recognize Christ as Messiah led to the rejection of the Jews themselves? Here the New Testament authors equivocate. While reflection on this question sometimes issues in angry vilifications of "the Jews" (better read, scholars tell us, as "elements of the Jewish leadership which are opposed to Jesus"), some texts emphasize the ironic and tragic nature of a Jewish Messiah who is rejected by God's favored people. In Paul's letter to the Romans (especially chs. 9–11), the conflicted Christian mind is on open display. Paul laments the "mystery" of Israel's unbelief despite its unique role in the economy of salvation, elaborates the humility required of Gentiles who have replaced Israel only temporarily, and voices his conviction that "all Israel will be saved" (Romans 11:26). The New Testament, then, is an important source for the ambivalence toward Jews that is a hallmark of the witness-people myth since it provides solid bases for both the reprobationist and preservationist dimensions of witness-people thinking.

B.   The Church Fathers

The witness-people myth assumed more definite shape in the second and third centuries as the activity of Providence was perceived in the misfortunes of the church's significant other and co-claimant to the patriarchal promises. Much has been written in recent years concerning the patristic *adversos Judaeos* tradition and the dispositions of individual church fathers toward the Jewish people.[3] Although Augustine of Hippo (354–430) was the theologian who first articulated a witness-people doctrine, he was working in a tradition already established by his predecessors.

Clear expressions of witness-people ambivalence are often lacking in the writings of the church fathers of the second to the fourth centuries. This seems to be because witness-people thinking is suspended or degenerates into outright hostility when the Jew is perceived as an obstacle to the dream of a Christian society, or when a vibrant Judaism is regarded as a missionary competitor.[4] In the wake of imperial persecutions, the rivalry between religious antagonists could issue in bitter conflict and harsh polemic. Even after the ascendancy of Christianity in the Roman Empire, knowledge of local tensions between Christians and Jews aids us in comprehending the anti-Jewish diatribes of a man like John Chrysostom (344–407), who responded to the policies of Julian the Apostate and his own congregants' apparent fascination with Judaism.

Portrayals of the Jews in the writings of the church fathers are often quite negative. But in their very obsession with Jews' past, present and future these texts suggest the presence of the witness-people myth. Hardly a theologian of the patristic era whose writings survive fails to address the relationship of Christianity with Judaism, despite the fact that these men lived after the final exit from the synagogue, which was complete by 135 CE at the latest. The compulsion to understand and to condemn Jews and Judaism well after this fateful break probably reflects lingering hopes of a mass Jewish turning to Christ. But it also evinces an inability on the part of Christian theologians to refrain from considering the mystery of Jewish existence. The church fathers typically place all ancient Hebrews, first-century Palestinian Jews and Jews of their own place and time into a single mythical category – "the Jews." This, and the various allegorical schemes utilized by the patristic authors to make theological sense of the relationship between the "two peoples" are further examples of the Christian mind's continual struggle to comprehend the significance of the Jewish people.

Augustine – in light of three hundred years of Jewish failure to recognize its Messiah, under the pressure of his own systematizing mind, and informed by a new situation of political influence and empowerment for Christianity – gave theological expression to the witness-people myth. Although there are traces of a witness-people doctrine in the writings of Lactantius (d. 330),[5] Augustine created the definitive witness-people theology. While Augustine never devoted an entire work to explicating his theology of the Jews, he sketched outlines of a witness-people doctrine in a number of his writings.[6] Edward Flannery maintains that Augustine's original contribution

> resides in his theory of the Jews as a witness-people, a theological construction by which he attempts to solve the apparent dilemma of the Jews' survival as a people and their increasing misfortunes. The role of the Jews, in his opinion, is still providential; they are at once witnesses of evil and of Christian truth ... they subsist "for the salvation of the nation but not for their own." They witness by their Scriptures and serve as "slave-librarian" of the Church; and likewise they give witness by their dispersion and their woes. Like Cain, they carry a sign but are not to be killed (Gen. 4: 15).[7]

Augustine's witness-people theory was a theological instrument used to account for the worsening of Judaism's status in the third and fourth centuries as the fortunes of the church were improving. Augustine's task was not to demonstrate that Christianity was a more genuine interpretation of the Hebrew Scriptures than post-biblical Judaism. He assumed this to be the case. Absent from Augustine's witness-people theology, in fact, is the sort of anti-Jewish rhetoric which belittles Jews from the perspective of a competing and persecuted sect. Nor is Augustine's witness-people doctrine simply another elaboration of the charge of deicide that had been developed in the writings of earlier church fathers.[8]

By Augustine's time, the battle for ascendency in the Roman Empire had been won by Christians, and the recognition, security and influence which were the spoils of victory had been attained. Augustine's task is to explain the theological import of Jewish history from the victors' perspective. He relates the story of the defeated religious foe with whom Christians identify most closely. In the process, he must discern a complex plot that can account for the fortunes of Jews and Christians in the past, present and future. But Augustine is no more aware of being a composer of theology than he is of being a transmitter of the witness-people myth.

In Augustine's theology of Israel, both form and content reflect the ambivalent tension that is characteristic of the witness-people myth. On one hand, Augustine emphasizes that the Jewish people are guilty of the murder of Christ, their brother and awaited Messiah, and have paid for this act of deicide by being exiled from their homeland and living a tenuous existence everywhere. On the other hand, Augustine contends that this very dispersion is a sign of God's providence, that the Jews' stubborn adherence to "Old Testament" serves to disseminate the truth of the Christian religion among the nations and, most importantly, that since the unique witness Jews provide must remain they will be preserved by God (and, by implication, should be protected by Christendom) until their final conversion at the end of the age.

A crucial though not original assumption of Augustine's witness-people theology is that God has dispersed the Jews over the face of the earth as punishment for their role in the crucifixion of Christ:

> For these two cities [Babylon and Jerusalem], according to the letter, in reality are two cities. And the former Jerusalem indeed by the Jews is not now inhabited. For after the crucifixion of the Lord vengeance was taken upon them with a great scourge, and being rooted up from that place where, with impious licentiousness being infuriated, they had madly raged against their Physician, they have been dispersed throughout all nations, and that land hath been given to Christians.... That they might not lose their place they killed the Lord; and they lost it, even because they killed.[9]

Augustine emphasizes that Jewish dispersion, though penal, is also providential since it functions to spread the knowledge that God will not tolerate false worship:

> And if they [the Israelites] had not sinned against God by turning aside to worship of strange gods and idols, seduced by impious superstition as if by magic arts, if they had not finally sinned by putting Christ to death, they would have continued in possession of the same realm, a realm exceeding others in happiness, if not in extent. If today they are dispersed over almost all the world,

amongst almost all the nations, this is part of the providence of
the one true God, whose purpose is that when in any place the
images of the false gods are overthrown, with their altars, sacred
groves and temples, and when their sacrifices are forbidden, it
may be proved that this was prophesied long ago; so that when
this is read of in our Christian Scriptures there may be no ground
for believing it a Christian invention.[10]

The Jewish diaspora, then, is a realization of the many warnings in
the Jews' own Scriptures. It represents the consequences of infidelity
in a very succinct manner, since the Old Testament testifies so
clearly to Christ:

But the Jews who killed him [Christ] and refused to believe in
him, to believe that he had to die and rise again, suffered a more
wretched devastation at the hands of the Romans and were
utterly uprooted from their kingdom [in 70 CE], where they had
already been under the dominion of foreigners. They were dispersed all over the world – for indeed there is no part of the
earth where they are not to be found – and thus by the evidence
of their own Scriptures they bear witness for us that we have not
fabricated the prophecies about Christ. In fact, very many of the
Jews ... have come to believe in him ... But the rest of them were
blinded ... It follows that when the Jews do not believe in our
Scriptures, their own Scriptures are fulfilled in them, while they
read them with blind eyes ... [and] we recognize that it is in
order to give this testimony, which, in spite of themselves, they
supply for our benefit by their possession and preservation of
those books, that they themselves are dispersed among all
nations.[11]

Jewish dispersion testifies simultaneously to the ultimate destiny of
those who are faithless and to the truth of Christian belief. This second point becomes clearer still in Augustine's writings. In his comments on Psalm 40, he declares that "the Jews are our attendant
slaves, who carry, as it were, our satchels, and bear the manuscripts
while we study them ... when we argue with the heathen we adduce
the predictions found in manuscripts written by Jews."[12]

A crucial aspect of Augustine's witness-people theology, and one
apart from which the history of the Jews in Europe cannot be properly understood, is the conviction that the Jews' providential mis-

sion and their role as the church's "slave-librarians" require that they remain alive. Augustine finds support for this belief in the Scriptures themselves:

> In fact, there is a prophecy given before the event on this very point in the book of Psalms, which they also read. It comes in this passage: "As for my God, his mercy will go before me; my God has shown me this in the case of my enemies. Do not slay them, lest at some time they forget your Law; scatter them by your might"... And this is the reason for his forbearing to slay them – that is for not putting an end to their existence as Jews, although they have been conquered and oppressed by the Romans; it is for fear that they should forget the Law of God and thus fail to bear convincing witness on the point I am now dealing with. Thus it was not enough for the psalmist to say, "Do not slay them, lest at some time they forget your Law," without adding, "Scatter them." For if they lived with that testimony of the Scriptures only in their own land, and not everywhere, the obvious result would be that the Church, which is everywhere, would not have them available among all nations as witnesses to the prophecies which were given beforehand concerning Christ.[13]

> Therefore you [Jews] do not forget the law of God, but carry it everywhere, a witness to the nations, a shame for you, and without understanding it you give it to the people that has been called upon from sunrise to sunset.[14]

In another place Augustine brings together the various elements of his witness-people doctrine, including the Jews' perpetual existence:

> Therefore, [the Jews] roam about anywhere and everywhere, their darkened eyes a most remarkable proof for our cause, so that through them our arguments are upheld at the very time that this same people is rejected.
>
> ...
>
> This same sect ... was scattered over the earth so that, by carrying about with it the prophecies of grace conferred upon us, it might everywhere be beneficial to us for a more firm convincing of unbelievers. Accept that which I am saying in the manner in which it was prophesied: "Slay them not, lest at any time my

people forget thy law. Scatter them by thy power." They have not been killed, therefore, for this reason, that they have not forgotten what things were read and heard among them.... For this reason they have not been exterminated, but dispersed; although they do not possess the faith whence they might be saved, they still retain in memory that whereby we are aided. They are our supporters in their books, our enemies in their hearts, our witnesses in their scrolls.[15]

The Jews are also to be spared annihilation since as a people they possess a *telos* in history, one that Augustine never forgets, as his words attest:

The belief [suggested by Malachi 4:5f] that in the final period before the judgment this great and wonderful prophet Elijah will expound the Law to the Jews, and that through his activity the Jews are destined to believe in our Christ, this is a very frequent subject in the conversation of believers, a frequent thought in their hearts.... Well then, when he comes, he will explain in a spiritual sense the Law which the Jews now take in a material sense, and by so doing he will "turn the heart of the father toward the son," ... [then] the sons, that is, the Jews will interpret the Law as their fathers – that is, the prophets, including Moses himself – interpret it.
...
The meaning [of "he will turn the heart of the father toward the son"] is that Elijah is to turn the heart of God the Father towards the Son ... by teaching men that the Father loves the Son, so that the Jews also, who first hated the Son, will love this same Son, who is our Christ.... And so, in their thought God's heart will be turned towards the Son when they themselves have their hearts turned by conversion....[16]

This supreme confidence in the ongoing role of the Jew in salvation history issues in what might be confused with a humanitarian concern for Jews' welfare. Augustine counsels Christians: "let us preach to the Jews, whenever we can, with a spirit of love.... It is not for us to boast over them as branches broken off ... We shall be able to say to them without exulting over them – though we exult in God – 'Come, let us walk in the light of the Lord.'"[17] Yet Augustine's positive feelings are motivated by theological considerations, namely the Jews' promised conversion and the conviction that they have yet to fulfill their role in God's plan.

By now it should be easy to apprehend the dialectical structure that animates Augustine's thinking about Jews. Augustine's theology of Israel is steeped in ambivalence: Even as they are judged by God for the rejection of their Messiah, the Jews retain a unique relationship with God and thus with the City of God as represented in Christendom. But there is no ambivalence concerning whether the existence and fate of the Jews in the era after the crucifixion of Christ remain important data for Christian reflection. This is taken for granted in Augustine's witness-people theology.

C. The Witness-People Myth in the Middle Ages

Expressions of the witness-people myth in medieval Christianity are manifold. It is behind social legislation affecting Jews, papal encyclicals and bulls, sermons, and special appeals on Jews' behalf. What follows is a broad but far from exhaustive survey of witness-people thinking in the medieval world.

1. Fourth to Sixth Centuries

The two-sided witness-people theology articulated by Augustine animated social legislation affecting Jews from the fourth to sixth centuries.[18] Running through the Theodosian Code, a fifth-century compilation of laws issued in the reigns of emperors from Constantine to Theodosius I, is the assumption that Jews are a separate and vanquished people. Yet what rights they have are established very clearly, and toleration is the general tenor of this legislation with very few exceptions. Judaism possessed full rights as a lawful religion in the Empire, and in terms of secular rights such as the ownership of property, Jews fared better than Christian heretics.[19] James Parkes's summary of the Jews' status in the fourth century reveals the extent to which preservationist thinking undergirded imperial legislation in this period: "The books of the heretics were burnt. The Torah of the Jew was a sacred book of the Church. In a word, the heretic could be forbidden to exist. The Jew could not."[20]

This situation was altered somewhat by the time the Justinian Code was compiled in the sixth century. Justinian had suspended many of the economic and civic privileges enjoyed by Jews under the Theodosian Code, but, as Parkes observes, Jews remained better off than Samaritans and members of heretical sects. And even though Justinian revoked the Theodosian law establishing Judaism's legal right to exist, his code took for granted that Jewish worship would continue undisturbed. Otherwise, the stipulation that the Jews read their Scriptures "correctly," that is, as prophesying the coming of Christ, is inexplicable:

> Necessity dictates that when the Hebrews listen to their sacred texts they should not confine themselves to the meaning of the letter, but should also devote their attention to those sacred prophecies which are hidden from them, and which announce the mighty Lord and Saviour Jesus Christ.
> ...
> Those who resist [this law] or try to put any obstruction in its way, shall first suffer corporal punishment, and then be compelled to live in exile, forfeiting also their property, that they flaunt not their impudence against God and empire.[21]

Novella 146 of the Justinian Code amounts to a theologically-motivated encouragement for Jews to convert themselves. It assumes that the Scriptures "carried" by the Jews witness to Christian truth and thus requires Jews to read and maintain their sacred texts in a manner which will hasten their conversion. As Parkes notes, Justinian's stipulations regarding the reading of the Hebrew Scriptures in the vernacular are not "anti-Semitic," but "grand-motherly."[22] They stem from a triumphant certainty that Christians alone can grasp the essence and destiny of Judaism. This law reflects witness-people theology inasmuch as it regards Jews as a unique people who are worthy of toleration not on universal moral grounds but because, despite their present state of rejection, they are the original depositories for divine revelation who will eventually come to recognize its fulfillment in Christ.

The Justinian Code contains another interesting adaptation of witness-people theology: the principle that because their religion and way of life have been judged by God, Jews should not occupy positions of authority over Christians.[23] This became a familiar principle in the Middle Ages, although some popes and emperors enforced it with greater vigor than others. In any case, the formal insistence on Jewish degradation arises from the belief that Jewish existence does and should illustrate the vanquished status of Judaism. Once again legislation is employed to insure that social reality reflects theology.

In the Byzantine East, where the tradition of Roman law remained more firmly anchored than in the West, stable conditions helped maintain the relatively benign status of the Jews prescribed in the Justinian Code. But also in the West a tradition of tolerance built on the theological foundation of the witness-people doctrine informed the policies of the civil authorities throughout the Middle Ages. Alfonso the Wise of Castile's description of the fate of Jews in the West seems quite familiar:

> And the reason why the church and the emperors and the kings and the other princes suffered the Jews to live among the Christians is this: because their living as in harsh captivity always would be a reminder to men that they come from the lineage of those who crucified our Lord Jesus Christ.[24]

Gregory the Great (540–604) is the first pope about whose attitude toward the Jews we know anything of substance.[25] Like the imperial legislation we have considered, Gregory's writings are informed by witness-people theology. On one hand, Gregory forbids violence to Jews or their property, noting that they are Roman citizens according to imperial law. He also objects to forced baptisms, preferring conversions that are the result of preaching motivated by love. Like Augustine, Gregory is confident that the Jews will ultimately find salvation.[26] At the same time, however, Gregory's biblical commentaries reveal that he regards Jews as killers of Christ who are punished for this crime by their historical misfortunes.[27] Gregory's formula for dealing with the Jews is one that was repeated by popes for generations after him until it finally became the official policy of the Catholic church.[28] It allows him to maintain in tension the two sides of the witness-people myth:

> Just as one ought not to grant any freedom to the Jews in their synagogues beyond that permitted by law, so should the Jews in no way suffer in those things already conceded to them.[29]

2. Carolingian Empire

In the Western part of the Empire, the Jews' situation became more dangerous than in the East. The anti-Judaism institutionalized in the Justinian Code took on an "erratic and personal" character in the West as distinct economic and social considerations led to popular pogroms.[30] The Jews of Visigothic Spain had a particularly difficult existence between the end of the sixth century (when the Visigoth kings were converted from Arianism to Catholicism) and the Arab conquest in the eighth century.[31] Likewise, the experience of Christendom was distinct for the Jews of Frankish Gaul. After policies of forced conversion were suspended for trade considerations, the Jews became favored and were protected by Frankish kings. In Gaul, the church upheld the witness-people theology and its legal implications, while the Carolingian kings extended even greater favor to the Jews than this theology called for.

In response, the church felt obliged to emphasize the congenital perfidy of Jews and their proper state of exile and degradation. For instance, in the ninth century the Roman liturgy was modified to reflect the unique dimensions of Jewish unbelief.[32] During this time the church increasingly played on popular feelings of envy and loathing toward the Jew, for instance in the development of liturgical drama at the end of the tenth century. Through the dramas connected with Christian festivals a loathing for Jews was disseminated among the populace. Thus, the masses were indoctrinated with the negative aspect of the theological conviction that the Jews are a unique people with a special role in history.[33]

Although this negative version of witness-people thinking ultimately would triumph among the masses in the form of a multifaceted anti-Judaic myth, positive elements of the witness-people tradition were not without effect through the Carolingian period. Respect for Jews and Judaism remained strong among many Christians toward the end of the millennium. Pagan converts to Christianity were receptive to what authorities called "Jewish propaganda" and, according to the complaint of Archbishop Agobard (779–840), tended to "regard the Jews as the only people of God ... cherished because of the patriarchs from whom they are descended."[34] Agobard was disturbed by Jewish influence among his flock and appealed to Louis the Pious to enforce existing anti-Jewish legislation, which Louis refused to do. Agobard's theological polemic was aimed mainly at assuring separation of Christians and Jews. He reasoned that "since they live among us, we should not be hostile to them or injure their life, health or wealth."[35] Agobard remains under the influence of the witness-people myth:

> for all [his] impassioned indignation nowhere does he accuse the Jews of those diabolical practices – profanation of the Host, ritual

murder, poisoning of the wells – that in later times will constitute the leitmotiv of the anti-Jewish campaigns.[36]

Thus, the preservationist aspect of witness-people thinking remained visible in Carolingian Europe even when relations between Christians and Jews were strained. High church dignitaries, including an Italian bishop who became a convert, continued to be attracted by Judaism. Overall, Carolingian Europe was characterized by peaceful cohabitation between Jews and Christians without outbursts of popular hatred. Soon after the year 1000, however, rumors that the "prince of Babylon" had caused the destruction of the Holy Sepulchre in Jerusalem at the instigation of Jews led Christians to seek revenge. This was the harbinger of a turning point.

3. Crusades

The Crusades mark a turning point in Jewish–Christian relations, whether one speaks of popular Christian perceptions of Jews or their actual security within Christian Europe. At the time of the First Crusade the degraded but relatively secure position specified for Jews in the witness-people tradition suddenly broke down with the massacres carried out by Crusaders and local citizens.

Rosemary Ruether observes that "the fine points of the Church's theory that the Jews, though damnable, are to be physically preserved to the end of time, although in a state of 'misery,' to witness the triumph of the Church, eluded the comprehension of the mobs." She suggests that the purveyors of this witness-people theology did not understand the mobs were acting out a hatred it had taught, and that the theory itself kept the church from creating social conditions in which the Jew would be more secure.[37] But two facts have been obscured by analysis of the terrible suffering of Jews during this period. First, the "theological view of the Jew" *per se* should not be blamed for the pogroms associated with the Crusades. Also implicated is a state of societal crisis – precipitated in this case by rapid social change within and perceived threats from without Christian Europe – which encouraged people, educated and peasant alike, to think of the "enemy within" as somehow to blame for the unsettling state of things.

A second important observation to be made about the Crusade period is that the preservationist side of witness-people theology continued to be implemented by bishops, popes and theologians in order to protect Jews from popular hostilities. At times local bishops personally sheltered Jews and protected them from rioting burghers.[38] A fortuitous invocation of the witness-people myth came in 1146 when Bernard of Clairvaux (1090–1153) was summoned by the archbishops of Cologne and Mainz to assist in quelling anti-Jewish riots associated with the Second Crusade. Bernard recalled Radulf, a Cistercian monk who had fomented anti-Jewish sentiments in the Rhineland, and preached against the madness. According to a Jewish chronicler of the period, Bernard was a symbol of divine grace:

> In His great mercy and grace, He [The Lord] sent a decent priest, one honored and respected by all the clergy in France, named Abbe Bernard of Clairvaux, to deal with this evil person [Radulf]. Bernard, too, spoke raucously, as is their manner; and this is what he said to them: 'It is good that you go against the Ishmaelites. But whosoever touches a Jew to take his life, is like one who harms Jesus himself. My disciple Radulf, who has spoken about annihilating the Jews, has spoken in error, for in the Book of Psalms it is written of them: "Slay them not, lest my people forget."'[39]

Bernard's understanding of the Jewish people's place in Christendom, and its basis in witness-people theology, are also captured in his "Letter to the People of England":

> The Jews are not to be persecuted, killed or even put to flight. Ask anyone who knows the sacred Scripture what he finds foretold of the Jews in the Psalms. "Nor for their destruction do I pray, " it says (Ps. 59:12). The Jews are for us the living words of Scripture, for they remind us always of what our Lord suffered. They are dispersed all over the world so that by expiating their crime they may be everywhere the living witnesses of our redemption. Hence the same psalm adds, "only let thy power disperse them" ... If the Jews are utterly wiped out, what will become of our hope for their promised salvation, their eventual conversion?[40]

It would be difficult to find a more succinct or sincere rendition of the witness-people theology as it had come to inform Christian thinking. Fortunately, Bernard's pastoral letters forbidding harm to Jews were for the most part heeded.[41] We may consider his approach wrong-headed since his comments only encouraged a kind of mythical apprehension of the Jewish people and reinforced their dependence on Christian charity. The point is that Bernard naturally resorted to the witness-people myth in a situation of theological and social crisis.

In the following century we discover another incident in which the witness-people myth is pressed into service to preserve Jewish life. In a letter of Gregory IX (1148–1241) written in response to Crusader massacres in France, the pope railed against those who take up the Cross, and yet

> plot impious designs against the Jews, and pay no heed to the fact that the proof for the Christian faith comes, as it were, from their archives, and that, as the prophets testified, although they should be as the sands of the sea, yet in the end of days a remnant of them shall be saved, because the Lord will not forever spurn His people.[42]

4. Thirteenth Century

Whether or not Jews were as well off as the rest of Europe's population before the thirteenth century, they undoubtedly were recognized members of European society who had an important place within it.[43] While the church's official attitude toward Jews remained as it had been since the time of Gregory I, the thirteenth-century popes implemented both sides of Gregory's witness-people principle with a striking consistency. In particular, Jewish degradation became a preoccupation of these popes, especially Innocent III.

Innocent is notorious for a policy of exclusion which relegated the Jews to a position as outsiders who should exist physically and symbolically apart from Christians. One of his prescriptions was the infamous badge decree of 1215. Innocent's philosophy of exclusion created tangible evidence of Jewish inferiority which would counteract what he called their "insolence." This term connoted the tendency of Jews to hold positions of authority over Christians, to remain religiously attractive to the faithful, to intermingle with and remain indistinguishable from Christians, and to receive preferential treatment from government.

Overall, canonical legislation affecting Jews in the thirteenth century expressed a principle that had informed legal thinking in Christian lands since the fourth century. This legal principle, which came to be known as *Servitus Judaeorum*,[44] has roots in the witness-people myth and shares in the myth's ambivalence. Despite the unprecedented degree of social isolation foisted upon the Jews in the thirteenth century by Christians who feared "contamination," the two sides of witness-people thinking remained in force.

In fact, the primary architect of the new policy of isolation continued to view the existence of Jews as a theological necessity. In classic witness-people style, Innocent argued that:

> the Lord made Cain a wanderer and a fugitive over the earth, but set a mark upon him, making his head to shake, lest any finding him should slay him. Thus the Jews, against whom the blood of Jesus Christ calls out, although they ought not to be killed, lest the Christian people forget the Divine Law, yet as wanderers ought they to remain upon the earth, until their countenance be filled with shame, and they seek the name of Jesus Christ, the Lord.[45]

Unlike his predecessors, Innocent concluded from the necessity of the Jews' survival that they required no defenders.[46] Innocent's papal successors, however, responding to the Jews' worsening status in many parts of Europe, employed both "reasons of humanity" and "reasons of piety" in arguing that they receive protection.[47-] The reasons of piety include arguments that the existence of Jews is proof of the truth of the gospel, that their degraded state is proof of the triumph of Christianity,[48] that although the Jews fail to understand their Scripture, they are its guardians,[49] that Jesus demanded the Jews' conversion be awaited patiently,[50] and that a remnant of the Jews will be saved.[51] Each of these "reasons," of course, are fundamentals of witness-people theology.

The positive, preservationist aspect of witness-people theology is especially prominent in the *constitutio pro Judaeis*, the standard bull of protection for Jews issued by all thirteenth-century popes. The *constitutio pro Judaeis* provided protection from Crusaders, from forced baptism, from the disruption of legal worship, from the charge of ritual murder, and from attacks by nobility and burghers. The spirit animating the offer of protection for Jews was the very one articulated by Gregory I seven hundred years earlier: "if no new privileges are to be granted Jews, they should not suffer restriction of rights already theirs."[52] The *constitutio pro Judaeis* was first issued by Calixtus II (1119–24), was repeated by Eugene III (1145–53), Alexander III (1159–81), Clement III (1187–91), and Coelestine III

(1191–98), and reiterated five times between 1199 and 1250. The same principle was reaffirmed at the Lateran Council of 1179.

Like the ages which precede it, the thirteenth century confronts us with an ambiguous record of Christian attitudes toward the Jewish people. Christian thinkers in the High Middle Ages developed theological justifications for a policy of exclusion and isolation, and many lower clergy contributed to mass notions of the Jew as a demonic enemy of Christendom. But beginning in the papacy of Calixtus II in the twelfth century and continuing through the fifteenth, papal bulls threatened excommunication for mistreatment of Jews not condoned under the law.[53] This pervading ambivalence toward Jews is evident also in the words of the greatest theologian of the thirteenth century, Thomas Aquinas. In his response to queries by the Duchess of Brabant, Aquinas wrote:

> Your Excellency asked, 'whether at any time and if so when, it is permissible to exact tribute of the Jews.' To such a question, put thus in general terms, one may reply that it is true, as the Law declares, that Jews, in consequence of their sin, are or were destined to perpetual slavery; so that sovereigns of states may treat their goods as their own property; with the sole proviso that they do not deprive them of all that is necessary to sustain life. But because we must bear ourselves honestly, even to those who are outcasts, lest the name of Christ be blasphemed, (as the Apostle warns us by his own example, to give no offence either to Jews or to Gentiles or to the church of God), it would seem more correct to forego what is permitted by the law ...[54]

D.   Interpreting the Shift

Historians and theologians alike recognize that the period from the late eleventh to the late thirteenth century marks a fateful shift in the nature of the Christian–Jewish relationship. Discriminated against and excluded to a greater extent than ever by official church policy, the Jews of Europe became the objects of popular delusions and paranoias that are well-documented by historians of anti-Semitism. Some have attempted to locate the turning point in the chronology of historical events. They point out that following the massacres associated with the First Crusade, blood libel, host desecration, poisoning, and sorcery charges became commonplace. An atmosphere of demonization and dehumanization took shape in which the Jew was commonly associated with the Devil and with Antichrist. Yet despite the obvious deterioration in Jewish fortunes after the late eleventh century, the causes of this change remain obscure.

There have been many attempts to isolate the social and economic factors that precipitated the shift, but several historians have sought the explanation in theological developments. Amos Funkenstein was a pioneer in this regard. In the 1960s Funkenstein contended that the theological turning point in the Christian attitude toward Jews should be located in the twelfth century. Funkenstein detected there a twofold shift in the nature of Christian theological polemics. First, according to Funkenstein, Christian writings aimed at Jews underwent a shift from reliance on christological *testimonia* extracted from the "Old Testament" to the utilization of rational proofs for the truth of Christianity. Second, increasing familiarity with contemporary Judaism encouraged Christian exploitation of and attacks upon post-biblical rabbinic literature. Funkenstein believes this move to a "rationalist stage"[55] in anti-Jewish polemic, which is especially evident in the writings of Peter the Venerable (1092–1156), was ultimately influenced by Anselm (1033–1109). Significant is the fact that the danger level for Jews increased as Christian polemics moved into the realm of rational argumentation, since opponents unmoved by rational arguments were considered *irrational*, and thus inhuman. A similar conclusion could be reached on the basis of "irrationalities" supposedly discovered in the Talmud.

In the 1980s, Jeremy Cohen offered a critique of Funkenstein's thesis when he pointed out that several heirs to Anselm's teaching do not reflect the important novelty in anti-Jewish polemic Funkenstein had elaborated. Cohen contended that even Peter the Venerable had adhered to Augustine's witness-people perspective on the Jews at crucial points in his writings.[56] Cohen's own hypothesis was that the sea change in Christian anti-Jewish polemic occurred in the thirteenth century with the emergence of a new "mendicant anti-Judaism" among Dominican and Franciscan friars. According to Cohen, novel and more virulent thinking about Jews gradually replaced the Augustinian model as the friars were enlisted by a newly dominant papacy to eliminate religious dissent within Christendom. In other words, the preservationist impulse was suspended in the thirteenth century as "the Dominicans and Franciscans developed, refined, and sought to implement a new

Christian ideology, one that allotted the Jews no legitimate right to exist in European society."[57] According to Cohen, Latin Christendom's new strategy was to rid itself of Jews through missionary activity, forced expulsions and physical harassment designed to induce conversion or flight. Cohen's argument is credible inasmuch as it takes for granted the Augustinian witness-people tradition and reveals awareness that the expulsions of the thirteenth century and beyond are inexplicable on the basis of that tradition alone:

> given the influence and involvement of the Church in all avenues of medieval life, one still wonders if the expulsion of the Jews from most of Western Europe could have proceeded as smoothly as it did, without interference or voiced opposition from the clergy, had Christian thought of the later Middle Ages remained steadfastly committed to Augustinian teaching.[58]

More recently, Gavin I. Langmuir, Jeffrey Richards and Hyam Maccoby have advanced provocative explanations of the discernible change in medieval Europe's perception and treatment of Jews. Their work complements and challenges the ideas of Funkenstein and Cohen. As discussed in the previous chapter, Langmuir regards the all-important change in the Christian attitude toward Jews as one that occurred in the transition from nonrational conflicts over incompatible religious beliefs to the irrational fantasies which stemmed from suppressed doubts. According to Langmuir, such fantasies are evident in the first charges of ritual murder, which commenced in the mid-twelfth century.

Building on the arguments of Cohen, Richards attempts to elucidate the increasing equation of Judaism and heresy in the late Middle Ages, a trend he believes was the basis for the Jews' diminished security in Europe.[59] Richards notes the role of the mendicant orders in the hereticization of the Jews and suggests that thirteenth-century Talmudic inquiries by Christians may have been a source of heretical belief. According to Richards, these inquiries also nurtured the view that Judaism was actually a heretical perversion of the "Old Testament." He cites the work of several mendicant polemicists who associate Jews, heathen and heretics, and argues that a similar conflation is reflected in papal policy:

> The medieval Papacy continued officially to advocate the protection of the Jews, but only Jews who conformed to the

Augustinian concept of the 'bearers of the Old Testament', and that protection was increasingly ineffective. The friars were more in touch with the developing popular opinion and their rabble-rousing sermons accompanied changes in the artistic and folklore representations of the Jew and a rising tide of violence against Jews.[60]

Richards also attributes the flourishing of anti-Jewish feeling in Europe to a growing medieval nationalism, the need for scapegoating which accompanied societal disasters like the Black Death, and the burgeoning preoccupation with the end of days encouraged by the writings of Joachim of Fiore. Richards observes that initially this situation was ameliorated by the patronage and protection of Christian rulers, but that the Jews' financial value to these rulers ultimately deteriorated.

In *The Sacred Executioner*, Hyam Maccoby proffers an explanation for the medieval shift in Christian attitudes toward Jews by illuminating two stages in the development of the ritual murder accusation. Maccoby claims that the first stage, in which the Jews were accused of abducting and crucifying a Christian child, was modelled on the New Testament story of Jesus' crucifixion and was associated with the Christian festival of Easter. The second stage, however, emphasized Passover and was characterized by allegations that the victim's blood was used in Passover ceremonies. According to Maccoby, "once the notion of the use of blood had entered the picture, all kinds of wild, bizarre fancies were introduced."[61]

In the first phase in the history of the ritual murder canard, the Jew was perceived as continuing his role as sacrificer, a role Maccoby views as central to the Christian myth of sacred execution. But in the second phase the Jew became "a kind of demon or werewolf or vampire." According to Maccoby, "the ancient identification of the Jews as the people of Satan here amalgamated with Christian and pagan nightmares about bloodsucking demons."[62] Maccoby regards it as significant that medieval ritual murder charges always involved the murder of a child. He interprets this as more evidence of a "significant psychological shift in the twelfth and thirteenth centuries in Christendom ... in the way in which the Jew as sacrificer was envisaged."[63]

Other scholars have traced the fateful shift in Jewish fortunes to the fifteenth century, where they discern a transition in the Christian mind from theological to racial images of the Jew. Bernard Lewis is among those who view the fifteenth century as a turning point for Christian ideology and the history of anti-Semitism:

> In medieval times hostility to the Jew, whatever its underlying social or psychological motivations, was defined primarily in religious terms. From the fifteenth century onward this was no longer true, and Jew hatred was redefined, becoming at first partly, and then, at least in theory, wholly racial.[64]

According to Lewis, religious hostility acquired racial overtones in the fifteenth century when, amid the reconquest of Muslim Spain, Spanish Jews were forced to choose between exile, conversion and death. It was not merely the rechristianizaton of Spain, however, that directed attention to Jewish "blood," for converts from Judaism had been objects of suspicion for some time. In 1449, a generation before the Spanish edict of expulsion was pronounced in 1492, a blood-purity statute was promulgated in Toledo. Initially the papacy opposed laws that discriminated against converts from Judaism, but eventually these were tolerated and approved by the church. While it is clear that the concern with "purity of blood" in pre-modern Christendom was religiously inspired, Lewis and others interpret this concern as a harbinger of modern racial anti-Semitism.[65]

Scholars continue to supplement and dispute the conclusions of pioneers like Funkenstein and Cohen, but none have offered more compelling *theological* explanations for the transformation in Jewish–Christian relations in the High Middle Ages. To the extent that they offer plausible reasons for the temporary suspension of witness-people thinking during this era, the work of Funkenstein and Cohen is especially useful. For any explanation of the changes considered here must address the fact that witness-people theology did not come to an end in the twelfth or thirteenth century. As we shall see, it is operative in every subsequent era of church history, including the present one.

E. Reformation

A great deal of recent literature on the Reformation and the Jews has focused on the anti-Jewish diatribes of Martin Luther (1483–1546) and their part in preparing the German soul for the Nazi "Final

Solution." This is understandable, since the Lutheran tradition of anti-Judaism seems to have made the German people particularly receptive to Nazi anti-Semitism. Because he has been the object of so much attention by historians and theologians, we will consider in some detail Luther's relationship to the witness-people myth.

When describing his view of the Jewish people, it is important to place Luther and his contemporaries in the proper context. But this historical context at times is obscured by Luther's assumed role as the prototypic German anti-Semite, a role Heiko Oberman calls an "orthodox [historical] canon."[66] When the proper context for Luther's writings is retrieved, however, a major caveat becomes necessary: Luther's basic anti-Jewish outlook was common to most humanists and reformers of his time, and his overall attitude to Jews actually compares favorably to some of his contemporaries, including Johannes Eck and Erasmus.[67] This proviso does not mitigate the virulence of Luther's own anti-Judaism, but it reminds us that the problem of anti-Judaism in the Reformation era is not limited to the writings of Martin Luther.

Many have been perplexed by an apparent contradiction in Luther's writings: How could the Luther who penned *Jesus Christ Was Born a Jew* (1523), a tract in which he is sympathetic to the Jews' plight and rails against Christians for treating them "as if they were dogs and not human beings,"[68] also be responsible for the incitements to mob violence which pepper *On the Jews and Their Lies* (1543)? A standard answer is that in the earlier text Luther labored under the illusion that when the Jews were shown brotherly compassion and made aware of the true gospel they would convert to Christianity as promised in Scripture. By the 1540s, however, Luther came to regard this hope as naive and in *On the Jews and Their Lies* vented his personal anti-Jewish sentiments and a frustration over the Jews' failure to convert.

Whatever explanation is offered for this change, it is on the basis of *On the Jews and Their Lies* that post-Holocaust researchers assume Luther to be without ambivalence toward Jews. He is often portrayed, in fact, as the source of a pure, genocidal hatred. While it is true that in places Luther exemplifies the "mendicant" sort of anti-Judaism described by Jeremy Cohen (and its suspension of the witness-people theory), witness-people theology is not absent from his writings on the Jews. While the witness-people doctrine is never neatly outlined in Luther's writings, there is present the kind of ambivalence toward Jews which characterizes theology influenced by the witness-people myth.

At the heart of Luther's theology of the Jews are two beliefs crucial to witness-people thinking. One is the realization that "Jesus Christ was born a Jew," and that as a result there is an organic connection between contemporary Jews and biblical Hebrews, and thus a special relationship between Jews and followers of Jesus the Jew. Another is the conviction that for their blasphemy and unbelief Jews must suffer collective dispersion and exile. However, this foundation of the Augustinian witness-people doctrine is not tempered in Luther's writings by the corollary belief that since their dispersion is a result of divine providence Jews should enjoy protection from secular and spiritual powers. Luther does stress the importance of Jewish conversion as a harbinger of the last things. But even on this matter Luther differs from many of his predecessors and contemporaries, since he does not think this conversion will occur as a mass event. Because any Jewish conversion seemed unlikely to Luther toward the end of his life, he leaned increasingly toward the option of expulsion. Yet even Luther's pleas for expulsion were based in his theological conviction that the homelessness of surviving Jews was indubitable proof of the their rejection by God.

Particularly interesting in this regard is Luther's rationale in *On the Jews and Their Lies* for the oft-quoted advice that Jews' synagogues and houses be razed, that their books be confiscated, their safe travel restricted, their usury prohibited, their worship restricted, and that personally they be subjected to expulsion. Luther's prescription is intended to bring home to Jews the theological realities that they are "living in exile and captivity," and are not "masters in our country." But Luther also contends that because Christians have failed to convert the Jews they instead should practice a "sharp mercy" which may ultimately bring salvation to a few. This is necessary, Luther writes, because "God's anger with them is so intense that gentle mercy will only tend to make them worse and worse...."[69] Christians cannot force Jews to believe, but neither can they risk confirming them in their blasphemy, which they should have recognized during their "fifteen-hundred-year exile." Later in *On the Jews and Their Lies* Luther employs the same term "sharp mercy" in describing his prescription for treating the Jews: Our rulers "must act like a good physician who, when gangrene has set in, proceeds without mercy to cut, saw, and burn flesh, veins, bone and marrow."[70]

This metaphor, as offensive as it is to modern sensibilities, reveals that Luther's ultimate intention is to bring healing. And unlike

Hitler, it is the salvation of Jews (as well as the German *Volk*) which he seeks. Luther provides a *theological* rationale for his harsh ravings against the Jews and this rationale is fraught with the ambivalence of witness-people thinking. Luther warns that despite their providential suffering at the hands of God Christians are prohibited from avenging themselves upon Jews. Yet it is easy to understand how the nuances of witness-people theology might be overwhelmed by Luther's extreme advice to the governing authorities.

Ambivalence *vis-à-vis* the Jews also is perceptible in Luther's contemporary Johannes Reuchlin (1455–1522). Reuchlin evinces a genuine respect for the Hebrew language, argues for a (Christianized) cabalistic method of reading the Scriptures, and views Jews as "co-citizens" with equal civil rights whose conversion must be sought "gently and kindly." On the other hand, he argues for a separation of the Hebraic tradition from Judaism, and a thoroughgoing rejection of the Talmud.[71] In fact, Reuchlin believes that conversion offers the only relief for Jewish suffering and exile, conditions he was sure were a divine punishment for their collective guilt.[72] While Reuchlin is commonly viewed as a friend of the Jews, he actually displays the same ambivalence (Oberman refers to Reuchlin's policy toward the Jews as "Janus-faced") found in other Christian thinkers of his time, including Luther.

In his characterization of the age of Renaissance and Reformation, Heiko Oberman highlights the essential ambivalence toward Jews that we have noted: "Hatred of the Jews did not exist apart from protection of the Jews; these were two sides of the same coin...."[73] Oberman observes that Christian anti-Jewish fanaticism often vacillated between the options of mass conversion and mass expulsion of Jews. This observation is confirmed in Luther's final written statement, penned three days before his death: "We ought to practice Christian love and beg them to convert, ... if they refuse we should neither tolerate them nor suffer their presence in our midst."[74]

Can Luther be said, then, to "conform to the classical position of Christendom"[75] with regard to the Jews? The answer must be yes and no. For Luther, as for nearly every Christian theologian who preceded him, the Jews are both the people of God and deniers of God's Son. Luther retained this Augustinian ambivalence: On one hand, he viewed Jews as a unique people to whom God had given the prophets, the sacred writings and Jesus Christ the Messiah. This implied a special bond with Christians, and Luther believed that, unlike heretics, Jews could be tolerated in Christendom. He spoke out against the burning of Jewish books in 1514, and wrote in the 1520s that "the Jews are the blood relatives, the cousins and brothers of Our Lord...."[76] Luther also expressed an ardent hope in the salvation of a Jewish remnant through conversion, which he thought Christians should encourage by treating Jews in a friendly manner. On the other hand, Luther was convinced that Jewish exile signified divine punishment upon their unbelief and blasphemy.

Yet in Luther's writings on the Jews there is much which does not correspond to the witness-people tradition. When Luther interprets Jewish misfortune as a "proof" of God's providence, he also sees in it proof of the Jews' displacement from salvation history:

> for one dare not regard God as so cruel that he would punish his own people so long, so terribly, so unmercifully, and in addition keep silent, comforting them neither with words nor with deeds, and fixing no time limit and no end to it. Who would have faith, hope, or love toward such a God? Therefore this work of wrath is proof that the Jews, surely rejected by God, are no longer his people, and neither is he any longer their God.[77]

Luther also severely weakens (if he does not sever altogether) the assumption underlying witness-people theology that the original elect people of God and contemporary Jews belong to one and the same people. In *On the Jews and Their Lies* Luther contends that there are "two classes of Jews or Israelites," those of Moses and those of "the emperor." This latter group is dated from the time of Pilate and includes those who according to the gospels shouted "We have no king but Caesar!" It is from these Jews who soon were exiled throughout the empire, Luther concludes, that "the present remnant of Jews descended, of whom Moses knows nothing."[78] Simply put, Luther denies that the Jews of his day are "Hebrews." Thus, they are not due the sort of respect owed the true people of God.

In places, Luther also dissents from the witness-people principle that the Jews possess a permanent home in Christendom, and seems to adopt the view that the adherents of rabbinic Judaism do not warrant preservation. In this Luther seems to have been influenced by the apocalyptic *Zeitgeist* which severely tested the patience regarding Jewish conversion that had previously characterized Christian attitudes. Luther lived in an era of turmoil in which Christians, especially those allied with the Reformation, felt threatened by internal and external forces. Reflecting this atmosphere, Luther lumped together all perceived enemies of true Christianity – Jews, heretics, the heathen, sinners and Turks – as associates of Antichrist, adopting this "chain of iniquity" as a key to biblical exegesis and theology in his later writings.[79] His later writings on the Jews, then, should be regarded as "an expression of Luther's assessment of the condition of the church at the close of history."[80]

While this portrayal of the Jews as agents of the Devil rings of popular superstition rather than of theological reflection, it is nevertheless pervaded by the witness-people notion that the Jews are "signs" and "keys." The Jews serve Luther "as precise coordinates for charting evil's invasion of the church in [his] own day.... The critical issue is that the Jews are a prototypic 'compass' for determining the devil's points of penetration into the contemporary church."[81] For Luther the Jews are "the key to the interpretation of the age," a people with an "exemplary, diagnostic and deterrent function."[82] In his writings, anti-Jewish sentiments and apocalyptic expectations are indissolubly tied together.

F. Restorationism

The apocalyptic atmosphere which animates the later writings of Luther existed in parts of Europe into the seventeenth century. R.H. Popkin describes the mood that permeated these times:

> For quite a few Protestant leaders the Reformation itself indicated that the culmination of Christian history was at hand. For some Counter-Reformers the purification of the Church indicated that the final act of world history would shortly occur. Other developments such as the Thirty Years War, the Turkish invasion of central Europe, the Puritan Revolution, the preaching of the Gospel in America, Asia and Africa all reinforced this expectation.[83]

Yet post-Reformation apocalypticism issued in a considerably more positive understanding of the Jews and their future than was common during the sixteenth century. The change was rooted in three perceptible shifts in theological thinking. The first concerned the expected arrival of the so-called millennium. The majority of sixteenth-century reformers had accepted the Augustinian view of the thousand-year period referred to in Revelation 20, which equated the millennium with church history itself. Both Luther and Calvin rejected the connection of religious revival and chiliasm as this was manifest among the radical reformers of their day.[84] Within a century of Luther's death, however, millenarian expectation of every kind characterized Protestant Christianity in America, Britain, Holland and Germany. Especially in Cromwellian England millenarian speculation tended to be postmillennial – that is, Christ's Second Coming was expected after a millennial kingdom had been established on earth.

A second theological shift concerned hopes for Jewish conversion. While conversion of the Jews had been awaited for centuries, expectations of a corporate Jewish conversion that would yield great blessings for the church were rekindled by allusions to the salvation of "Israel" in Romans 11:25ff.[85] Some thinkers of this period optimistically predicted a "latter-day glory," an outpouring of the Spirit that would accompany the promised conversion of the Jews. A third theological change that affected thinking about Jews was the development of Protestant Restorationism. "Restorationism" denotes the Christian belief that Jews will be restored to their homeland in biblical Israel as a sign of God's impending millennial reign, usually just before, after or during a mass conversion of Jews to Christianity.[86] Restorationist thought was a feature of nearly all millenarian thinking in the sixteenth through eighteenth centuries. It was central to Puritan theology in Holland, Britain, and America, where the Mathers and Jonathan Edwards were among its notable proponents.

Restorationism is an eschatological hope animated by the promise of a peaceful future rather than the threat of an insecure present. Unlike the apocalyptic eschatology of the late Middle Ages and Reformation which highlighted Satan's plot to destroy Christendom, the identity of Antichrist and the world's end, seventeenth-century Restorationist thought focused on promises of latter-day glory, conversion of the Jews, inauguration on earth of God's millennial reign, and Christ's Second Coming.[87] It recognized Jews as partners in waiting rather than colleagues of the Devil. To the present day, Christians influenced by Restorationist thought perceive in the experience of contemporary Jews unambiguous signs of Israel's ultimate salvation.

In the seventeenth century the Restorationist impulse was most pronounced in "Reformed" societies. This is because Calvinist Christians were wont to identify their struggle and mission with those of

biblical Jews.[88] In fact, many carriers of Calvinist theology were refugees from Germany, France and the Netherlands who were familiar
with a diaspora existence. As Heiko Oberman observes,

> One of the outstanding features of the 'Third [Calvinist]
> Reformation' was the new stance taken toward the 'miserable'
> Jews. Exile, and not the castigation of the Jews, became the
> distinctive mode of existence for God's people in all ages."
> ...
> Once the homeless, fugitive Christians were compelled to share
> the destiny of the Jews, expulsion no longer bore the unambigu-
> ous marks of a God-sent punishment. The destiny of worldwide
> diaspora, formerly the proof of the obstinate Jew's guilt, was now
> the badge of faith of the avowed Christian.[89]

Significantly, when they came under Calvinist control in the late
sixteenth century, the Low Countries became a refuge for Jews experiencing persecution in Spain and elsewhere.[90] And in the
seventeenth century Jews were granted new civil rights in lands
influenced by the Calvinist Reformation. Although Reformed
Christians retained a conversionist attitude, their Calvinist emphasis on the "Old Testament" and its (moral) law established a special
ideological bond between them and the Jewish people.

Restorationist theology had emerged in England in the late
sixteenth century, with the first developed plan for the restoration of
the Jews being published by Sir Henry Finch (1558–1625) in 1621.[91]
Restorationist ideas gained wide circulation in England by the
1640s, with the restorationist outlook being found among both
traditionalists and freethinkers. Eventually it took hold in other
parts of Europe, including Germany and France. But it was the
English Puritans among whom general interest in the Jews was
greatest at this time. Largely due to Puritan influence, "by 1600
Jewish law and history had earned a central place in British
culture."[92] Puritans evinced a special sympathy for Jews that was
rooted in a sense of shared persecution and perceptions of a similar
faith and common philosophy of life.[93]

The American Puritans who settled New Plymouth and Massachusetts Bay colonies exemplified this attraction to things Jewish:

> New England Puritans patterned their laws upon the Mosaic
> codes of the Old Testament, and they adopted the experiences of

the early Hebrews as a model on which to shape their own lives. Like the Jews of old they conceived themselves to be chosen by God to perform a special mission in the wilderness of the New World.[94]

Along with their sense of being set apart by God for a unique mission, many American Puritans possessed a love for the Hebrew language, a sentiment that in Christian Europe had been limited to biblical scholars and humanists. Intense interest in Jewish conversion and restoration as a prelude to the end of days and the Second Coming also marked the thinking of American Puritans, including Increase Mather, John Davenport, William Hooke and Samuel Willard.[95] While New England had few Jews who could serve as objects of the Puritans' conversionist fervor, some missionized the Native Americans, whom it was commonly believed were members of the "ten lost tribes" of Israel.[96]

It is not difficult to discern the ambivalence of the witness-people tradition in Puritan attitudes toward the Jews. On one hand, Jews were regarded as important signs of – and even instruments for bringing about – God's millennial reign.[97] On the other hand, the negative witness-people notions of providential dispersion and ultimate conversion to Christianity were central to the hopes of many Puritans. A particularly lucid example of Puritan ambivalence may be found in the apocalyptic writings of Jonathan Edwards, whose postmillennial eschatology unmistakably reflects the witness-people myth:

> when [the Jews'] unbelief ceases, their dispersion, the dreadful and signal punishment of their unbelief will cease too.... And as they have hitherto continued as a distinct nation, that they might continue a *visible monument of his displeasure*, for their rejecting and crucifying their Messiah, so after their conversion [which will occur before the arrival of the Lord] will they still be a distinct nation, that they may be a *visible monument of God's wonderful grace and power* in their calling and conversion.[98]

The majority of Puritan and non-Puritan Restorationists in the seventeenth century were convinced that restoration would follow a mass conversion of the Jews. Yet Christian approaches to conversion assumed a more friendly tenor in this era. Many Christian Restorationists in England and Holland heeded Augustine's advice to "preach to them in love" by working to make Christianity less offensive to Jews, and by assisting Christians in understanding and appreciating Judaism in its contemporary forms.[99] These goals were realized through close cooperation between Jews and philosemitic Christian millenarians.

Thus, in many ways Jews actually encouraged Christian Restorationist thinking in the post-Reformation era. They did so indirectly through the influence of their own messianic expectations. These burgeoned following the expulsion of Jews from Spain in 1492, were encouraged by Isaac Luria's (d. 1572) cabalistic teachings in the sixteenth century, and culminated in the seventeenth-century pseudo-messianic appearance of Sabbatai Zvi.[100] Some well-known Jews, including the Amsterdam Rabbi Menasseh ben Israel, welcomed the Restorationists' support for their own messianic longings. They worked side by side with Christians in seeking the Jews' readmission to England, and developed a joint "Judeo-Christian" outline of the future – a two-Messiah theory that affirmed both Jewish and Christian eschatological hopes.[101]

Jewish scholars also cooperated with Restorationists in disseminating knowledge of post-biblical Judaism among them. Christians of a millenarian bent acknowledged that contemporary Judaism was based primarily on the Mishna and Talmud rather than the Christian "Old Testament." But this realization only encouraged Restorationists' hopes that a better informed Christianity would be a Christianity less offensive to Jews, and thus less of an obstacle to Jewish conversion and restoration. Jewish–Christian symbiosis also received impetus in the Christian discovery of the Caraites, a Jewish sect which rejected post-biblical developments in Judaism.[102]

To summarize, ambivalence toward the Jewish people continued to define Protestant thought in the post-Reformation era. A striking example of this fact is the seventeenth-century campaign by British Restorationists to have Jews readmitted to that country – a campaign motivated, ironically, by their desire to see fulfilled the prophecy that the Jews would be dispersed to all corners of the earth as a prelude to final restoration in the land of Israel. There was a corresponding ambivalence toward Jews in popular attitudes as well. Frank Felsenstein has observed that "by a curious paradox, the diabolical stereotype and the view of the Jews as God's chosen people were to exist side by side in the England of the later Renaissance."[103]

The age of millenarian and Restorationist thinking saw an intens-ification in the positive side of the witness-people tradition: It was widely agreed that the conversion and restoration of the Jews was the most important sign or precondition of the promised millennial kingdom. Also, in encouraging a favorable response to the Christian message among Jews, Christian Restorationists downplayed the witness-people notions of Jewish degradation and exile, viewing these as relics of a past age.[104] Finally, Jews became the objects of intense curiosity and respect for many who were wont to emphasize that contemporary Jews were living descendents of the biblical Hebrews.

Overall, Protestant Christians experienced a heightened sense of identification with Jewish failure and Jewish promise in the sixteenth and seventeenth centuries. But if this period saw a Christian transformation of witness-people thinking which high-lighted its positive elements and diminished its emphasis on Jewish degradation and suffering, a transformation in the opposite direction ultimately characterized the modern, post-Enlightenment world.

II.   MODERN AND SECULAR VERSIONS OF THE WITNESS-PEOPLE MYTH

A.   Enlightenment and Emancipation

Despite an increase in toleration for the Jew in certain countries of Western Europe immediately after the Reformation, it was only in the secularized world spawned by the Age of Reason that Jews gradually won Emancipation. The price of secular emancipation, however, was a loss of recognition for collective religious identity. The sacrifice of Jewish peoplehood is symbolized by a French version of the terms of Emancipation: "Jews should be denied everything as a nation, but granted everything as individuals."[105]

In place of a popular Christian ideology that depicted Jews as a deicide race paying for their momentous crime, the new rationalists disseminated the notions that Judaism was a crude superstition and the Jews an eternally perverse race.[106] For eighteenth-century *philosophes* like Voltaire, Christianity became an object of enlightened disdain and hostility. But their anti-Christianity did not make these men pro-Jewish. In fact, they often clung to the sort of degrading stereotypes of Jews which had characterized Christian polemic at its worst. Many influential Enlightenment figures brutally rejected Judaism as the root of Christianity. As Bernard Lewis remarks, "if for Christians, the crime of the Jews was that they had killed Christ, for the new anti-Christians it was rather that they had nurtured him."[107]

Another aspect of the mixed blessing which the Enlightenment brought Europe's Jews was even more insidious. For Enlightenment rationality had the effect of fostering the growth of racism. Historian of anti-Semitism Leon Poliakov elaborates the relationship between the triumph of Enlightenment ideas over the primitive dogmas of the church and the apotheosis of anti-Semitism in the first half of the twentieth century:

> At a period when the nascent sciences of biology and anthropology classified living beings in fixed and immutable genera and species, such views contained the germ of a racism *avant la lettre.* Thus the grandiose edifice of the church was breached and a historian of ideas could readily reconstruct the thread that leads from Spinoza to Herder, Fichte and Hegel, and also to Schleiermacher and Harnack. It is in this context that the "divine" interpretation was replaced by the "racial" one: the prerogative of an elite in the eighteenth century, the property of the masses in the nineteenth, and in the twentieth affording an ideological justification for the crematory ovens.[108]

Modern anti-Semitism had its roots in non-religious and quasi-religious movements as diverse as eighteenth-century linguistic research and nineteenth-century Romanticism, socialism, and Social Darwinism. Is there any connection, then, between Christian witness-people theology and so-called modern anti-Semitism?

1.   The Witness-People Myth and the Transition between Religious and "Enlightened" Thinking about Jews

The witness-people conception of the Jews continued to influence European history into the nineteenth century. For instance, as Napoleon anticipated the conquest of Jerusalem in the 1798–99 campaign, he assumed the persona of a modern day Cyrus, summoning the "Israelites" to return to their ancestral home and claim "the unlimited right to worship Jehovah in accordance with [their] faith, publicly and most probably forever."[109] Evidence of the witness-people mentality's admixture with modern, racial notions of Jewish peculiarity is plenteous as well.

One example of this phenomenon is Johann Eisenmenger's book *Entdektes Judentum*. In the midst of an era which sought to "subvert the fundamentals of theological thought and reject the conclusions based on it,"[110] Eisenmenger reasserted classical Christian thinking about Jews. Although its title ("Judaism Uncovered") suggested his book was a work of scientific inquiry, Eisenmenger actually recapitulated the oldest Christian interpretation of Jewish existence. He transmitted the witness-people tradition in his convictions about the significance of Jewish exile, his pleas for Jewish degradation, and his hopes for Jewish salvation. And despite his accusations of ritual murder, Eisenmenger sought only to place restrictions on Jews, not to have them expelled or annihilated. As Jacob Katz comments,

> the primary reason for Eisenmenger's relative tolerance is that one should not give up the hope that the Jews will one day see the truth and acknowledge the Christian religion.... Indeed, one of the reasons that Eisenmenger sought to worsen the degradation and suppression of the Jews was to make them feel the burden of their lowly position and to see that they had no salvation from it but through Christianity.[111]

Eventually, however, even de-theologized forms of witness-people thinking lost their power and popularity in the nineteenth century as a corresponding secular myth gained in influence. Recent research suggests that the truly fateful ideas about Jews in the post-Enlightenment era cast them as arch-conspirators plotting to control or destroy Western civilization. This modern myth and its effects have been analyzed incisively by Norman Cohn in his study of "The Protocols of the Elders of Zion" and its mythic progenitors.[112] Cohn elucidates how the Jewish world-conspiracy myth arose as a reaction to societal changes, to the "revolution" of 1848, and to the mysterious forces of evil associated with large cities like Paris.

There are connections, of course, between traditional Christian notions about Jews and the conspiracy myth which reached its apotheosis in the *Protocols*. In fact, post-Enlightenment conspiracy theories adapted the Christian legend of a council of rabbis who meet periodically in Moorish Spain to plot war against Christendom, and utilized medieval images of Jews as waiting for

Antichrist, as servants of Satan, and as mortal enemies of Christendom.[113] But as is true of modern anti-Semitism in general, some elements of Christian theology are incorporated while others are excluded. In particular, modern conspiracy thinking transmits the witness-people perception of Jews as a unique people and as key players in history who determine society's fortunes, while notions of the Jews' eschatological significance and the importance of their preservation within society are lost. While post-Enlightenment anti-Jewish conspiracies utilize medieval Christian fantasies like the Wandering Jew and blood libel, they emphasize the Jews' exclusion and annihilation, not the theological significance of their survival. The theological hope for conversion and restoration and the related teaching of preservation simply lost much of their credibility with the failing prestige of the church. In the mental universe of the conspiracists, Jews retained the mysterious quality they had acquired in the Christian imagination, but came to personify the sinister and frightening qualities of the modern world.

The Jew's signifying function in the modern mind also is suggested by the popularity of what might be called the "Jews, your majesty!" legend. The legend is recorded by a variety of modern writers, among them historians of anti-Semitism and Christian fundamentalists, and is attributed to a variety of sources. In his definitive history of anti-Semitism, Leon Poliakov reports that the physician of Frederick II of Prussia, when asked for proof of God's existence, replied "the Jews, your majesty."[114] Similarly, speaking at the International Prophecy Conference in Boston in 1901, William G. Moorehead related that "'the Jews, your majesty' was the pertinent reply of the believing courtier when Frederick the Great asked him for the credentials of the Bible."[115] American evangelist Pat Robertson tells a version of the story involving Queen Victoria and her Prime Minister Disraeli. According to Robertson, when asked to cite the "greatest evidence of God's existence," Disraeli responded "the Jew, your majesty."[116] In the 1930s, American evangelist Louis S. Bauman recounted essentially the same story, without ascribing a source:

> An eminent man once said, "the universal dispersion of the Jews throughout the world, their unexampled sufferings and their marvelous preservation, would be enough to establish the truth of the Scriptures if all other evidence was cast into the sea."[117]

In other versions of the tale, the monarch seeking confirmation of God's existence in a world of nascent rationalism is Peter the Great or Napoleon.[118]

In its many variations, the "Jews, your majesty!" legend is a post-Enlightenment version of a conviction that is deeply imbedded in the Western (Christian) imagination: The Jews are a unique people and their dispersion, survival, and very existence are a "miracle." For Christians the miracle of Jewish life has always indicated God's providential care. But in a deistic or agnostic environment where God's involvement with the world is not taken for granted, the Jews become invoked as proof of God's very existence.

2. Witness-People Thinking, Christianity and the Holocaust

To what extent did Christians and Christianity contribute to the Holocaust? Anyone answering this question confronts both historical and emotional difficulties, but answers must be sought. A standard response to the question is that while Christian anti-Judaism was not a sufficient condition for Nazi genocide, it was indeed a necessary condition. It is beyond debate that in every country in which the Nazi terror gained a foothold Christian participation made the *Shoah* possible. But what effect did "Christian" theology have on the decisions of individual Christians to welcome or tolerate the Nazi solution to the "Jewish question"? Certainly many Christians were led to complicity in Nazi crimes by Christian stereotypes and myths about Jews and Judaism. And yet other Christians, some of whom risked their lives to rescue Jews, cite their Christian convictions as the basis for their opposition to the Nazis and their Jewish policies.[119]

It is often difficult to determine the motivations of persons who were actively involved in perpetrating or resisting the Nazi "Final Solution." If the mixed record of Christians during the Holocaust allows for any general conclusions, however, perhaps they are these: First, teachings of Jewish exile and degradation made European Christians susceptible to the rhetoric and propaganda of modern, racial anti-Semites, including Hitler and his followers. Second, some Christians perceived in the persecution of Jews, especially the public degradations inside Germany in the thirties, confirmation of the accursed state which Christian theology seemed to require for the crucifiers of Jesus. Third, many Christians who resisted the Nazis' treatment of Jews were motivated by reservations that were theological.

The first and second conclusions are supported by the "pseudo-religious and pseudomessianic"[120] rhetoric through which Nazism attempted to appeal to the Jew-obsession of many Christians. But in the shift from theology to ideology out of which the Nazi universe of pseudo-religious symbolism came into being, Christian witness-people thinking ceased to function. This fact is borne out in Hitler's own speeches and writings. In describing the Jew, Hitler was wont to use religious images that appealed to the popular German imagination and its anti-Jewish bent. According to Hitler,

> No one need be surprised if among our people the personification of the Devil as the symbol of all evil assumes the living shape of the Jews.

> Hence today I believe I am acting in accordance with the will of the Almighty Creator: by defending myself against the Jew, I am fighting for the work of the Lord.

> Two worlds face one another – the men of God and men of Satan! The Jew is the anti-man, the creature of another god. He must have come from another root of the human race. I set the Aryan and the Jew over and against each other.[121]

These quotations offer a glimpse of Hitler's apocalyptic – even Manichean[122] – conception of the conflict between the worlds of "Aryan" and "Jew." But while Hitler's vision was apocalyptic, it was not millennial in the Christian sense, a sense that requires Jews to remain until God has finished working through them to consummate history. Thus, Nazi racial law – and modern racial anti-Semitism in general – is incompatible with Christian Jew-hatred to the extent that they deny that Jews are redeemable through conversion.[123] It is true that some of Hitler's sentiments have demonstrable roots in the Christian tradition, from the Gospel of John to the Antichrist hysteria of the Middle Ages and Luther's anti-Jewish apocalypticism. And yet the positive dimensions of the Christian view of the Jew are missing. In fact, the "Jew as sign" premise of witness-people thinking has been transformed so that the unique significance of Jews is now purely negative. No ambivalence remains.

A story that is narrated as a way of establishing continuity between Christianity and Nazism actually illustrates how Hitler stealthily redefined the Christian theological notion of the Jew.

According to Hitler's *Table Talk*, when two bishops visited the Führer to dissent from his racial policies, Hitler cleverly but mistakenly claimed he was only putting into effect the policies Christianity had preached for two thousand years.[124] Hitler's transformation of the witness-people tradition is also discernible in *Mein Kampf*. Hitler follows Christian interpreters in regarding the remarkable survival of the Jews as a "proof." But it is a proof of their profound instinct toward self-preservation, not of the reality of divine providence. And while Hitler utilizes the Christian image of the Jew as exile and wanderer, he is careful to point out that the Jew is no "nomad." The nomadic life, which for Hitler is an early stage in the history of creative races, is substituted by the image of the Jew as "parasite." Furthermore, Jews are not witnesses to God's punishment upon unbelievers, but are *themselves* "the scourge of God." In his most important departure from the classical Christian approach, Hitler denies that the Jews' religious identity is important to understanding their true nature. The Jews, he says, are a not a religious community at all, but a "race."[125] Exploiting traditional prejudices as they fit his plan, Hitler is determined to counteract any tendency on the part of his readers to think of Jews as a religious community or the "Jewish problem" as solvable in religious terms.

But what about the statements by Christians who seemed to believe that Christianity and Nazism had essentially the same plan for the Jew? Careful examination of the words of Christian leaders who fostered anti-Semitism in Nazi Europe reveals the extent to which they were corrupting classical Christian theology. As an example, we may take the statements referred to by Irving Greenberg in his seminal article "Cloud of Smoke, Pillar of Fire: Judaism, Christianity and Modernity After the Holocaust."[126] Greenberg cites Slovakian Archbishop Kametko's response to the pleas of the Nietra Rebbe in 1942:

> It is not just a matter of deportation. You will not die there of hunger and disease. They will slaughter all of you there, old and young alike, women and children, at once – it is the punishment that you deserve for the death of our Lord and Redeemer, Jesus Christ – you have only one solution. Come over to our religion and I will work to annul this decree.[127]

Greenberg also cites German Archbishop Grober, who in a pastoral letter blamed the Jews for the death of Christ and added that "the self-imposed curse of the Jews, 'His blood be upon us and upon our children,' had come true terribly, until the present time, until today."[128]

Responding to such sentiments, Greenberg concludes that "in general there is an inverse ratio between the presence of a fundamentalist Christianity and the survival of the Jews during the Holocaust." But this claim is greatly misleading. It does not account for the thousands of committed Christians who rescued Jews throughout Europe, often acting out of their religious convictions. But even more importantly, it implies that anti-Semitic Christians (of whom there were perhaps millions in Europe) embodied the "fundamental" essence of Christian faith. Clearly, the statements cited by Greenberg recapitulate popular Christian notions about Jews being accursed, exiled and reprobate, and reflect the conviction that the Jews' contemporary misfortunes confirm God's providential ordering of history. But just as clearly, both statements obscure the preservationist impulse that is part and parcel of the witness-people myth. The first statement, in fact, has precious little continuity with traditional Christian thinking, since it approves of Jewish slaughter and treats forced conversion favorably.

Tragically, during the Holocaust there were influential Christians whose failure to maintain both sides of the witness-people doctrine contributed to the suffering of Jews. Yosef Yerushalmi emphasizes this point, observing that the reprobation element in Christian thinking about Jews remained entrenched in the 1930s and 40s while the preservationist element somehow became inoperative. Analyzing the behavior of the papacy during the Nazi era, Yerushalmi writes:

> ...my private *J'accuse* is based on the fact that [Pius XII] *broke*, in essence, with the tradition of the medieval popes. It is precisely because the medieval papacy managed to speak out for the Jews *in extremis* that the silence of the Vatican during World War II is all the more deafening.[129]

Claiming that "European Jewry from 1933 to 1945 could have lived under the formulations of the *Siete Partidas*" [a medieval Spanish document outlining the classical Christian view of the Jew], Yerushalmi concludes that the church's behavior during the Nazi era was a modern, not a medieval phenomenon.

Recognizing the discontinuity between classical Christian anti-

Judaism and the history of the Nazi era does not lead to a denial of Christianity's share of responsibility for the Holocaust. The evidence for responsibility is dreadfully clear. Many Christians were directly involved in genocide, and Christian theology contributed to an intellectual ethos of hostility to Jews which affected even those perpetrators who were not believing Christians. The history of the Nazi era seems to yield the disturbing conclusion that while Christianity was not a sufficient condition for the Holocaust, it did little if anything to stem the Nazi onslaught against the Jewish people.

The Christian witness-people myth placed Jews at the center of a mythology of history; but this myth was impotent to insure the Jews' preservation when a competing Jew-centered mythology was spawned in the modern era. For many European Christians, the positive side of the Christian witness-people myth (the preservationist teaching) was suppressed during the Nazi era, while the negative side (the degradation teaching as well as the popular notion of the Jew as the enemy of Christendom) was activated and intensified. But does the Holocaust represent the end of the witness-people tradition in Christian theology? The chapters which follow demonstrate that the witness-people myth is still the grid through which many, many Christians interpret Jewish existence and envision the Jewish future.

4

Karl Barth, the German Church Struggle and the Witness-People Myth

The aggravating image of Judaic Christianity must remain in the German Church as a living monument ... that Christian faith is not a national religion.

Hans Ehrenberg, Letter to Gerhard Jacobi, July 5, 1933

After the death of Christ, Israel was dismissed from the service of Revelation ... and from that time forth Assuerus wanders, forever restless, over the face of the earth. Even after the death of Christ the Jews are still a "mystery," as St. Paul says (Rom. 11:25); and one day, at the end of time, for them too the hour of grace will strike (Rom. 11:26).

Michael von Faulhaber, "Judaism, Christianity and Germany."

I. BARTH AND "ISRAEL"

In another place I have described Barth's "theology of Israel" as simultaneously radical and traditional.[1] Barth displayed the radical side of his Israel doctrine when he spoke out against Jewish persecution and declared that anti-Semitism was anti-Christian, when he emphasized the continuing and irrevocable nature of Israel's divine election, when he engaged in private and public dialogues with rabbis and Jewish intellectuals, when he pronounced Christian mission to the Jews "theologically impossible," and when he took to task the authors of the Vatican's "Nostra aetate" for its classification of Judaism as a "non-Christian religion."

Barth revealed his debt to a traditional understanding of the Jewish people when he defined Israel as "the people of the Jews which resists its divine election," when he viewed the goal of Israel's existence as integration into the church, when he reiterated aspects of the patristic and medieval anti-Jewish tradition, when he gave credence to the deicide charge and the notion that the Jews remain in the world as a witness to God's judgment, and when he acknowledged a "totally irrational aversion" to Jews which he conceded probably influenced his theology.[2] At several distinct points, and especially in its overall ambivalence, Barth's theology of Israel reflected the influence of the Christian witness-people myth.

A. Barth's Early Theology

In the work that signalled his abrupt entrance onto the stage of German theology, his *Der Römerbrief* of 1918, Barth displayed a preference for theological over strict historical interpretation. This preference is especially evident in Barth's treatment of Israel. In *Der Römerbrief* "Israel" signifies not merely the Jewish people, but the theological entity that came into being when a group of ancient Hebrews became the objects of God's self-revelation. The history through which he lived, however, eventually frustrated Barth's desire to treat Israel purely as a theological phenomenon.

In the decade following the publication of *Der Römerbrief*, the question of Israel's theological significance was superseded in Germany by the "Jewish question." Anti-Semitism, though it had a long history in Europe, nevertheless flourished in the wake of the same cultural apocalypse that made *Der Römerbrief* so salient. Popular hostility toward Jews was nourished by resentment at Germany's war defeat and by the subsequent foundering of the Weimar Republic. In 1928 Barth was responding to this rising tide of anti-Semitism when he exhorted the Protestant church to remember its roots:

> We are persuaded that the Anti-semitic movement, which in the aftermath of the world war has had so mighty a boom, is irreconcilable with the Christian point of view and is incompatible with our debt of gratitude to the cradle of Christianity.[3]

A more sustained response to anti-Semitism was required in the spring and summer of 1933 when some Christians sought to make the Nazi "Aryan paragraph" official policy in the German Evangelical Church. In July Barth met the challenge by publishing the first of what became an important series of pamphlets under the title *Theologische Existenz Heute.* Barth publicly opposed the introduction of Nazi ideology in the church by contending that

> The community of those belonging to the church is defined not through blood and therefore also not through race, but through the Holy Spirit and through baptism. If the German Evangelical Church excludes the Jewish Christians, or if they are treated as second class citizens, they will have stopped being the Christian Church.[4]

With these words Barth declared a *status confessionis* over opposition to the Aryan paragraph and officially entered the German Church Struggle. Barth quickly became the leading figure in the "Confessing Church" movement, whose members dissented from Nazi ideology but found their *raison d'être* in resisting the Nazification of the church. Their primary struggle was with the "German Christians" who embraced Hitler and viewed the church's task as acceptance and support of Hitler's policies. The threat they posed was revealed in November 1933 when at the infamous "Sportpalace Rally" the German Christians demonstrated their intention of wedding the cross and the swastika and rendering Hitler their unquestioning support.

In May of 1934 Confessing Church delegates gathered at the Synod of Barmen to register their opposition to the German Christian heresy.[5] Composed mainly by Barth, the "Declaration" which emerged from Barmen is typically regarded as a symbol of the heroic stance which the Confessors assumed *vis-à-vis* the Nazis. The document has become part of the confessional tradition of the Reformed churches where it is often considered a landmark of theologically-grounded political opposition.[6] The Barmen Declaration was not a summons to direct resistance against the Nazi state's totalitarian aims, however, but a vilification of German Christians' "false doctrine" and "alien principles." Significantly, Barmen's condemnation of the German Christians

> did not lead on to a theological statement of the promise and tribulation of Israel's election, let alone any expression of solidarity with the Jews in their suffering.[7]

Toward the end of his life Barth acknowledged his failure to produce a statement of solidarity with the Jews, and offered this intriguing explanation:

I have long since regarded it as a fault on my part that I did not make this question a decisive issue, at least publicly in the church conflict (e.g., in the two Barmen declarations I drafted in 1934). A text in which I might have done so would not, of course, have been acceptable to the mindset of even the "confessors" of that time, whether in the Reformed or the general synod. But this does not excuse the fact that since my interests were elsewhere I did not at least formally put up a fight on the matter.[8]

This candid admission that he had failed on so crucial a matter suggests Barth's great personal integrity. But his *mea culpa* does not explain why Barth "did not at least formally put up a fight on the matter," and why a statement of solidarity with persecuted Jews would have encountered resistance from "even the 'confessors' of that time." Were Barth and his colleagues simply occupied with other matters, as he suggests? Or were they influenced by the way Christians in general think about Jews and their travail?

One thing is certain. Despite having "interests elsewhere," Barth was not unconcerned with the theological import of the Jewish persecution that was then taking place in Germany. In December 1933 Barth had preached a sermon on Romans 15: 5–13 in the Castle Church at Bonn. His words unmistakably reflected the political upheavals of the previous year:

It is not self-evident that we belong to Jesus Christ and he to us. Christ belongs to the people Israel. The blood of this people was in his veins the blood of the Son of God. This people's form he adopted, while he adopted the being of man.... Jesus Christ was a Jew, but in taking up and taking away the sins of the Jews, the sins of the whole world and even our own, the salvation of the Jews has come also to us. How can we, each time we think about this, not be obliged to think above all of the Jews?[9]

Although Barth claimed during this time that the "Jewish question" did not belong in the pulpit, in this sermon he attacked the Nazis and German Christians with their own weapons,[10] utilizing references to blood and race in order to stress Christ's solidarity with the Jews and Christians' debt of love to Israel.

In conversations with Jewish acquaintances during the 1930s, Barth interpreted the Nazi onslaught as an event of tremendous theological import. In 1934 Barth wrote to Rabbi Emil Bernard Cohen:

You will expect from me nothing other than that thought on the essence, the way, and the mission of your people under the great riddles of our time occupies me with a great depression. We are also in agreement on the fact that the terror which befalls your people today in Germany – I can as a Christian think about it only in shame and horror – is so terrible because in this, known or unknown, the final mysteries of divine grace are touched upon and because with it the Synagogue just as well as the church is called to an entirely new hearing of the divine word and an entirely new responsible decision.[11]

In other pieces of personal correspondence with Jewish leaders Barth evinces the same tendency to view the travail of the Jewish people through a theological lens.[12]

After refusing to sign the oath of loyalty required of employees in a German university, Barth returned to his native Switzerland in 1935. In an address to a Swiss audience soon after *Kristallnacht* in November 1938, Barth referred explicitly to Jewish suffering in Germany:

When that takes place which has in Germany now been manifestly determined – the physical extermination of the People of Israel ... an attack is being made on the Christian church at its very roots ... He who is on principle an enemy of the Jews ... is to be recognized as on principle an enemy of Jesus Christ.[13]

This passionate statement shows that well into the 1930s Barth continued to think and write about Jews and the intensification of anti-Semitism in a theological idiom. World War II and the Holocaust only exacerbated this tendency, as we shall see.

Barth's apprehension of the Jewish people was not only theological, but also reflects profound ambivalence. Despite forcefully arguing that ill-treatment of Jews was a denial of Christ, Barth seems to have understood the Jews of his day as a people in whose sufferings God's mysterious providence was working. Curiously, Barth's reflections on the religious significance of Jewish suffering occur in the midst of his campaign to head off Nazification of the church's rules of membership. As was demonstrated in the previous chapters, it is precisely a conception of Jews that is theological and ambivalent that is the chief characteristic of witness-people thinking.

B. "Israel" in *Church Dogmatics*

Amid the tumultuous 1930s Barth was at work on the multi-volume systematic theology that is recognized as the great achievement of his career. However, in the first three half-volumes of *Church Dogmatics*,[14] Barth devoted very little space to "Israel" as a topic for theology, and what he did say did not directly reflect current events. Barth merely reaffirmed the same abstract solidarity between Christians and Jews which characterized his pronouncements during the German Church Struggle. Yet from the beginning of *Church Dogmatics* there are anticipations of Barth's paradoxical approach to Israel which invests his mature theology with formal and substantive connections to the witness-people tradition.

In *CD* I:2 (first published in 1938), Barth considers the relationship between the "testaments." He asserts that the church and synagogue are bound together, with the church of the New Testament being joined inseparably to the people whose forgiveness is proclaimed in the Old Testament.[15] Later in the same volume, however, Barth's words resound with the canards of patristic and medieval anti-Judaism:

> The Jewish people is a hard and stiff-necked people, because it is a people which resists its God. It is characterized as the people which in its own Messiah finally rejected and crucified the saviour of the world and therefore denied the revelation of God ... What has later Anti-Semitism to say, compared with the accusation here levelled against the Jews? And what can it do compared with the judgment under which they have been put at the hand of God himself long ago?[16]

While Barth's insistence upon the bond linking Christians and Jews is a positive aspect of witness-people theology, his recitation of anti-Jewish polemic reflects the negative side of the witness-people tradition. These two competing sides of Barth's theology of Israel, one advocating solidarity between Israel and the church, the other apparently legitimizing Jewish suffering as a result of Israel's resistance to God's will and the crime of deicide, remain in dialectical tension throughout his writings.

Barth's first extended treatment of Israel appears in *Church Dogmatics* II:2 (first published in 1942). Within a lengthy chapter on "the election of God," Barth discusses "the election of the community." After contending that humanity's divine election is actually its election in Jesus Christ – since Jesus simultaneously represents electing God and elected humanity – Barth explicates the election of the community of God,

> by the existence of which Jesus Christ is to be attested to the whole world and the whole world summoned to faith in Jesus Christ. This one community of God in its form as Israel has to serve the representation of the divine judgment, in its form as the Church the representation of the divine mercy.... To the one elected community of God is given in the one case its passing, and in the other its coming form.[17]

Here are contained in microcosm the assumptions underlying the Israel doctrine Barth elaborates in *CD* II:2. First, Barth reminds us that election's focus is Jesus Christ. The indissoluble unity of the one community in its two forms (Israel and church) is based in the one who is both "crucified Messiah of Israel" and "secret Lord of the church."[18] Second, Barth insists that Israel's election is permanent and inescapable despite its refusal to believe the gospel. Barth cautions against referring glibly to Jews as "rejected" and Christians as "elected," since the object of God's election is the one community of God. This caveat does not remove the stigma of Israel's presumed disobedience, however, since Israel's continuing election is perceived in the light of Jesus' crucifixion and God's judgment.[19] Third, Barth contends that Israel's special service within the elected community is to hear, receive and accept the divine promise.[20] When Israel is obedient to its election, this service will mean its "rising to life in the church." But because presently Israel hears but does not believe (and, therefore "refuses to hear properly and perfectly") it places itself in a "vacuum" at the very point where it could and should enter the church. Fourth, Barth maintains that in the election of Jesus Christ God "appoints for man a gracious end and a new gracious beginning."[21] Israel, on the other hand, represents the passing and setting aside of the "old man," of the man who resists his election.

These assumptions illuminate the ambivalent and even paradoxical character of Barth's Israel-doctrine. Ambivalence is evident, in fact, in Barth's very definition of Israel as the people of God which resists its divine election.[22] This definition has positive and negative implications. It includes Jews before and after the coming of Christ and thus it is anti-supersessionist. Barth acknowledges as part of "Israel," in other words, not only biblical ("Old Testament") Israel but also contemporary Jews who remain in the synagogue. But Barth's definition of Israel is a negative one since Israel's rejection of Christ is not coincidental, but reflects its very essence and determines its relationship to God and the church.

Barth's view of the relationship between Israel and the church is also steeped in ambivalence. In *CD* II:2 Barth posits the theological unity between church and synagogue to which he alluded in the *Römerbrief* and which he emphasized in sermons and tracts during the early 1930s. This vision of unity is rooted in his understanding of Israel and church as separate forms of the single elect community of God. "A most unnatural severance in God's community," however, has resulted from Israel's rejection of its Messiah. Barth insists that when the church ignores its unity with "the people of the Jews" it ceases to be the church.[23] In fact, Barth claims, "the church leads no life of its own beside and against Israel. It draws its life from Israel, and Israel lives in it."[24]

But in order to explain the actual separation of two religious communities that share "unity in principle," Barth must point to the Jews' "unbelief." Israel's disobedience to its election "creates a schism, a gulf in the midst of the community of God" through which it disrupts the community and punishes itself.[25] But Barth reminds us that Jewish "unbelief" has had other effects as well. According to Barth, since it was "the Jews" who delivered Jesus up to be crucified,[26] Israel should be considered the "people of its arrived and crucified Messiah":

> The Synagogue cannot and will not take up the message: "He is risen!" But it must still pronounce all the more clearly the words: "He is not here!" It speaks of the darkness that fell upon the world in the hour of Jesus' passing.[27]

Here as elsewhere in Barth's systematic theology, the cross of Christ is the symbol of Israel's judgment. Barth alleges that even "the Jews of the ghetto ... involuntarily, joylessly, ingloriously ... have nothing to attest to the world but the shadow of the cross of Jesus Christ that falls upon them."[28]

Still, despite implied responsibility for the death of the Messiah, neither Israel's unbelief nor its initiation of a schism in the community of the elect, nor even its loud "No" in response to divine election, can release Israel from the role it is to play in salvation history. At the present time, Barth observes, Israel discharges its role "involuntarily." But it cannot evade its "appointed service," which is to represent the judgment of God in the same way the church represents God's mercy. In its representation of judgment Israel is a vessel of dishonor,[29] and the synagogue is bound to give "wretched testimony." But because "God only kills to make alive" Israel is the object of God's "Yes" as well as the "No" that is manifest in its sufferings. This "Yes" will rest upon Israel when it becomes obedient to its election and takes its place within the church. Thus, Jesus Christ is "already the secret of Israel's history which has its goal in Him."[30]

In paradoxical fashion, the church–Israel relationship Barth elaborates in *CD* II:2 is simultaneously affirming of Jews and triumphalist. As in Barth's earlier writings, the church and Israel are conceived as interpenetrating realities which are ultimately inseparable. However, Israel is always viewed from the perspective of its proper *telos* – entrance into the church through faith in its Messiah.[31] While Barth denies that the church has become a new Israel, he avers that Israel is obedient to its election – it truly becomes "Israel" – only when it has entered the church. Barth does not explain how Israel is to enter the church and remain Israel, but he is emphatic that only when this occurs can the "indissoluble unity" of the one community of God be realized.

In *CD* II:2 an integrationist[32] understanding of Israel's future exists in dialectical tension with affirmations of its "eternal election." The Israel-affirming element in Barth's teaching underlies his emphases on Israel's eternal chosenness, on its ongoing role in salvation history, and on its appointed service within the community of the elect. Anti-Jewishness finds expression in his depictions of Israel as a passing form of the community of God and of the synagogue as a witness to judgment. In the paradoxical Israel doctrine developed in *Church Dogmatics* II:2 we encounter the most developed twentieth-century version of witness-people theology.

In *Church Dogmatics* III:3 (first published in 1950) Barth reveals a new interest in comprehending the mystery of anti-Semitism and Jewish suffering. The Holocaust seems to have led Barth from a purely theological consideration of the Jewish people to the kind of historical and social analysis which was notably absent during the German Church Struggle. In *CD* III:3 Barth once again underscores the continuity between Israel and church, this time referring to the

Christian God as the "King of Israel." This King is "continually to be rejected by Israel," however, so that Israel's history is "simply a series of the predicted and inevitable judgments of this King."[33]

In a prolonged consideration of "the history of the Jews,"[34] Barth writes that Jewish history provides the most convincing indication (it is almost a "demonstration," he says) of God's world-governance. Barth observes that this history possesses a "very special cogency" that is "enlightening," and echoes his earlier claim that the history of the Jews represents the only convincing "natural" proof for God's existence.[35] Barth also contends that Jewish history can be divided into two parts – one preceding and one following Israel's visitation by its King, Jesus of Nazareth:

> After the death of Jesus there was a significant interval of some forty years – a kind of final period of grace, a last opportunity for repentance. Then the real history of the Jews began.... The definitive destruction of the old form of Israel [in the destruction of the temple in the year 70] was the negative side of the death of Jesus as a saving event.[36]

For Barth, in other words, Jesus' crucifixion exists in a correlative – if not explicitly causal – relationship with the commencement of "Jewish history." Like many Christian theologians before him, Barth interprets Jewish existence as falling under the shadow of events in the first century (especially Jesus' crucifixion and the Fall of Jerusalem). Yet while these fateful events explain the suffering of Jews since the time of Christ, they do not explain how Jews have survived these "1900 years" and continue to survive.[37]

While Barth wishes to infer from their seemingly miraculous survival a uniqueness for Jews, he is aware how problematic it has become in the post-Holocaust world to ascribe special characteristics to the Jewish people. Barth clearly intends to distance himself from the racial anti-Semitism that animated the Nazi "Final Solution" when he writes that "the idea of a specifically Jewish blood is pure imagination."[38] But his rejection of racialism does not in the least deter Barth from attempting to penetrate the mystery of Jewish survival.

Barth declares that Jews can in no way be considered one people among others: Because they have appeared in world history only in a "negative" way, they comprise a problem *sui generis*. In fact, since Jews do not share a common language, a common culture, a unified religion or a single history they must be regarded as "a people which is not a people." But this sociological cul-de-sac only highlights the "providential significance" of Jewish history and makes Barth more determined to discover the theological rationale for the Jews' "mysterious persistence."[39] The special character of Jewish life, Barth concludes, is rooted ultimately in their divine election which is "still valid."[40]

In the Jews' election Barth locates an explanation for their remarkable history of suffering: "It costs something to be the chosen people, and the Jews are paying the price."[41] To estimate the price the Jews must pay for divine favor, Barth engages in a theological/ historical analysis of anti-Semitism. How can we explain, Barth asks, this strange disease from which every non-Jew appears to suffer? His answer contains characteristic ambivalence: It is explicable "only if as strangers – the Jews are still the elect of God."[42] The thing which is annoying about Jews, Barth contends, is not that they are better or worse than other peoples (for they are not), but that they are actually a "mirror" in which we see reflected "who and what we all are, and how bad we all are."[43] Continually revealing the essence of sinful humanity, then, is part of the price the Jew pays for the privilege of being God's elect. Each person's true stature before God is disclosed in the Jew, while it is "suppressed and concealed" in others.

And why is human sinfulness not suppressed and concealed more effectively in the Jew? Barth only repeats that the Jew displays "the primal revolt, the unbelief, the disobedience in which we are all engaged."[44] Non-Jews become annoyed with Jews because they force them to recognize the pitiful nature of the human condition. "Obviously," Barth says, "it is because they are this mirror that the Jews are there."[45] The mysterious function of Jewish presence has been arranged by divine providence, and thus this "mirror" will never be taken away. It is true that the "sign and testimony" offered to humanity in the Jew often issues in anti-Semitic hatred, but anti-Semites only demonstrate that they have encountered in the Jew a trace of divine world-governance.

Barth argues that in addition to their role as witnesses to God's providence, Jews also serve as mirrors of God's free electing grace. Human beings naturally resist this grace, and from the Jew non-Jews learn that the particularity of divine election has completely overlooked them. The persistence of the Jews, then, becomes a constant and irritating symbol of divine grace and mercy. Is it any wonder, Barth asks, that non-Jews fail to appreciate "the message or those who deliver it," that they become anti-Semites and that they "desire that the mirror should be removed?"[46]

CD III:3 is another text in which Barth's debt to the witness-people tradition is tremendous. Barth connects divine providence with Jewish survival, and divine judgment with Jewish unbelief. He emphasizes the inevitability of anti-Semitism while affirming God's eternal love for Israel. He even speaks of Jewish history as a sign and witness: "The Jew Jesus Christ" appears indirectly in the "desolation and persistence" of Jewish existence. According to Barth, this sign may be misunderstood, but there it remains.

C. Occasional Theology

In a radio broadcast in 1949 Barth addressed his theological inter-pretation of anti-Semitism to a wider audience. This broadcast was subsequently published as "The Jewish Problem and the Christian Answer."[47] Barth begins by condemning anti-Semitism as anti-Christian and claiming that it represents a "breakdown of Christian values." He advocates brotherly cooperation between Christians and Jews and welcomes the Jewish bid for independence in Palestine. He also declares that the commandment to "love thy neighbor" must be applied in Christian relationships with Jews. However, Barth quickly observes that admonitions to love the Jew cannot "do justice" to the Jewish problem. In fact, he argues, a Christian answer to this problem must take several theological considerations into account.

First, a "decisive Christian answer" to the Jewish problem must acknowledge the surprising fact that the Jewish race is still in existence. The Jews should really not have survived after the Fall of Jerusalem in the year 70 CE, Barth says, and the Christian explana-tion for the Jews' "surprising position of historical permanence" is located in salvation history. Jewish persistence is a "mystery of faith ... a sign of what the one true God has done once for us all, once and for all in this one Jewish person [Jesus Christ]."[48] Jewish life after the crucifixion of Christ and the fall of Jerusalem witnesses to God's perpetual world-governance and mercy, though to be sure the Jews are "reluctant witnesses."

Second, Barth contends that anti-Semitism, which "seems to be just as inexplicable as the very existence and character of the Jews," only makes sense if we perceive in Jews "mirrors" that reflect human misery, evil and insecurity.[49] We dislike the Jew and dislike being told that the Jews as a whole are a chosen people; yet it is "in the 'lost-ness' and in the persistence of the Jews that that Other One looks down on us."[50] A natural response is to turn the Jewish "mirror" to the wall, or even to smash it. In fact, Barth suggests that the folly of smashing the mirror may represent "the only bit of sense in all the nonsense of Antisemitism."[51] But none of this can alter the picture of ourselves which the mirror reveals.

Finally, Barth reaffirms that the Jews are "to this very day the chosen people of God in the same sense as they have been so from the beginning...."[52] Christians, on the other hand, have the promise of God only as branches engrafted in the Jewish tree. Ironically, the solidarity between the Jewish and Christian communities which this engraftment implies is revealed in Jesus Christ, who also represents the barrier between church and synagogue.

In "The Jewish Problem and the Christian Answer" Barth condenses for a popular audience the major themes in his mature theology of Israel. Barth argues that Christians are "one with the Jews," but laments that this unity is not recognized or accepted by Israel. He maintains that Jewish existence following the time of Christ is a sign of divine election and the sustaining power of divine grace, although Jews refuse to acknowledge the very message which their existence signifies – that they can live only by God's grace. Finally, Barth denies that a human ethical response can constitute an appropriate Christian answer to the "Jewish problem":

> We can all admit the truth of the fine words on this subject which we heard at the beginning. It is doubtful, however, whether they are specifically Christian, whether they give to the Jews the honor due to them, and whether they have the power to accomplish anything practical in the matter of the Jewish problem. This problem opens a gulf which is too wide to be bridged by mere human reason and ethics.[53]

"Mere human reason and ethics" must fail because the Jews are not mere human beings. They are signs of God's presence, mirrors of human sin, reluctant witnesses to the truth of Christianity.

New windows on Barth's ambivalent theology of Israel were opened during the last years of his life. One of these was Barth's book *Ad Limina Apostolorum*, which appeared in 1967 just a year before his death.[54] In 1965 Barth had been invited by the Secretariat for Christian Unity in Rome to attend the final two sessions of the Second Vatican Council as an "observer." Unfortunately, illness prevented Barth from visiting Rome until after the Council had ended. In preparation for his visit in September 1966 Barth devoted himself to "serious study" of the sixteen Latin texts produced by Vatican II and produced lists of "clarifying" and "critical" questions for his hosts. Among these were queries directed to the authors of the "Declaration on the Relationship of the Church to Non-Christian Religions" ("Nostra aetate"):

6. On what grounds does the Declaration (4, 1ff) speak of the past and present history of Israel in the same breath with Hinduism, Buddhism and Islam as a "non-Christian religion," while

a) the Old Testament does not present a religion at all but the original form of the one revelation of God

b) and in the existence of later and contemporary Judaism (believing or unbelieving) we have the sole natural (i. e., in terms of world history) proof of God?

7. Would it not be more appropriate, in view of the anti-Semitism of the ancient, the medieval, and to a large degree the modern church, to set forth an explicit confession of guilt here, rather than in respect to the separated brethren?[55]

Also toward the end of his life Barth came to perceive in the State of Israel confirmation that divine providence was active in Jewish history. In the later volumes of *Church Dogmatics* and elsewhere[56] Barth reveals that he was particularly impressed by the establishment of Israel in 1948 against what he called great historical odds. Barth was even more interested in the fate of this tiny nation in the 1960s. During a debate with American Rabbi Jacob Petuchowski in 1962 Barth was asked to respond to the establishment of the State of Israel in light of his view that Jesus represents the fulfillment of Old Testament prophecy. Relying on the kind of paradoxical thinking about Jews which had guided Christian minds for centuries, Barth reported finding no final contradiction between a superseded and a symbolically resonant Israel:

A possible explanation is that it is another and new sign of the electing and providentially ruling grace and faithfulness of God to that seed of Abraham, a very visible sign, visible for every reader of the papers, the whole world – a sign which is not to be overlooked.

After the horrors of Hitler's time the reappearance of Israel ... may well be called a miracle for all that have eyes to see this evidence, and a scandal for all those who have not eyes to see.[57]

He also observed that the Jews have always owed their existence to the power of God alone and that the Jewish state is simply another example of this divinely dependent existence. He added that the "Jews, your majesty!" legend associated with Frederick the Great might well be updated with the words "your majesty, the State of Israel."[58]

Thus, Barth increasingly ascribed theological significance to the State of Israel in the last years of his life. In 1950 Barth described the Jewish state as "the remarkable representative remnant of Israel."[59] And reflecting on Israel's stunning victory in 1967, Barth was cautious, but enthusiastic:

Of course the foundation of the state of Israel [is] not to be seen as an analogy to the conquest under Joshua and thus as a sign that God cannot let his people be defeated. Yet we can read in the newspapers: "God keeps his promise."[60]

Concerning a declaration by the Christian Peace Conference which condemned Israel following the war, Barth declared it a "scandal" and considered signing a counter-declaration.[61]

D. Barth and the Witness-People Theory

It should be evident by this point that Barth's theology of Israel evinces distinct parallels with classical Christian apprehensions of the Jews as a witness-people. As was argued in the preceding chapters, it is the dual-sided, ambivalent interpretation of Jewish existence that is the distinguishing mark of witness-people thinking. And ambivalence with regard to "Israel" is the quintessence of Barth's theology of Israel.

On one hand, Barth accentuates Israel's irrevocable election, asserts the church's own dependence on this election, reaffirms the hope that Jews will enter the church through conversion, stresses the bond shared by Jews and Christians through the Jew Jesus, condemns anti-Semitism as anti-Christian, asserts that the existence of the Jews is the only legitimate natural proof for God's own existence, contends that Jewish history provides a "trace of the divine world-governance" and implies that Israel's rebirth as a nation-state is providential. On the other hand, Barth recapitulates ancient anti-Jewish stereotypes and canards, including Jewish stubbornness and defiance, Jewish responsibility for Jesus' crucifixion,[62] Israel's dispersion as punishment for its failure to acknowledge its Messiah, and Israel's role as a "witness to judgment" in salvation history. Barth describes the synagogue as lifeless, the unbelieving Jew as the "passing man," and the Jews' dark travail through history as bearing the shadow of Christ's cross.

Besides contributing to the ethos of ambivalence in Barth's theology of Israel, each one of these themes has its own roots in the soil of the witness-people myth. Even the language of "sign" and "witness" which Barth utilizes in speaking of the Jews is reminiscent of earlier versions of witness-people theology. The following passage from "The Jewish Question and the Christian Answer" suggests the extent of Barth's dependence on witness-people vocabulary:

> They [the Jews] could and can disappear just as little as God's faithfulness can come to an end ... This continued existence of the Jews which is so puzzling is a sign which cannot be ignored.... Yet they are no more than the shadow of a nation, the reluctant witnesses of the Son of God and Son of Man ... whom they rejected, yet who has not ceased to call them.[63]

Such passages provide a vivid glimpse of Barth's Israel as a witness-people: It is a unique chosen nation, destined to be preserved forever by divine providence, its existence a "puzzling sign which cannot be ignored" by the Christian, its people resisters of God's call and rejecters of Christ, in their dispersion and survival "reluctant witness" to Christian truth.

Even Barth's apparently novel conception of the Jew as a mirror of human sinfulness which irritates and threatens the non-Jew[64] is a clever expression of the witness-people myth. For Barth, as for witness-people thinkers from Augustine to Enlightenment courtiers, the Jew represents a mysterious and even miraculous sign of God's presence and activity in history. True, Barth's claims that the Jewish "mirror" is neither better nor worse than the rest of us, since what are reflected there are the failures of humanity in general. But it is because they are the quintessential witness-people that Jews are able to perform this unique revelatory service of reflecting divine favor and disfavor among non-Jews.

Perhaps not surprisingly, Barth's implication in the Christian witness-people tradition has not received critical attention. This lacuna in Barth scholarship can be illuminated with reference to a recent study of Barth's "doctrine of Israel" by Katherine Sonderegger. In *That Jesus Christ Was Born a Jew* Sonderegger correctly notes the ambivalence that is a hallmark of Barth's theology of Israel. She observes that Barth reveals both "the Christian obsession with Judaism" and "the controlling ambivalence of deep hostility and deep, unshakeable attachment."[65] Sonderegger even acknowledges that this ambivalence toward Jews and Judaism is a chief characteristic of the Christian tradition, one displayed in Barth's writings with uncommon clarity. However, Sonderegger is not interested in exploring the implications of Barth's reliance on this tradition, and to that extent contributes to its perpetuation.

Perhaps the most incisive critique of Barth's understandings of Israel, anti-Semitism and Jewish history is to be found in a work that is not directly concerned with Barth at all. In 1966 Richard L. Rubenstein expressed severe reservations concerning the prevalent Christian notion that despite their misfortunes Jews remain special and chosen people. In *After Auschwitz*[66] Rubenstein reflects upon Christian theologies which assume an objective relationship between Jewish behavior and anti-Semitism on the one hand, and a "special providential relationship" between Jewish history and the will of God on the other. Although he does not specifically mention Barth's theology, Rubenstein was in fact reacting to the Barthian version of witness-people theology he had encountered with disturbing frequency among churchpeople in post-war Germany. In particular, Rubenstein was struck by the widespread belief that "nowhere in the world [are] the fruits of God's activity in history more evident than in the life and the destiny of the Jewish people."[67]

Actually, Barth's theology of Israel provides a graphic illustration of Rubenstein's claim that Christian thinking tends to relegate Jews to "mythical, magic and theological categories." Like Christian writers since the first century, Barth too invests "the Jew" with an exceedingly mythical character. His desire to interpret the history of the Jews and the persistence of anti-Semitism theologically compels him to posit both a mythicized "Jew" and a fictional "Jewish history." What Barth calls "Jewish existence" is actually the Jews' fate viewed from the perspective of their alleged role in salvation history before and after their "rejection" of Jesus. His version of "Jewish history" is a fable in which an eternal anti-Semitism discovers increasingly destructive ways to reveal its contempt for the Eternal Jew. Barth's "Jew" is a stereotype of human depravity, of the person who is chosen and called by God but who defiantly remains steeped in sin.

In the *Church Dogmatics* and elsewhere Barth forges an "Israel" that is pure theological abstraction.[68] In doing so, Barth adapts elements of both popular medieval anti-Judaism and Neo-Romantic anti-Semitism.[69] But the crucial source for his Israel-doctrine is the ancient witness-people myth, which Barth recapitulates in both form and substance. In his endeavor to oppose the Nazi myth of "Jewish blood" Barth unconsciously resorts to an older myth, one generated by the earliest Christian attempts to understand God's way with the Jew. Thus, his vocal opposition to the Nazis notwithstanding, Barth's revivification of the witness-people myth played directly into Nazi hands. It is true that Barth opposed blatant anti-Semitism and remained confident that God would insure the survival of the chosen people. But Barth lent credence and authority to the beliefs that the Jews were a powerful force in history and that travail and dispersion were the destiny of this people he called "witnesses to judgment." Barth reawakened some of the oldest instincts in the Christian imagination and in the process helped make it even easier for the Jews' enemies to cast them as "other."

II.   THE CHURCH STRUGGLE AND THE WITNESS-PEOPLE MYTH

Amid the European crisis of the 1930s and 40s Karl Barth recapitulated the witness-people myth as he interpreted the "Jewish problem" and articulated a "Christian answer." But Barth was not unique in this regard. Other German Christians of the interwar period employed the language and concepts of the witness-people tradition as they reflected upon the situation of the Jewish people. What is more, examples of this phenomenon are found in the writings of both supporters and resisters of the Nazis.

A.   Dietrich Bonhoeffer

Another well-known leader in the Confessing Church was Barth's younger colleague and early theological apprentice Dietrich

Bonhoeffer. Bonhoeffer ultimately resolved to resist Hitler in tangible and very dangerous ways. But in the early days of Nazi rule Barth and Bonhoeffer were equally reluctant to present a frontal challenge to the state or its policies. As a result, in the decisive period 1933–4 the Confessing Church's opposition to Nazi totalitarianism took the form of a campaign to block application of the Aryan paragraph in the church. The declaration drafted at the Confessing Synod of Barmen in May 1934 warned of idolatry, but alluded to the state only in an oblique reference to "the responsibility of those who rule." In September 1933 Bonhoeffer declared that the looming Nazification of the church had precipitated a *status confessionis* (literally, a "confessional situation"), but cautioned that the church of the Reformation had no right to address the state in its "history-making actions."[70]

Like Barth, Bonhoeffer was assured that Jewish tribulation was fraught with religious significance and that Christians could discover in it a sign of God's providential activity. In "The Church and the Jewish Question" (1933), Bonhoeffer proclaimed that

> the measures of the state toward Judaism stand in a quite special context for the church. The church of Christ has never lost sight of the thought that the "chosen people," who nailed the redeemer of the world to the cross, must bear the curse for its action through a long history of suffering. "Jews are the poorest people among all nations upon earth, they are tossed to and fro, they are scattered here and there in all lands, they have no certain place where they could remain safely and must always be afraid that they will be driven out..." (Luther, *Table Talk*). But the history of the suffering of this people, loved and punished by God, stands under the sign of the final home-coming of the people of Israel to its God. And this home-coming happens in the conversion of Israel to Christ.... The conversion of Israel, that is to be the end of the people's period of suffering.[71]

This passage foregrounds the dialectic between dispersion/punishment and restoration/salvation that is a defining feature of witness-people theology. According to Bonhoeffer, Israel's redemption is a theological drama before which the church stands in awe, remembering that through all their sufferings the Jews' destiny remains in God's hands:

From here the Christian church sees the history of the people of Israel with trembling as God's own free, fearful way with his people. It knows that no nation of the world can be finished with this mysterious people, because God is not yet finished with it. Each new attempt to 'solve the Jewish problem' comes to nothing on the saving-historical significance of this people...[72]

The church also perceives in Israel's history a message for itself:

As [the church] looks at the rejected people, it humbly recognizes itself as a church continually unfaithful to its Lord and looks full of hope to those of the people of Israel who have come home, to those who have come to believe in the one true God in Christ.[73]

The influence of the witness-people tradition is unmistakable in these passages from Bonhoeffer's "The Church and the Jewish Question." They embody not only the formal ambivalence of the witness-people myth, but also several of the specific beliefs associated with it.

Witness-people thinking also pervades the "Bethel Confession" of 1934, a document which Bonhoeffer was instrumental in shaping. The confession's section on "the church and the Jews, " in fact, is a veritable primer in witness-people theology.[74] It begins with a rehearsal of the myth's negative side: Despite God's free choosing of Israel, the Jewish people rejected the Christ in favor of a national Messiah they believed would bring them world rule. Jesus died at the hands of the Jews and thereafter the "Old Testament" people was replaced by a church called from among the nations. The positive, preservationist dimension of the witness-people myth is apparent in the "Bethel Confession" as well: The Jews' faithlessness notwithstanding, God keeps faith with "Israel after the flesh" and will someday work through them to consummate the world's salvation. For this reason God preserves a holy remnant bearing the "indelible stamp of the chosen people," and this remnant can be neither assimilated nor exterminated. Furthermore, the confession forcefully denies that Israel's commission in sacred history can be usurped or that any nation is commissioned to avenge the Jews' deicide.

Although at one point the confession discounts "the religious significance of the Jewish people," this is merely an attempt to offset a racialized understanding of Jewish Christians: "The special element in the Jewish Christian does not lie in his race or his character or his history, but in God's special faithfulness towards Israel after the flesh and in that alone."[75] While Nazi racial theories are implicitly repudiated, the unique theological import of the Jew is affirmed. The Jewish Christian, in fact, is a "*living memorial* of God's faithfulness within the church and is a sign that the barrier between Jew and Gentile has been broken down..."[76]

Furthermore, the language Bonhoeffer employs to combat "German Christian" ideology communicates a profound anti-Judaism. For in both the "Bethel Confession" and "The Church and the Jewish Question" Bonhoeffer accuses those who wish to adopt Nazi racial principles in the church of proclaiming a Judaistic heresy! The principle on which Bonhoeffer stands is theologically sound: "The community of those who belong to the church is not determined by blood and therefore not by race, but by the Holy Spirit and baptism."[77] But in defending this principle Bonhoeffer utilizes rhetoric whose anti-Jewish implications appear to elude him. He contends that those who wish to exclude Jewish Christians from the German Protestant church will actually be creating a "Jewish-Christian community," since "to raise the racial unity of the church to the status of a law which would have to be fulfilled as a presupposition for church membership" is to create "the Jewish-Christian idea of a religion based on law." This, according to Bonhoeffer, would amount to "modern Jewish Christianity."[78]

Tragically, Bonhoeffer's opposition to the Aryanizing of the church did not compel him to repudiate, or even acknowledge, his own deep-seated anti-Judaism.[79] This fact is one more reflection of the troubling ambivalence with which the best Christian minds reflected upon the Jewish people during the decisive early years of Nazi rule.

B. Martin Niemöller

Another leader in the German Church Struggle, one less well known than Bonhoeffer in the English-speaking world, was the pastor and decorated war hero Martin Niemöller. After exhibiting initial enthusiasm for the Nazi movement (he voted National Socialist in the elections of 1931 and 1933), Niemöller formed the "Pastors Emergency League" to aid Christian victims of Nazi racial laws. Niemöller was also a leading figure at the Barmen Synod, and a member of the church delegation that gained an audience with

Hitler in January 1934. He became a consistent and outspoken critic of Hitler's church policies and made himself such a nuisance that the Nazis finally arrested him in July 1937. In 1941 Niemöller was imprisoned at Dachau where he remained until the end of the war.[80]

A sermon preached by Niemöller in 1937 elucidates his understanding of the Jewish people's sufferings under Nazi rule:

> This is a day [the tenth Sunday after Trinity] which for centuries has been dedicated in the Christian world to the memory of the destruction of Jerusalem and the fate of the Jewish people, and the passage of Scripture provided for this Sunday throws light upon the dark mystery that envelopes the sinister history of this people which can neither live nor die, because it is under a curse which forbids it to do either. We speak of the "Eternal Jew" and conjure up the picture of a restless wanderer who has no home and who cannot find peace ... [but] we have no licence empowering us to supplement God's curse with our hatred.[81]

In this sermon is visible the very same pattern of reflection about Jews and their fate which distinguishes the theological writings of Barth and Bonhoeffer. Ambivalence is betrayed in alternating affirmations of rejection and salvation. Jewish reprobation (expressed in references to the destruction of Jerusalem and the dispersion of Jews) fails to displace the "Eternal Jew" from the center of salvation history. Likewise, the objects of divine preservation are described as a "people which can neither live nor die." Further, despite the "dark mystery" of the Jews' "sinister history," Christians are forbidden from taking their own vengeance on this people.

As was the case with Barth and Bonhoeffer, Niemöller's opposition to the Nazis seems to have coexisted very comfortably with deeply held notions about Jews which are part and parcel of the witness-people tradition.

C. Theologians under Hitler

One of the striking aspects of this period is that the writings of Christians who embraced Hitler and his discriminatory policies in the early 1930s contain interpretations of Jewish existence that are remarkably similar to those articulated by the leaders of the Confessing Church. Among the men who commended Hitler to the Christian community in Germany were biblical scholar Gerhard

Kittel and Lutheran theologian Paul Althaus. In their theological apprehensions of the Jewish people both men exhibit the influence of the witness-people myth.

Kittel's is a complex case, as Robert P. Ericksen's recent analysis has shown.[82] Kittel had a wide reputation in Germany as an expert on Judaism and Jewish backgrounds to the New Testament. His career during the Nazi era has led some to vilify him as a despicable collaborator and others to defend him for bringing reason, tolerance and courage to an environment in which chaos reigned. Although a negative shift in his attitude toward Judaism is detectable after 1933, Kittel's Nazi and pre-Nazi writings share in common a conception of the Jewish people that is rooted in the ambivalent witness-people tradition.

Kittel affirmed that the Jews were at the same time God's chosen people and a nation disobedient and cursed. Especially in his earlier writings, he emphasized the Jewishness of Jesus and his teachings, elucidated Christianity's roots in the "Old Testament," and sought to dissociate the pristine religion of the ancient Hebrews from the degeneration of modern Judaism. On the other hand, however, Kittel portrayed Jews as players in a "God-willed tragedy" that had been brought upon them by their disobedience.

How did his loyalty to the Nazi regime affect Kittel's view of Jews? Before 1933 Kittel ascribed to a standard Christian view of Judaism as an outmoded religious phenomenon. After the Nazi revolution, however, Kittel's scholarship increasingly reflected the modern anti-Semitic views popularized by National Socialist propaganda. Kittel even spoke of "world Jewry as a demand for power." But even as his portrait of Judaism started to reflect Nazi racial fantasies Kittel was adamant that his position on the "Jewish Question" stemmed from the instruction of Jesus and the Apostles.[83] In making this claim, Kittel was concerned to distinguish himself from so-called vulgar anti-Semites. For unlike them, Kittel insisted on discriminating between secular Jews and pious Jews, for whom he held considerably more respect. The real failure of Judaism, Kittel believed, was its failure to remain true to its religious roots. Having succumbed to assimilation and decadence, Judaism was now a taproot of modern atheism and relativism.[84]

In the post-Holocaust environment the career of Gerhard Kittel is sometimes invoked as a leading example of German Christianity's infatuation with Nazism. But despite his profound anti-Judaism and the ideological assistance he supplied the Nazis, Kittel retained a posture toward Jews that was typical of most Christian thinkers during this time.[85] Even when he adopted Nazi racial ideas and read race into every stage of Jewish history, Kittel could not overcome a native ambivalence concerning God's chosen people. He could not relinquish the notion of the Jews' central role in God's plan. Thus, he counseled Jews to "accept the role of alien as God's judgment on the Jewish people for their disobedience," though he could not countenance Jewish extermination, which he concluded would be "unchristian."[86]

Paul Althaus was a noted German Protestant theologian who opposed the Weimar Republic and applied a favorable theological status to the Nazi movement. Despite the political and religious commitments which separated him from his contemporaries in the Confessing Church, Althaus shared their reliance on the witness-people myth. In an important lecture at the University of Leipzig in May 1937, Althaus undertook to construct a theology of the German *Volk* by combining *völkisch* ideas with a Lutheran "orders of creation" theology. In the same speech, however, Althaus consciously dissented from more radical versions of *völkisch* ideology in order to defend the Jews as a unique people, irrevocably chosen by God.[87]

Elsewhere Althaus warned that the German *Volk* could not usurp the cardinal role in salvation history that was reserved for the Jews, and characterized Jewish history as "unique, incomparable and unrepeatable."[88] In fact, it was their tendency to downplay Jesus' Jewishness which made Althaus uncomfortable with the "German Christians." Althaus consistently resisted the Aryanization of Christianity "by defending the Old Testament, the uniqueness of the Jewish people, and the ultimate supremacy of Christian over *völkisch* concerns."[89] Despite being a vocal supporter of the Nazis and many of their measures against the Jews, Althaus held fast to the theological conviction that the Jewish people were God's revelatory vehicle in world history. As we have seen, this conviction was an invisible link between Nazi sympathizers like Althaus and Kittel and their opponents on the other side of the German Church Struggle.

III. CONCLUSION

It is disturbing to encounter signs of the subtle and not so subtle anti-Judaism with which leaders in the Confessing Church like Karl Barth and Dietrich Bonhoeffer were apparently infected. While they condemned Jewish persecution and retained a belief in the ultimate sacredness of Jewish life, these men were convinced that the suffering of Jews was fundamental to God's unfolding plan. It causes greater dismay to realize that the same Christians who vigorously opposed Nazi racial anti-Semitism inadvertently aided Hitler's campaign against the Jews by denigrating Judaism and substantiating Hitler's fantasy that the Jew is a key for comprehending the flux of history. But the preceding analysis of writings by combatants on either side of the German Church Struggle yields an observation that is even more puzzling and unsettling: Christians who opposed and Christians who supported the Nazis often employed the very same language and concepts when expounding the fate of the Jewish people.

Several historians and scholars of the Holocaust have commented on this phenomenon. Uriel Tal notes that in the controversy between Heinrich Vogel and Friedrich Gebhart, the former a leader of protests against Jewish persecution and the latter a spokesman for the German Christians, both men "adhere to the same traditional Christian view that the Jews are in a state of rejection (*Verwerfung*)."[90] Marc Saperstein observes that during the Nazi era a number of Christian leaders proclaimed "the worst anti-Jewish teachings of their tradition, yet refus[ed] to endorse Nazi anti-Semites, and sometimes even us[ed] the traditional doctrine to attack Nazi policies."[91] In an anthology of texts related to the Jewish-Christian encounter, Frank Talmage provocatively juxtaposes a section of Barth's *Church Dogmatics* with a selection from the writings of Gerhard Kittel, commenting that when the subject is the Jews, "the thinking of a Christian anti-nazi [Barth] and that of a Christian nazi [Kittel] ... are not very far apart."[92]

Richard Rubenstein in particular has expressed surprise and dismay at the congruity of Christian thought across the Nazi divide. In *After Auschwitz* Rubenstein describes the fateful meeting with Heinrich Grüber which he would later recognize as a personal turning point. Rubenstein was expecting to meet a political maverick who had earned official recognition as a "Righteous Gentile" for risking his life to rescue Jews; what Rubenstein discovered was a devout Christian seized by the idea that as God's chosen people Israel lives under a special obligation to behave in a manner consistent with their election. Grüber unabashedly asserted his belief in a "very special providential relationship between Israel, what happened to it, and God's will, that this had been true in the time of the Bible and that the *Heilsgeschichte* of the Jewish people had continued to unfold to this very day."[93] Compounding his guest's consternation, Grüber continued to aver in the 1960s that Hitler had been a rod of God's anger against the Jews. In *After Auschwitz* Rubenstein marvels at the irony of Heinrich Grüber – a man who actively resisted the Nazis and nearly lost his life helping Jews escape their murderous anti-Semitism, but who remains "incapable of seeing Jews simply as normal human beings with the same range of failings and virtues as any other group."[94]

The persistence of traditional notions about Jews in persons who responded so differently to Nazi rule suggests the witness-people myth's deep influence on the Christian imagination. We have seen that Barth's theology of Israel reflects this ancient myth at every turn. But it appears that many other Christians in Germany in the 1930s – in sermons, lectures, articles and confessions – instinctively portrayed Jews in terms adopted from the witness-people tradition. It is this tradition's profound ambivalence *vis-à-vis* Jews that made it a suitable vehicle for conveying a variety of conflicting positions on the "Jewish Question."

The repeated allusions to the Jews as a witness-people in the texts of German theologians active in the 1930s suggest that in periods of social crisis – and especially when Jews are persecuted or threatened – Christians may automatically revert to this primal religious mythology concerning the Jewish people. In fact, the witness-people myth is so prominent in their theological imaginations that if there were no evidence for its powerful influence in the nineteen centuries between the birth of Christianity and the German Church Struggle, we might infer its existence solely from their writings.

As we shall see in the following chapters, the tendency to perceive Jews as a witness-people actually characterizes twentieth-century Christian thinkers across a wide spectrum of theological perspectives. The fact that witness-people thinking is particularly evident in German theological discourse tempts us to regard it as a German phenomenon. Thus, Richard Rubenstein attributes much of what he hears from Dean Grüber to "a typically German incapacity to place the concrete empirical facts of day-to-day life before an overwhelming ideology." Rubenstein finds solace in the fact that "most Americans and Britons simply don't think the way Dean Grüber does."[95] Unfortunately, the chapters that follow cast considerable doubt on this judgment.

5

Walker Percy and the Witness-People:
Signposts in a Strange Land

[Once there was] the belief that man was created in the image of God with an immortal soul, that he occupied a place in nature somewhere between the beasts and the angels, that he suffered an aboriginal catastrophe, the Fall, in consequence of which he lost his way and, unlike the beasts, became capable of sin and thereafter became a pilgrim or seeker of his own salvation, and that the clue and the sign of his salvation was to be found not in science or philosophy but in news of an actual historical event involving a people, a person, and an institution.

Walker Percy, "The Delta Factor"

This chapter will explore selected writings of the American novelist and philosopher Walker Percy (1916–90). I have chosen Percy because he is a "Christian" thinker and novelist in the broadest sense of that term, and because his work expresses with peculiar clarity the same witness-people myth described in the preceding chapters. One persistent thread in Percy's writings is his portrayal of the Jewish people as unique, wandering, suffering, and eternal witnesses – a people who individually and collectively symbolize God's existence, presence and activity in the world. Just as striking as Percy's decision to utilize this theme again and again in his work has been the failure of Percy's critics to analyze it critically.

I do not attempt here an exhaustive analysis of Percy's references to Jews, anti-Semitism and the Holocaust, though such a study would be welcome. Rather, I desire to trace in varying detail the narrative dimensions of Jewish existence in three of Percy's novels and several of his essays, my main concern being to clarify Percy's debt to the Christian witness-people myth. After a biographical introduction and a consideration of his writings, I will attempt to elucidate Percy's connection with the witness-people tradition.

I. PERCY'S LIFE AND TIMES

Walker Percy was born in 1916 in Birmingham, Alabama. After his father's suicide in 1929 Percy moved to Athens, Georgia and resided with his mother's family. In 1931 Percy's mother was killed in a car accident, after which he was adopted by his father's first cousin, William Alexander Percy of Greenville, Mississippi. In "Uncle Will's" house, Percy imbibed an atmosphere of humanistic learning and *noblesse oblige* typical among the planters of the Mississippi Delta.[1] After graduating from the University of North Carolina at Chapel Hill in 1937 with a B.S. degree in chemistry, Percy attended medical school at the College of Physicians and Surgeons of Columbia University in New York. He received his M.D. degree in 1941, but the following year contracted tuberculosis while serving his residency in pathology at Bellevue Hospital. During his three year convalescence, Percy discovered the writings of the modern existentialists – first Dostoevsky, then Kierkegaard, and finally twentieth-century thinkers including Heidegger, Marcel, Sartre and Camus. Percy's immersion in existentialism and his temporary inability to practice medicine contributed to his eventual decision to pursue a career as philosopher and novelist. In 1946 Percy returned to the South, was married, and along with his new wife converted to Roman Catholicism in 1947. In 1950 the Percys relocated from New Orleans to nearby Covington, Louisiana where Walker Percy lived and wrote until his death in 1990.

Percy's work is best known in America and the English-speaking world. But editions of his novels have been published in all the major European languages, and *The Moviegoer* has even been translated into Turkish and Japanese.[2] In a literary career spanning four decades, Percy developed something of a dual authorship. From the 1950s on Percy's philosophical writings are characterized by a "recurring interest ... [in] the nature of human communication and, in particular, the consequences of man's unique discovery of the symbol. "[3] His concerns with symbolic communication and what he called its "triadic" dimension are particularly evident in the essays collected in *The Message in the Bottle*.

The fictional side of Percy's authorship was launched in 1961 with the publication of *The Moviegoer*. This first novel was a critical success and Percy was honored with the National Book Award in 1962. Over the next three decades, Percy published a new novel every three to seven years: *The Last Gentleman* in 1966, *Love in the Ruins* in

1971, *Lancelot* in 1977, *The Second Coming* in 1980, and *The Thanatos Syndrome* in 1987. Not surprisingly, Percy's philosophical concerns are consistently reflected in his novels. His interest in the nature of language, for instance, finds narrative expression in *The Second Coming* and *The Thanatos Syndrome*. In both novels the human capacity for symbolic communication functions as a kind of *imago dei*. The seminal role of existentialism in Percy's thinking is also apparent in his novels. Seemingly all of Percy's leading characters are in search of themselves and God in a world that has become empty and absurd. Most Percyan antagonists, however, are able to triumph over their own destructive instincts and the modern world's fecklessness, "coming to themselves" more or less by novel's end.

Some recurrent themes in Percy's fiction have autobiographical roots. One leitmotif is the uncertain future of the American South in an age of increasing cultural homogenization; and related to this regional uncertainty are the personal struggles of Southern gentlemen who feel they are caught between a secure, but unjust and dying past and a future animated by the promise and threat of modernity.[4] The struggle with suicide is another topos in Percy's fiction which grows out of his own experience. Percy's father took his own life, as did the first of Percy's male ancestors to arrive in America.[5] Similarly, a number of Percy's male characters are haunted by the impulse to self-destruction, and it is a major sub-plot in *The Second Coming*.

Another aspect of Percy's biography that must be recognized to properly appreciate his fiction is his self-understanding as a "Christian novelist." While using this term, Percy wished to define it as precisely as possible:

> As it happens, I speak in a Christian context. That is to say, I do not conceive it my vocation to preach the Christian faith in a novel, but as it happens, my world view is informed by a certain belief about man's nature and destiny which cannot fail to be central to any novel I write.[6]

If there is a religious thread uniting his fictional corpus, it is Percy's utilization of the Christian world view to diagnose the malaise which he believed afflicted late twentieth-century America. As Percy once noted, historic Christianity speaks not only to the contradictions of individual existence, but to the apocalyptic flavor of life in the postmodern age:

Being a Christian novelist nowadays has certain advantages and disadvantages. Since novels deal with people and people live in time and get into predicaments, it is probably an advantage to subscribe to a world view which is incarnational, historical, and predicamental, rather than, say, Buddhism, which tends to devalue individual persons, things, and happenings. What with the present dislocation of man, it is probably an advantage to see man as by his very nature an exile and wanderer rather than as a behaviorist sees him: as an organism in an environment.... And if it is true that we are living in eschatological times, times of enormous danger and commensurate hope, of possible end and possible renewal, the prophetic-eschatological character of Christianity is no doubt peculiarly apposite.[7]

Perhaps the term "diagnostic" – a term used by Percy himself on occasion[8] – is fitting as a label for Percy's fiction. Not only does it allude to Percy's theological intentions, but it reminds us that his training as a scientist and physician was a legacy he never relinquished. Referring to Percy as a "diagnostic" novelist also helps explain his interest in the Jewish people. In 1986 Percy wrote that in serious fiction

what is being explored or should be explored is not only the nature of the human predicament but the possibility or non-possibility of a search for signs and meanings. Depending on the conviction of the writer, the signs may be found to be ambiguous or meaningless – or perhaps a faint message comes through, a tapping on the wall heard and deciphered and replied to.[9]

It is in the context of his career-long concern with signs and meanings that Percy's fictional treatment of the Jews must be investigated.

II.   PERCY AND THE JEWS

Although Percy's fictional corpus includes six published novels,[10] only three – *The Moviegoer*, *The Second Coming*, and *The Thanatos Syndrome* – will receive attention here. But because this list includes his first and last published works of fiction, it seems reasonable to conclude that Percy's interest in the sign represented by Jewish existence was an abiding preoccupation.

A. *The Moviegoer*

Already in *The Moviegoer* (1961) Percy communicates his peculiar fictional treatment of "the Jews." In Binx Bolling, the novel's narrator and hero, the reader encounters a young man who is self-consciously engaged in a "search." Bolling has recently abandoned his "vertical search" (a scientific and objective quest that has yielded only abstract knowledge), and is now embarking on a "horizontal search" for clues to the meaning of his existence. About one-third of the way through the novel, Binx Bolling discovers an initial clue on his horizontal search:

> An odd thing. Ever since Wednesday I have become acutely aware of Jews. There is a clue here, but of what I cannot say. How do I know? Because whenever I approach a Jew, the Geiger counter in my head starts rattling away like a machine gun; and as I go past with the utmost circumspection and with every sense alert – the Geiger counter subsides.
>
> There is nothing new in my Jewish vibrations. During the years when I had friends my Aunt Edna, who is a theosophist, noticed that all my friends were Jews. She knew why moreover: I had been a Jew in a previous incarnation. Perhaps that is it. Anyhow it is true that I am Jewish by instinct. We share the same exile. The fact is, however, I am more Jewish than the Jews I know. They are more at home than I am. I accept my exile.
>
> Another evidence of my Jewishness: the other day a sociologist reported that a significantly large percentage of solitary movie-goers are Jews.
>
> Jews are my first real clue.
>
> ...
>
> [W]hen a man awakes to the possibility of a search and when such a man passes a Jew in the street for the first time, he is like Robinson Crusoe seeing the footprint on the beach.[11]

Bolling, the self-exiled solitary moviegoer who claims he is a Jew "by instinct," discovers in actual Jews a "real clue" to begin his existential search.[12] But a clue to what? The reader is not yet told.

Reflecting on his transformed posture from vertical to horizontal searcher Binx, notes that "before, I wandered as a diversion. Now I wander seriously and sit and read as a diversion."[13] In the narrative world of *The Moviegoer*, then, wandering is anything but purposeless. Binx's wandering – his exile – makes him "more Jewish than the Jews [he] know(s)," since he embraces his exile rather than pretending to be at home in an alien and threatening world. Upon accepting the National Book Award for *The Moviegoer*, Percy confirmed that his novel "attempts a modest restatement of the Judeo-Christian notion that man ... is a wayfarer and pilgrim."[14]

But *The Moviegoer* traffics in images that are mythically charged in ways of which Percy seemed unaware. It is clear that Percy employed the phrase "wayfarer and pilgrim" to refer to the Western notion of earthly life as a journey unto God. But Percy's portrayal of the Jews in *The Moviegoer* as archetypal wanderers has deeper and more sinister roots in the West's collective unconscious. If Percy believed that the image of the Wandering Jew would cease being religious mythology when it was applied as a philosophical metaphor he was no doubt mistaken. Percy's use of the adjective "Judeo-Christian" is also misleading, since this glib hyphenation obscures the fact that in the West Jews and Christians have lived very different histories.

In *The Moviegoer* Jewish existence signifies exile. And exile, of course, connotes suffering. Percy intends precisely these connections in his characterization of Binx Bolling, whose instinctual exile is accompanied by existential suffering. But in the theological tradition within which Percy works, exile is believed to result from a God-willed dispersion which is providential punishment for sin. While Binx Bolling's non-Jewish wanderings[15] symbolize the personal search for God and self, the Jewish wanderings Binx mimics correspond to a real history beyond the bounds of the novel's narrative world.

If Percy does not seem to have been troubled by the connection between real and instinctual Jews, neither have his critics. They are fully aware that *The Moviegoer* depicts Binx Bolling as a Wandering Jew who suffers in his exile from humanity,[16] that Binx's mission is a "Hebraic" one which requires him to suffer, exile himself from the unchosen, and wait expectantly for a sign,[17] and that Binx recognizes the Jews' testimony to humanity's mission as wayfarers under God.[18] But none of these critics has expressed surprise or concern that Percy uses the myth of the Wandering Jew to portray Binx's spiritual state. None acknowledges this myth's pernicious history or the fact that it is part and parcel of an anti-Semitic tradition that has contributed to Jewish suffering. Thus, none recognizes the irony that Roman Catholic Christianity, which is the religious *telos* of

Binx's search, is also the historical source for this legend of a Jew who is condemned by Jesus to roam the earth until his return.

B. *The Second Coming*

In *The Second Coming* (1980), we encounter a second Percyan character who nurtures a private obsession with Jews.[19] But while Binx Bolling is struck by the presence of Jews, Will Barrett is impressed by their absence. On a golf course in "Christian Carolina" the middle-aged Barrett is suddenly seized by a visual memory of his first love, a Jewish girl named Ethel Rosenblum. Shortly after her reemergence into his conscious mind, the agnostic Barrett begins to consider the religious meaning of Jews living in a Gentile world. The following conversation between Barrett and his physician and golf partner Vance Battle takes place on the links. Barrett speaks first:

> "I just realized a strange thing."
> "What's that?"
> "There are no Jews up here."
> "Jews?"
> "I've been living here for two years and have never seen a Jew. Arabs, but no Jews. When I used to come here in the summer years ago, there used to be Jews here. Isn't that strange?"
> ...
> "Come to think of it, how many Jews are left in the state of North Carolina?"
> ...
> "Think about it. Weren't there Jews here earlier? You're a native,"
> "Well, there was Dr. Weiss and Dutch Mandelbaum in high school who played tackle."
> "They're not here now?"
> "No."
> "You see."
> "See what?"
> "You know, my wife, who was very religious, believed that the Jews are a sign."
> "A sign of what?"
> "A sign of God's plan working out."
> "Is that so?" Vance's eyes strayed to his wristwatch. He pretended to brush off a fly.

"But what about the absence of Jews? The departure of Jews?" he asked, ... "What is that a sign of?"[20]

At this point the novel's narrator interrupts the dialogue, noting that "it is not at all uncommon for persons suffering from certain psychoses and depressions of middle age to exhibit 'ideas of reference,' that is, all manner of odd and irrational notions about Jews, Bildebergers, Gypsies, outer space, UFOs, international conspiracies, and whatnot. Needless to say the Jews were and are not leaving North Carolina."[21]

Readers do not know whether this voice is to be trusted, or why the narrator wishes us to believe that Will Barrett is insane. The reader who has visited Percy's fictional universe before may not feel that Barrett's attention to the comings and goings of Jews qualifies him for the asylum. Crazy or not, Will Barrett remains capable of applying elementary logic: if the existence of Jews is a sign of divine providence, then the absence of Jews must be a harbinger of chaos. And Barrett recognizes the marks of chaos when he sees them: "When the Jews pull out, the Gentiles begin to act like the crazy Jutes and Celts and Angles and redneck Saxons that they are. They go back into the woods ... socking little balls around the mountains, rattling ice in Tanqueray, riding $35,000 German cars...."[22] Like everyone else who has become lost in the postmodern age, Will Barrett is engaged in a search for himself and for God; and like any serious searcher he is groping for clues.

Barrett is convinced that the crucial clue to self-understanding lies just out of reach in some forgotten corner of his fading memory. Throughout the novel he is straining to recall his dim childhood past, hopeful that it will aid him in deciding whether or not to continue with his life. He remembers just enough to suspect that his father once took him on a hunting trip in order to kill them both in a murder-suicide. Though Barrett survived the ordeal, the legacy of self-inflicted death lives on for him. He is reminded that suicide is an option, in fact, every time he thinks of the German Luger which sits in the glove box of his Mercedes. As it turns out, the combination of images of death and German technology is anything but coincidental.[23] For during one of Barrett's internal soliloquies we learn that his father had accepted the Luger from a German SS colonel at the end of the Second World War.

Will's father has left behind not only the Luger but a picture of himself standing in the hatch of a Sherman tank. Still, he never disclosed what Will later discovered on his own – that his father's division had witnessed the liberation of Buchenwald. Significantly, this is the clue that allows Barrett to comprehend his father's death-wish: "Is not this in fact, Father, where your humanism ends in the end?"[24] Will comes to recognize two things: That his father's stoic humanism yielded a death-in-life that was less bearable than death itself, and which led there soon enough; and that the bankruptcy of this outlook on the world was pointed up in his father's oblique encounter with the Holocaust.[25] Now the question which up to this point has haunted him Will levels at his dead father:

> What if there is a sign? What about the Jews? Are the Jews a sign? And if so, a sign of what? Did you overlook something? There were the Romans, the Augusta Legion, yes. There was the Army of Northern Virginia, yes. There was the Afrika Korps, yes. But what about the Jews? Did you and the centurion overlook the Jews? What did you make of what happened to them?
> What to make, Father, of the Jews?[26]

In a further reference to the Holocaust, Barrett realizes that he himself is a survivor of his father's death-wish, "alive by a fluke like the sole survivor of Treblinka, who lived by a fluke, but did not really feel entitled to live."

Soon after these discoveries, Will Barrett has the chance to share his ideas on the Jews' significance with an Episcopal priest named Jack Curl. But Curl quickly adopts the narrator's perspective regarding Barrett's sanity, and is too sophisticated theologically to countenance the notion that Jews act as a sign in history: "Hopefully we've gotten past the idea that God keeps the Jews around suffering to avenge Christ's death," Curl replies condescendingly.[27] As a clergyman committed to "serious dialogue" with Catholics and Jews, Curl cannot accept the apocalyptic belief that the return of Jews to the Holy Land is a sign of the consummation of history. Will Barrett is not deterred by Curl's theological snobbery, however.

Yet while he cannot get free of his hunch that Jews are somehow witnesses to divine mystery, Barrett's concern with the Jews fails to yield a decisive result in his quest for existential balance. Midway through the novel, in fact, Barrett claims to have "given up his peculiar preoccupation with the Jews" in favor of a search for a more direct sign of God's presence. Barrett resolves to descend into an underground cave, where he will conduct the "ultimate scientific

experiment": he will ascertain final proof for or against God's existence and will not reemerge until such proof is in his possession. Not
surprisingly, however, Will's on-again-off-again Jewish obsession
and his new plot to force God's hand are closely related.

In the language of Percy the semiotician, Barrett desires to replace
an ambiguous sign ("Jews") with the signified itself ("God"), or at
least to discover a more definitive sign. Replacement has become
necessary because the previous sign has been devalued by a disturbing counter-sign:[28] "Now it appears," Will laments, "the Jews
may have not left North Carolina after all, and in fact are making
porno flicks and building condos and villas in Highlands, enjoying
the leaves, and in general behaving like everyone else. There goes
the last sign."[29] Underground, Will pleads with the Signifier to
"break his silence" and provide a clarification of distorted signs:
"Speak God, and let me know if the Jews are a sign and the Last
Days are at hand."[30]

In an example of Percy's wry narrative humor, Will Barrett's
experiment ends inconclusively when he is forced by an aching
tooth to exit the cave prematurely. His experiment does yield some
new information, however, for soon afterward Barrett is diagnosed
with a psychiatric disorder called "Hausmann Syndrome." Thus, it
seems, the narrator was right all along – Will Barrett suffers from
delusions and "inappropriate longings" which abate when his
blood pH imbalance is chemically normalized. He no longer
fantasizes about Ethel Rosenblum or the Jewish exodus from North
Carolina, and following some time in a convalescent home,
Will apparently is experiencing existential healing as well.

But at the end of the novel Percy surprises readers with another
reversal. Will meets Father Weatherbee, a decrepit Roman Catholic
priest who believes only in electric trains and apostolic succession.
In conversation with Weatherbee Will's Jew-obsession reemerges,
this time from the depths of a healthy mind. In contrast to Jack Curl,
Father Weatherbee does not dismiss Will's question about whether
"the historical phenomenon of the Jews ... may be said to be in some
fashion or another a sign."[31] As a result it is in Father Weatherbee's
presence that Will realizes that the Jews do signify: Since the Jew
Jesus was "a unique historical phenomenon, as unique as the Jews,"
and since Father Weatherbee's convictions about apostolic succession purport an actual connection with Jesus, the Jews are "the common denominator" between Will and the faith Father Weatherbee
represents.[32] Although he claims he is still an unbeliever, Will senses

he is on the track of something, and that "the Jews may be the clue."

In contrast to narrative voices in *The Second Coming* which interpret Will Barrett's concern with the presence and absence of Jews as a psychic delusion, Barrett finds in the Jews a mysterious sign with the capacity for illuminating meaning in the recesses of an apparently absurd world. Jews are the clue which guides Will's own circuitous search, and they are "the sign his father had missed."[33]

C. *The Thanatos Syndrome*

In Percy's final novel, *The Thanatos Syndrome*, the paradigmatic character of Jewish existence is again a dominant theme. In this work Jewish life and death are established as meaningful signs through a complex of subtle and unsubtle references to the Nazi "Final Solution." *The Thanatos Syndrome* was the sequel to an earlier novel entitled *Love in the Ruins* (1971). In both books, Percy's fictional "Feliciana Parish" in southern Louisiana opens a dystopic window through which readers are able to glimpse the American near-future.

In both novels Dr Tom More's researches with "heavy sodium" and his expertise in brain pharmacology sweep him into the story's action and make him a final obstacle to societal catastrophe. But in *The Thanatos Syndrome* the threatening disaster is not the result of visible societal breakdown as in *Love in The Ruins*, but of invisible forces working surreptitiously beneath society's exterior. The *Thanatos Syndrome*'s plot is driven by a conspiracy which threatens human tragedy on several fronts. The potential victims are the more vulnerable members of society: children, poor and minority populations, and the afflicted whose lives are judged as lacking quality. "Pedeuthanasia" and "gereuthanasia" have become quite legal in Feliciana and are practiced routinely at the Parish's "qualitarian centers." The narrative revolves, however, around a conspiracy to perpetrate an even grander violation of human freedom and dignity.

Utilizing federal funds and the umbrella of legitimacy provided by federal agencies, a group of Tom More's psychiatrist colleagues implement "Operation Blue Boy," a pharmacological attempt to contain violent crime and other social ills by leaking heavy sodium into the public water supply. To the conspirators' delight, their "treatment" dramatically reduces the incidence of street crime, child abuse, teen-age pregnancy and suicide, wife battering, homosexual activity and AIDS – social plagues which symbolize for them the "decay of the American social fabric." Given the astounding success of heavy sodium in allaying these societal ailments (crime in the streets is reduced by 85 per cent "overnight"), its therapeutic effects are naturally directed at the minority urban populations who are most affected.

As a program to engineer societal improvements which is under-girded by pseudo-science, Blue Boy reaches Nazi proportions; but it also achieves some desirable results. Previously hostile and aggress-ive segments of the population have become docile and peaceful. And while subhuman capacities for language and sexual expression are side effects of heavy sodium therapy, it also produces a super-human capability for information recall. Moreover, heavy sodium poisoning alleviates "such peculiarly human symptoms as anxiety, depression, stress, insomnia, suicidal tendencies, and chemical dependence." All this leads Tom More to characterize the mysteri-ous "syndrome" that is the result of heavy sodium poisoning "as a regression from a stressful human existence to a peaceable animal existence."

A consultant to the cabal who would repair Feliciana's social fabric by selectively toxifying the water supply is computer hack, soccer aficionado, and world-class bridge player John van Dorn. Van Dorn, too, is concerned with what he calls the "three social plagues" – crime, AIDS, and teen-age suicide and drug abuse – but he is a free-lancer with "bigger fish to fry." Van Dorn devotes much of his time to the hands-on operation of a private school called Belle Ame Academy, while citing as his personal mission "the sexual liberation of Western civilization."[34] Unfortunately, Van Dorn's *modus operandi* in this project of sexual liberation is the kind of abuse of his Belle Ame boarders that is sufficient to turn the stomach of a Louisiana redneck (as it does in the novel).

More's expertise in the pharmacology of radioactive isotopes makes him a natural for "joining the team" with the novel's conspirators; but it also puts him in a position to infiltrate Blue Boy and Belle Ame before a veritable human holocaust has been perpetrated. The term "holo-caust" is not unwarranted as a description of this threat. From the very beginning of the novel, explicit and oblique references of the Nazis and their racial ideology are to be found, most of them in descriptions of the conspirators. For instance, Bob Comeaux unravels his Hitlerian jus-tifications for Blue Boy as strains of German Romantic music fill the air inside his Mercedes. And John van Dorn, whose blue-eyed attractiveness gives him a vaguely Aryan persona, appears in Tom More's imagination as a "Prussian general," an "Afrika Korps Officer," and "a German officer standing in the open hatch of a tank and looking down at the Maginot Line." His fishing outfit includes a hat that resembles a "Wehrmacht Helmet."[35]

But the chief connection with the Nazis and the Holocaust in *The Thanatos Syndrome* is established through Father Rinaldo Smith, the whiskey priest who is Tom More's aged and addled friend. Smith is a secondary character who like his patron saint Simeon the Stylite has retreated from a corrupt world and become a contemporary pole-sitting desert father (he lives in a fire-tower). Father Smith, who like *The Second Coming*'s Will Barrett is portrayed as mentally unstable, is also preoccupied with Jews and their significance in the apocalyptic atmosphere of the late twentieth century. Smith, the reader learns, is convinced that Jews are "unsubsumable," are "the only sign of God which has not been evacuated by an evacuator," and are "a sign of God's presence" which constitutes a "proof."[36]

Smith reveals the extent of his fantasies concerning Jews – or, more accurately, the word-sign "Jew" – when Tom More ascends the fire tower which is Smith's work place, home and pulpit. Dr More has been sent to diagnose Smith's ministerial dysfunction, which it turns out is a problem not of intention or capacity, but of signification. For the peculiar nature of Smith's obsession is rooted in the failure of what Percy the philosopher called "triadic" communication. Their "dialogue" resists paraphrase, and thus necessitates this lengthy citation, in which Father Smith speaks first:

> "Words are signs, aren't they?"
> "You could say so."
> "But unlike the signs out there, words have been evacuated, haven't they?"
> "Evacuated?"
> "They don't signify anymore."
> ...
>
> [Father Smith "plays psychoanalyst" with Tom, giving him words and asking for More's free associations. To "Jew," More responds "Israel, Bible, Max, Sam, Julius, Hebrew, Hebe, Ben –"]
> ...
>
> "Unlike the other test words, what you associated with the word 'Jew' was Jews, Jews you have known. Isn't that interesting?"

"Yes," I say, pursing my mouth in a show of interest.

"What you associated with the word sign 'Irish' were certain connotations, stereotypical Irish stuff in your head. Same for Negro. If I had said Spanish, you'd have said something like guitar, castanets, bullfights, and such. I have done the test on dozens. Thus, these word signs have been evacuated, deprived of meaning something real. Real persons. Not so with Jews."

...

"That's the only sign of God which has not been evacuated by an evacuator," he says, moving his shoulders.

"What sign is that."

"Jews."

"Jews?"

"You got it Doc"...

"Got what?"

"You see the point."

"What's the point?

He leans close, eyes alight, "The Jews – cannot – be – subsumed."

"Can't be what?"

"Subsumed."

"I see."

"Since the Jews were the original chosen people of God, a tribe of people who are still here, they are a sign of God's presence which cannot be evacuated. Try to find a hole in that proof!"

...

"Try to subsume Jews under the classes of mankind, Caucasians, Semites, whatever. Go ahead, try it."

...

"The Jews as a word sign cannot be assimilated under a class, category, or theory. No subsuming Jews! Not even by the Romans."

"Right." I yank again [at the firetower's stairway door]. What's wrong with this damn thing?

"No subsuming Jews, Tom!"

"Okay, I won't."

"This offends people, even the most talented people, people of the loftiest sentiments, the highest scientific achievements, and the purest humanitarian ideals."

"Right."

...

"The Holocaust was a consequence of the sign which could not be evacuated."[37]

With his curious ideas regarding the unsubsumability of the word sign "Jew" as background, Father Smith goes on to condemn Dr More as a member of the first generation of physicians to turn their backs on Hippocrates. In prophetic tones, Smith announces that like the "enlightened" doctors of Weimar Germany More will end up killing Jews. He also makes the paradoxical claim that "tenderness always leads to the gas chamber."[38]

While this odd exchange may strike the reader as an inexplicable diversion from Percy's page-turner narrative, it actually contains clues necessary for understanding the book as a whole. Of course, Father Smith's bizarre ideas about Jews are not unfamiliar to readers of Percy's earlier novels. The priest gives a confident recital of the sorts of notions about Jews that Binx Bolling and Will Barrett generally kept to themselves. Father Smith believes that the Jews are God's original chosen people, that their continued existence is a sign and proof of God's presence, as well as a clue in the human search for divine truth, that as the unique people of God Jews can not or will not be subsumed by other peoples, and that non-Jews resist this fact, sometimes violently.

As the novel progresses it is made clear that Smith's strange aphorism about tenderness leading to the gas chamber actually derives from personal experience. In a second interruption to the main narrative entitled "Father Smith's Confession," Tom More listens to the maniacal priest relate the tale of his visit to Germany in the 1930s. Smith recalls being enthralled by the table talk of the Weimar psychiatrists who routinely gathered in the home of his father's cousin, himself a well-known child psychiatrist. Smith vividly remembers the psychiatrist's son, a boy about his own age who was at the time preparing to enter the SS training academy. On his departure, the young Simon Smith accepted a souvenir from his German friend – a bayonet etched with the words "blood and honor." Father Smith's cathartic admission is not that he found this would-be Nazi likable, or that he cherished the bayonet. Rather, he confesses that he would have joined Helmut Jäger as an SS cadet had he too grown up in Germany.

As difficult as this confession is for the aging priest, it seems insufficient in itself to precipitate a mental breakdown. But in a "footnote" to Father Smith's confession readers learn that there is much more to his German experience. As an American infantryman participating in the liberation of the Eglfing-Haar hospital near Munich, Smith made a terrifying discovery which has only bored its way into his soul after several decades. During the liberation, Smith ascertained that Dr Jäger, his relative and host in the 1930s, was personally administering Zyklon B to mentally ill children at Eglfing-Haar.[39] After this revelation, the narrative abruptly returns to Feliciana Parish and readers of *The Thanatos Syndrome* are left to ponder the well intentioned actions that ironically make murder and genocide possible.

Although the complexity of *The Thanatos Syndrome* is daunting, attention to its "German" and "Jewish" dimensions informs a reading of the novel as a parable of the Holocaust set in the American South. In Percy's parable we encounter Father Smith's outrageous notions about Jews, the "Blue Boy" conspiracy, and the stories of John van Dorn and Dr Jäger. Very cleverly, Percy ties these disparate elements together by novel's end. The chilling tales of of van Dorn and Jäger confirm Father Smith's admonition that the combination of a "lover of mankind" and a "theorist of mankind" is a recipe for genocide, and Smith's ravings about the unsubsumability of Jews allow us to comprehend why they were victims of our century's most notorious genocide.

Thus, in this book which ostensibly deals with crimes against children and the poor, "the Jews" are nevertheless principal characters. In fact, *The Thanatos Syndrome* is nearly unique among fictional works by non-Jews in its concern for Jewish life and the threats posed against it. Far from being a diversion from the plot, Father Smith's bizarre dissertation on the word-sign "Jew" is a pivotal exchange. It is pivotal because it reveals that Smith's experiences in Germany underlie his disabling obsession with Jews and Jewish suffering; but also because in it Percy indirectly addresses the problem of universalizing the Holocaust by de-Judaizing it. Through Father Smith Percy argues that attempts to view the Holocaust in non-Jewish terms will always fail for two reasons. First, because as representatives of the Hebraic principle the Jews were anything but accidental victims in the Nazi triumph of pagan mythology and Greek *techne*. Second, because the Jews cannot be subsumed under the abstract, universal categories that unite classical and modern Western thought.

Not surprisingly, Father Smith is also Percy's vehicle for communicating the centrality of the Jewish connection to authentic

Christianity. During his initial "confession," Smith refers to Helmut Jäger's cryptic fear that the Catholic Church is part of a "Judaic conspiracy." Upon reflection, Smith has come to realize that Helmut's parroting of Nazi ideology contained unwitting insight. Furthermore, in their first encounter Smith tells Tom More that the Romans, "who were not stupid people," mistook the early Christians for a Jewish sect. In doing so, Percy seems to be saying, the Romans grasped the historical bond between the two religious communities that modern Christians by and large ignore. Finally, at the very end of the novel, Smith recruits Tom to assist him in celebrating the Feast of Epiphany by leaving a coded message with Tom's wife Ellen: "Royalty, a visit, gifts – and a Jewish connection." "I think it's a valuable connection for you," Ellen comments unwittingly to Tom. And so it is.

For the perceptive reader Percy's message is clear: a Christianity allied with abstract ideals rather than rooted in unique revelatory events is likely to become another deadly ideology in the age of *thanatos*. True Christianity will retain its base in historical reality and will find its identity in the space-time advent of Jesus the Jew, in Mary the young red-faced Jewish girl, in its unique apostolic character, and in the penetration of matter by spirit.[40] These emphases can insure that Christianity will remain a "Judaic conspiracy" and have something meaningful to say again in the postmodern world. In the character of Father Smith Percy personifies a theology which speaks to the age of *thanatos*. It is a theology with the surviving Jew at its center.

Smith, in fact, is the Percyan character who seems to articulate Percy's own view of the Jews' relevance in the postmodern age.[41] Significantly, he is also the character who most clearly articulates Christian witness-people thinking. Smith echoes the witness-people notions that Israel and the church share an inseparable unity – he notes that "salvation comes from the Jews" and that the Romans first mistook Christians for a Jewish sect – and that the Jews "remain the beloved, originally chosen people of God."[42] And the fact that Father Smith's sanity is questioned even by his friends means – in the context of Percy's fictional corpus – that his witness-people approach to the Jews should be received as containing spiritual wisdom.

But Smith does not recapitulate the witness-people myth *per se*. In fact, several elements of the myth are conspicuously absent from his verbal ramblings, including the notions that Jews are cursed wanderers, Christ-killers, witnesses to judgment, and a people destined for restoration to their ancient homeland and conversion to Christ. As a result, Smith's apprehension of the Jewish people lacks the ambivalence that is characteristic of genuine witness-people theology. Yet Smith does give voice to a post-Holocaust version of the myth's fundamental tenet – that the Jewish people are a unique and unsubsumable entity whose survival comprises the only dependable sign of the divine presence in a world otherwise devoid of it. Most importantly, neither Smith nor Percy appear cognizant that this Christian view of the Jews is inseparable historically from the darker elements of the witness-people myth which pose a threat to the existence of the Jewish sign.

D. Reviews, Essays and Interviews

In some of his published nonfiction Percy offered direct evidence of his belief in the Jews' contemporary significance. In one of his earliest essays Percy displayed fascination at the remarkable survival of the Jewish people over time. He asks:

> Where are the Hittites?
> Why does no one find it remarkable that in most world cities today there are Jews but not one single Hittite, even though Hittites had a great flourishing civilization while the Jews nearby were a weak and obscure people?
> When one meets a Jew in New York or New Orleans or Paris or Melbourne, it is remarkable that no one considers the event remarkable. What are they doing here? But it is even more remarkable to wonder, if there are Jews here, why are there not Hittites here?
> Where are the Hittites? Show me one Hittite in New York City.[43]

In interviews Percy gave in the 1960s, he conveyed high esteem for the work of "Jewish novelists" like Bernard Malamud, Saul Bellow, Isaac Bashevis Singer and Joseph Heller. In fact, Percy claimed to possess more sympathy for the Jewish "renascence" represented by these writers than for the work of so-called Southern authors. What both groups share, Percy believed, is a desire to universalize from a particular culture, whether Southern or Jewish.[44] In a 1971 review of Walter M. Miller's *A Canticle for Leibowitz*, Percy described the "good vibes" given off by the novel as "Jewish – The coordinates of the novel are radically Jewish-Christian."[45] Percy is referring to what he believed was Miller's Jewish conception of time: there is "Something That Happened or Something That Will Happen" which defines everything before or after on the book's time line. Percy associated a historic, linear sense of time with "Israel," and contrasted this conception with the cyclical time of the Greeks and Orientals.[46]

But the most illuminating of Percy's nonfiction writings for comprehending his view of the Jewish people is "Why Are You a Catholic?," a short piece published in the last year of his life. Among the reasons cited in this essay for Percy's conversion to Catholic Christianity are the steadfastness of the church, which Percy describes as "Semitic." It is thanks to the Jews, Percy claims, that humanity has been able to emerge from the enchanted mists of the mythical past. The Jews are *not* mythical, for "[m]yths are stories which did not happen. But the Jews were there then are there now."[47] As a guide for the postmodern era, then, the Jew remains dependable, a sign *par excellence*:

> Semitic? Semiotic? Jews and the science of signs? Yes, because in this age of the lost self, lost in the desert of theory and consumption, nothing of significance remains but signs. And only two signs are of significance in a world where all theoretical cats are gray. One is oneself and the other is the Jews. But for the self that finds itself lost in the desert of theory and consumption, there is nothing to do but set out as a pilgrim in the desert in search of a sign. In the desert, that of theory and consumption, there remains only one sign, the Jews. By "the Jews" I mean not only Israel, the exclusive people of God, but the worldwide *ecclesia* instituted by one of them, God-become-man, a Jew.[48]

The central place of the Jews in Percy's religious vision is suggested by the fact that his view of the church is derived from his understanding of the Jews. As Percy implied in his fiction through characters like Father Weatherbee and Father Smith, it is the church's original and essential "Jewishness" which qualify it to be the sign of God's presence which it seeks to be: "a saving remnant, a sign of contradiction, a stumbling block, a transcultural phenomenon, a pilgrim church."[49]

III. PERCY SCHOLARSHIP AND THE WITNESS-PEOPLE MYTH

Since his death the number of new studies of Percy and his work has steadily grown. Oddly though, despite compelling literary evidence of Percy's career-long obsession with the modern meaning of the Jewish people, there exists no in-depth analysis of this side of his work. Many critics have acknowledged that in some of Percy's writings Jews are invested with a unique signifying power, but they are more likely to view this as a novelistic quirk than a window on Percy's religious imagination. Even intriguing clues that his characters' obsessions were also Percy's own have not generated much scholarly interest. Why do major characters in Walker Percy's novels speak in mythic terms of the Jews and their survival? What implications does this have for interpreting Percy's fiction? Such questions one expects scholars to seize on. But very few have.

Noted literary critic Harold Bloom is one in whom we might expect a sensitivity to Jew-obsessed authors. But while he counsels that Percy's Jewish images be treated carefully, his response to Percy's interest in the apocalyptic significance of the Jewish people is surprisingly magnanimous.[50] In his editor's "Introduction" to a volume on Percy's fiction, Bloom is content to distinguish Percy from his more fanatical co-religionists:

> With a stance very different from that of Protestant fundamentalists, he [Percy] regards the Jews as the eternal evidence for the reality of Yahweh, and the historical authenticity of the Roman Catholic Church. Like most of the Jewish people, I am normally rather wary of such a search for evidences, but Percy handles it with tact and humane wit.... Miraculously surviving, the Jews are the searcher's prime mark or sign of the promise of God that cannot be voided. The culmination of this sign in Percy is Will Barrett's humorous but obsessive concern with the supposed absence or flight of Jews from North Carolina in *The Second Coming*.... The saving difference between this madness [of Will Barrett] and the somber stuff I hear from television evangelists every night is that Barrett is only mad north-northwest, and Percy's apocalyptic wind is blowing at us from the south.[51]

Bloom's discussion of the Jew-obsessed in Percy's stock of characters is necessarily brief and superficial. I cite it because it contains one of the few evaluative references to this aspect of Percy's fiction in the critical literature. In general, interpreters of Percy's fiction who have considered his portrayal of Jews at all – and this is a small minority – do not pause even briefly to critique it.

Critics who do treat this theme typically do so with regard to its function within a particular novel. For instance, in a recent book on the apocalyptic element in Percy's fiction, Gary M. Cuiba offers the following comments on Father Smith's conviction that the Jews make God's word present in history:

> The Jews name the vital connection that seems lacking in the novel's lifeless world. As a tribe, they are united to each other by semiotic bonds; as a sign they collectively form the intersection between humanity and divinity. The beloved people of God incarnate the word of the Lord before the world. Their continued existence points to God's perduring presence, for despite the thanatos syndrome the Jews cannot be nullified either in semantics or in history.[52]

According to Cuiba, the novel's subtle and explicit references to Nazi genocide confirm the accuracy of Father Smith's view that Hitler's attempted destruction of God's chosen people was emblematic of the century of *thanatos*. Cuiba then adds a personal observation:

> Indeed, the twentieth century has replaced the Jewish sense of exile with mindless complacency; its fullness of speech with the emptiness of sounds; its incarnate existence with abstraction and slaughter; its salvation history with spiritual amnesia. The thanatos syndrome is another name for the truly mortal sin of the century: eliminating the inherent Jewishness that defines humanity.[53]

Cuiba not only fails to criticize Percy's theological vision of the Jewish people, he elaborates his own post-Holocaust version the witness-people myth, interpreting anti-Semitism in terms that are reminiscent of Barth's *Church Dogmatics*.

In an article entitled "Walker Percy, Flannery O'Connor and the Holocaust" John F. Desmond has offered an extended analysis of Jewish existence in *The Thanatos Syndrome*. Desmond contends that the novel was Percy's attempt to explain how something like the Holocaust was possible in the modern world, and refers to the book as a "long meditation on the meaning of the Jews in the history of the West...."[54] According to Desmond, Percy's views on the Holocaust are laid out in the dialogue between Father Smith and Tom More concerning language's deprival of meaning. Specifically, Smith's "Christian vision of history" elucidates the Nazis' rejection of this vision and its replacement by another myth: "The attempt to exterminate the Jews in the Holocaust is implicitly an attempt to exterminate God, the True Signifier, from history."[55] According to Desmond,

> The unique particularity of the Jews is linked to their unique historical character. Redemption history begins with the Jews and is defined by the Incarnation. Henceforth, Smith argues that because the Jews are the original chosen people of God, the focus of salvation in history, they are an ineradicable sign of God's presence in the world, one that cannot be evacuated of meaning.[56]

Desmond's analysis is incisive at two points. He notes that for Percy the Holocaust exists as "a sign of a much greater drama being acted out in history, the drama of the struggle with evil and the quest for salvation." Desmond also recognizes that in *The Thanatos Syndrome* "the Jewish experience in history and the Christ event which issues from it are the unique clues" needed to answer the theological question "what is man [*sic*]?"[57] Yet despite his insightful words about *how* the Jews function in Percy's final novel, Desmond fails to consider *why* the Jewish people must play such a central role in his narrative craft. Desmond's analysis of Percy's relation to the Holocaust ignores the possible connections between the *Shoah* and the mythological understanding of the Jews which Percy transmits. This failure is disturbing, but not uncommon among critics who share Percy's "Christian view of history."[58]

To date, the most extensive consideration of "the Jews" in Percy's fiction appears in a short article by Kathleen Scullin-Esser entitled "Connecting the Self with What is Outside the Self in *The Thanatos Syndrome*."[59] Though it too is concerned primarily with Percy's final novel, this essay includes a rare thematic treatment of his portrayal of Jews. In a long endnote, Scullin-Esser relates her surprise at the lack of scholarly attention this topic has received:

> No reviewer of *The Thanatos Syndrome* identifies the Jews as the crux of the novel. Of the fifteen reviews which I have seen, only

four bring up the topic, and of those, two reviewers regard the issue as unimportant.

...

It is safe to say, in fact, that the subject of the Jews as modern-day clues of God is generally bypassed in Percy criticism, despite the prominence of the theme in the two earlier novels: *The Moviegoer* and *The Second Coming*.[60]

But in her own comments on *The Thanatos Syndrome* Scullin-Esser laments Tom More's resistance to perceiving Jews as other Percyan characters do – "as a concrete way of recovering a sense of God's presence." She notes that unlike Will Barrett, More's scientific and objectifying mindset prohibits him from recognizing Jews as the "people who are seekers of signs, a people historically visited and sustained by God, and a people from whom arose the great sign of the Incarnation, the word made flesh."[61] However, More's apparent refusal to embrace Father Smith's perceptions of Jewish existence does not alter the fact that "the Jews – are a crux in this novel," since

they signify the possibility of recovering the signs of God – having been chosen to be such a sign in history, and to give birth to the sign, the Word of God. Yet they are also the natural targets of those who deny the signs of God and subvert the posture of the symbol-user, subsuming the other who is deemed valueless. They are at the center of the choice which, Father Smith tells Tom, "given a chance," one must in the end make – "life or death.[62]

Scullin-Esser argues that in *The Thanatos Syndrome* a failure of the symbolic partnership underlies the human holocausts which transpire in Germany and Louisiana:

Meaningful signs, the only means of connecting the self with what is outside the self are what the victims of the syndrome are deprived of; and ultimately they are then also deprived of the connection with God, who reveals Himself through signs.[63]

But why Jewish human beings are selected as the living signs of God's self-revelation Scullin-Esser does not explain. The answer lies in a Christian mythology of which she is apparently no more cognizant than Walker Percy. In fact, Scullin-Esser adds her own voice to Percy's song of celebration for the Jews' mysterious but permanent location at the center of salvation history. Despite uncovering a lacuna in Percy scholarship, Scullin-Esser's analysis takes us no further toward an understanding of Percy's treatment of the Jews, its sources or its implications.

Only a handful of critics have ventured to suggest a possible source for the Jew-obsessions in Percy's writings. Following Lewis A. Lawson, Martin Luschei notes that Kierkegaard's "absorbing interest" in the legend of the Wandering Jew – who typified doubt, sensuality and despair for the Danish philosopher[64] – is at the root of Percy's preoccupation with Jews, Jewish wandering, and Jewish suffering. Kierkegaard was undoubtedly an important influence on Percy's thinking, but the legend of the Wandering Jew is only one image of the alienated individual which pervades Kierkegaard's writings. It has also been proposed that Percy's reading of Gabriel Marcel provided the source for his "Christian notion of man as a wayfarer in search of his salvation...."[65] But this does not begin to explain why Percy consistently Judaized the castaway/wayfarer image in his fiction.

To date the most thoughtful explanation for Percy's treatment of the Jews has been advanced by Ralph C. Wood. In "The Alienated Self and the Absent Community in the Work of Walker Percy" Wood asserts that Percy's writings manifest an "existentialist understanding of Jews."[66] Wood contends that "for Percy the Jews have scandalous significance because they are the consummate peregrine people, the unsettled vagabond race." In their wanderings the Jews become "unwelcome reminders of the anguish that is intrinsic to human existence...." While this apprehension of the Jewish people may be typical among existentialist thinkers, it is fundamentally theological, as Wood intimates by employing Barthian language to describe it. Barth's "mirrors" could be substituted for "unwelcome reminders" without Wood's point being compromised.[67]

Ultimately, then, Wood obscures the deeply religious nature of Percy's thinking about Jews. While both Barth and Percy were influenced in their formative years by Kierkegaard and other existentialist writers, they shared much more than this. Both men operated within the intellectual world of orthodox Christianity; thus both men must be considered Christian existentialists if they are existentialists at all. These disparate minds share not only the search for meaningful signs in a world distorted by sin, but a conviction that the sign *par excellence* is to be found among the Jews.

IV.   CONCLUSION

As we have seen, despite the large and growing body of Percy scholarship now in existence, no critic has successfully explored the references to Jews and their unique capacity as human signifiers which proliferate Percy's writing. Even scholars who acknowledge this proliferation or seek to identify its sources have neglected to ask *why* Percy transmitted his Jew-images so consistently.

There are a few meagre clues in Percy's biography. Greenville, the Mississippi Delta town where Percy spent his formative years, was known for its tolerance of Jews and for the vital Jewish community which invigorated its civic life. Percy had Jewish friends and love-interests there, and his life-long friend, Greenville native Shelby Foote, is of partly Jewish descent.[68] The most promising bio-graphical clue to Percy's interest in the fate of Jews, however, is his excursion to Germany in 1934.[69] Although Percy mentioned this trip only in a few interviews toward the end of his life, some reviewers of *The Thanatos Syndrome* have considered it a key for interpreting his final novel.

As an eighteen-year-old college sophomore Percy spent seven weeks traveling throughout Germany and Austria. After a brief period in Bonn with the family of his German professor, Percy left the group with whom he had sailed and set out on his own. On several occasions, Percy's travels brought him into contact with European history in the making. He arrived in Vienna the day following the Nazi assassination of the Austrian chancellor; and while visiting Berlin, Percy found himself in a crowd that had gathered to catch a glimpse of Hitler. After being struck on the head by a man who demanded that he demonstrate his loyalty to the Führer, Percy also raised a salute to Hitler.[70] A less dramatic but apparently deeper impression was left on Percy during his stay in Bonn. In interviews in 1981 and 1988, Percy recalled the family of his German professor's nephew, with whom he lodged:

I spent a summer in Germany in 1934, and I lived with a family in Bonn. The father was a member of the S.A., *Schutz Abwehr*, and the son was a member of *Hitlerjugend*. There was a tre-mendous excitement at the "rejuvenation" of Germany, and the creation of new values in the Nietzschean sense: the death of God, the death of old values, and the creation of new values. I remember this young *Hitlerjugend* was very excited about the possibilities of the future. There was nothing about the Jews at the beginning.[71]

[My German professor's nephew's son] was dead serious, with his impressive uniform, and he was graduating from the Hitler Jugend and going to Schutzstaffel. I remember he talked about the Teutonic knights, and taking the oath at Marienberg, the ancient castle. There was a tremendous mystique there. I don't remember the Jews being mentioned the whole time. There was no particular thing about Jews. This was before Krystalnacht [*sic*] when they began to beat up Jews.[72]

These quotes, as any reader of *The Thanatos Syndrome* will recognize, are the germ for what became "Father Smith's Confession." Should we infer that Father Smith's admission that he might have joined the SS is Percy's own soul-baring? There is evidence that the young Percy did admire Willy Langnickel (his teacher's nephew's son in Bonn) and his devotion to the Nazi cause. Percy's biographer has concluded that he was much like the Smiths and Jägers in *The Thanatos Syndrome* in the sense that what truly impressed him in 1934 was

not National Socialism, not racial purity, not industrial recovery or territorial expansion, but the oldest strain of Teutonic romanticism, the *Lebenstod* that runs from the oldest German sagas, through the romances, Wagnerian opera, and Weimar culture before erupting with terrifying vividness in the mythology and symbolism of Nazism, particularly in the early and strongly cultural phase of Nazism.[73]

Following this line of interpretation, *The Thanatos Syndrome* reveals two things which remained profoundly disturbing to Percy as he considered the historical results of Nazism: First, his naïve fascination with the ethos of National Socialism, which according to one account left him "terribly impressed."[74] In *The Thanatos Syndrome* Percy's fascination is reflected in Father Smith's admission that in his youth he too was susceptible to the excitement sweeping Germany in the 1930s. A direct clue that Father Smith speaks for Percy is the teenaged Smith's acceptance of a bayonet from SS cadet Helmut Jäger, a gift that surely represents the souvenir bayonet Percy himself brought home in 1934. Percy intimates the momentous danger in this adolescent response to the call of patriotism and adventure when Father Smith says of Helmut Jäger that "what he hoped to do was not become a military policeman like many of the SS but a member of an SS division and incorporated into the Wehrmacht, the German army." Helmut's lack of overt anti-Semitism notwithstanding, his determination to serve in the Waffen-SS likely made him a cog in the killing machine that was the "Final Solution."

Just as disturbing as his youthful fascination with the myth of "blood and honor" must have been Percy's failure to recognize the real threat facing Jews by 1934. By the time of Percy's visit, the Nazis were already well on their way to systematically excluding Jews from every sector of German society. Dachau had been open for over a year, the German Church Struggle was in full swing, and Hitler had revealed his penchant for terror in his purge of the SA on June 30. Strangely, when he spoke of his German sojourn in the 1980s Percy made a point of reminding interviewers that "there was nothing about the Jews in the beginning [of the Nazi era]." Perhaps this not quite accurate reminiscence was Percy's way of rationalizing his obliviousness to the anti-Jewish campaign which was in full swing by the summer of 1934.

Perhaps, then, in *The Thanatos Syndrome* Percy portrayed the Jews as agents of mystery and signification in order to remind his readers of the "Jewish sign" he had so inexplicably overlooked as a young man. Reflecting for decades on his excursion to Germany at such a fateful moment in its history, Percy must have been troubled more and more by his inability to perceive the emerging Nazi threat, despite his vantage point. One response to this youthful myopia was his later refusal to de-Judaize the Holocaust, although he clearly intended to universalize its implications. As a result, *The Thanatos Syndrome* is distinguished among fictional works by non-Jews in that Jews are consistently portrayed as people with a historical, material and personal reality *sui generis*.

Yet despite the relevance of Percy's German experiences for understanding his focus on the Holocaust and the Jews in *The Thanatos Syndrome*, Percy's overall picture of "the Jews" can be appreciated only from a religious perspective. It makes sense, in other words, only if Percy is viewed as a Christian thinker, albeit one who was determined to translate the church's message for a generation that could no longer fathom traditional religious language. As a Christian writer, Percy unconsciously recapitulated elements of the witness-people myth, an ancient constellation of beliefs and hopes nurtured by the marvelous persistence of God's beloved people. Without doubt casual and professional readers of Percy will continue to conclude that his theological apprehension of Jews is innocuous. Jewish and non-Jewish interpreters alike have tended toward this view, with some casting him as a philosemite. But – and this is the matter on which Jewish and non-Jewish critics critics have exhibited a disturbing myopia – any conception of Jews which locates them at the center of a theological vision of history should be cause for concern in the post-Holocaust environment.

As has been argued in earlier chapters, the Christian philosemitism inherent in witness-people theology had the ironic effect of aiding the Nazi attempt to mythicize Jews and their role in history. In a post-Holocaust world, analysis of Christian texts must be newly sensitive to justifications for Jewish wandering or suffering that interpret these as signals of God's providence. It should also reflect an awareness of Christian discourse's potential for exacerbating Jewish vulnerability by portraying Jewish life as abnormal, theologically or otherwise. Very simply, texts which encourage non-Jewish readers to construe Jewish exile, Jewish suffering, and Jewish existence as symbols of divine mystery diminish the likelihood of a normalized and secure Jewish life.

Richard Rubenstein has argued that as long as the Jewish people are accounted for mythically, magically and theologically Jews will not be safe. Although Percy had philosemitic leanings and became increasingly conscious of the Holocaust's legacy as he grew older, his novels transmit precisely the kind of Christian mythologizing of Jewish existence which Rubenstein warns of. Thus, we can only conclude that many of Percy's texts render Jews in dangerous ways. Even ostensibly positive Jew-images are troublesome when, as Percy's character Father Smith recognizes, the word-sign "Jew" and real Jewish individuals are connected in the minds of anti- and philosemites alike. In fact, Percyan heroes like Binx Bolling, Will Barrett, and Father Smith have in common with Jew-obsessed denizens of the real world – including Adolf Hitler[75] – an acute awareness that the mythical "Jew" is incarnated in every Jewish person they encounter. This fact alone is sufficient cause for a new critical attitude to Walker Percy's fiction.

V. EPILOGUE: THE WITNESS-PEOPLE MYTH IN THE POST-HOLOCAUST WORLD

The preceding two chapters have elucidated parallels in the descriptions of Jewish existence in the systematic theology of Karl Barth and the novels and essays of Walker Percy. Binx Bolling's announcement that Jews are the "first real clue" in his horizontal search is reminiscent of Barth's contentions that Jews represent the sole natural proof for God's reality and that their history comprises a trace of divine world governance. Will Barrett's private musings – "Watch the Jews, their mysterious comings and goings and stay-ings!"[76] – resonate with Barth's conviction that Jewish persistence is a "mystery of faith" and a sign of Christ's Kingdom. In *The Thanatos Syndrome* Father Smith proclaims – in terms that echo Barth's discussion of Jewish history in *Church Dogmatics* III:3 – that society is offended by the unsubsumability of the Jewish sign and that anti-Semitism is born out of non-Jewish resentment of the truth that the Jew represents. And in his notion of the Jew as a mirror of sinful humanity Barth expresses Smith's view that "the Holocaust was a consequence of [this] sign which could not be evacuated."[77]

Yet despite these unambiguous similarities in their use of Jewish images, we need not search for direct lines of influence between the two men. For like the perennial myth of the Wandering Jew and the recurring "Jews, your majesty!" legend of Enlightenment Europe, the common perceptions of Jews in the writings of Barth and Percy are twentieth-century expressions of the Christian witness-people myth. This Swiss Protestant theologian and American Catholic philosopher/novelist shared a world view that was "Christian" in the broadest sense; this alone was apparently enough to determine that their work would mirror the witness-people myth whenever they wrote about the Jewish people.

Significantly, in neither case did consciousness of the Holocaust do anything to disabuse these men of their witness-people notions. In fact, the Holocaust seems to have only intensified their natural tendency to cast Jews in mythical dimensions. The radical evil of modern anti-Semitism and the Jews' miraculous survival of the "Final Solution" demonstrated for them the timeless salience of religious categories. Thus both sought to insure the physical security of the Jewish people in the future by reminding Christians of the Jews' unique theological significance. In this sense, Barth and Percy exhibit the same contradictions Richard Rubenstein discovers in

Dean Grüber. While working diligently to end the scourge of anti-Semitism among his compatriots, Grüber remains convinced that Jews live under a special obligation to behave like the people of God.

The cases of Barth and Percy suggest not only that the witness-people myth survives in modern Christian discourse, but that even the Holocaust has done little to deter Christian thinkers from apprehending Jews mythically. The writings of Barth and Percy do not provide enough evidence for drawing a general conclusion about the witness-people myth and post-Holocaust Christianity. Before arriving at that point, we must investigate other corners of the Christian imagination in which the myth continues to thrive.

6

Christian Holocaust Theology and the Witness-People Myth: The Jews' Fate as Sign, The Holocaust as Revelation, Israel as Message

> When we remember such historical periods as the Crusades, the Inquisition, pogroms or the Holocaust, we Christians must ever acknowledge our guilt in the eyes of others and in the eyes of God for the treatment of those we have also recognized as being among His Chosen People.
>
> Harry James Cargas, *Reflections of a Post-Auschwitz Christian*

> In a way mysterious and awesome, the Jews who perished in Hitler's Europe perished for a truth which Christians ... betrayed: that the Author and Judge of history was made manifest to us out of the Jews.
>
> Franklin H. Littell, "Church Struggle and the Holocaust"

> When we cut ourselves off from Judaism, we cut ourselves off from a living *heir of* and *witness to* biblical faith, from those in whom biblical faith lives on directly and, in many ways, less ambiguously than among ourselves.
>
> Clark Williamson, *Has God Rejected His People?*

> [T]heology that takes the "Holocaust" as a datum for Christian thought runs the risk of subsuming Judaism once again under the categories of Christian doctrine and experience.
>
> Katherine Sonderegger, *That Jesus Christ was Born a Jew*

> [I]f in the name of a struggle against the Shoah-*event*, we are left with the identical religious affirmation and drives that led to the Shoah, *and*

120

may contribute to a new Shoah, *our condition is like unto the man who was delivered of one unclean spirit only to be afflicted by seven more evil ones* (Matthew 12: 43–45).

A. Roy Eckardt, "Contemporary Christian Theology and
A Protestant Witness for the *Shoah*"

This chapter explores the phenomenon of Christian Holocaust theology as an instance of the witness-people myth's potency in contemporary theological reflection. In designating the concerns and tendencies of this theological movement, I will refer to a small group of thinkers whom I regard as "Holocaust theologians."[1] Although their number includes several Europeans, this chapter is concerned primarily with North American Holocaust theologians, especially John Pawlikowski, Paul van Buren, Franklin Littell, Alice L. and A. Roy Eckardt, Gregory Baum, Monika Hellwig, Robert Everett and James Moore. It is true that I am inferring the presence of an intellectual movement from the work of a few authors. I am emboldened to do so, however, by the surprising continuities in the writings of these men and women. While their visions for the future of Christian theology occasionally diverge, these theologians agree that the fundamental failure of Christendom in the past can be located in its conception and treatment of the Jew.

This chapter includes a definition of "Holocaust theology," some detailing of its character and presuppositions, and a discussion of the relationship between Christian Holocaust theology and the witness-people dynamic. Its role in assisting Christianity's repudiation of anti-Judaism generally has spared Holocaust theology from the kind of criticisms brought to bear in this chapter.[2] In asserting them here I do not intend to undermine or underestimate the contributions of Holocaust theologians in analyzing both the Christian tradition and the Christian mind. I only seek to illuminate the way Christian Holocaust theology itself is often a conduit for aspects of the Christian imagination it has helped to expose.

I.   CHRISTIAN HOLOCAUST THEOLOGY: A DEFINITION

Despite wide use, the term "Holocaust theology" is rarely provided with a concise definition. Such a definition is necessary, however, and is easily supplied: Holocaust theology is any sustained theological reflection for which the slaughter of six million Jews by the Nazis and their accomplices functions as a criterion, whether the *Shoah* displaces or merely qualifies traditional theological criteria and norms such as Scripture, tradition, reason and religious experience. Though precise, this definition would be more serviceable if theologians who embrace the Holocaust as a criterion for theology stated this fact explicitly.

Only in a few cases has the Holocaust's status as theological criterion been established axiomatically:

After Auschwitz, every theological "profundity" which is unrelated to people and their concrete situations must cease to exist.

... Auschwitz ... is not really a matter of revising Christian theology with regard to Judaism, but a matter of revising Christian theology altogether.

Never again should any theologian write anything that might even remotely reopen the path from supersession to genocide.[3]

More typically, the Holocaust theologians utilize the dramatic terminology of "endpoint," "interruption," "crisis," "break," "rupture," "paradigm shift" and *"metanoia"* to communicate the Holocaust's monumental impact on Christian faith. However, both approaches transmit the same message: The Holocaust signals the moral bankruptcy of any theology which lacks an awareness of anti-Judaism's deep roots in Christian faith and the ongoing complicity of Christians in Jewish suffering.

A simpler definition of Holocaust theology would include any theological discourse in which the Holocaust is an overriding concern. But this common sense approach is inadequate because the works explored here do not focus exclusively on the *Shoah*. Yet even when Holocaust theologians investigate the roots of anti-Semitism in Christian history and critique the history of doctrine in areas like election, covenant, providence, redemption, anthropology, Christology, sin, mission, and eschatology, they are laboring in the long shadow of the Nazi "Final Solution." Working here they are attempting to fashion a version of Christian faith able to make what Roy and Alice Eckardt call the "long night's journey into day."

As the Eckardts' description of their task implies, our technical definition of Holocaust theology fails to evoke its experiential and emotional dimensions. For that reason, any adequate description must draw attention to a conviction and a wager out which all Christian Holocaust theology proceeds. The conviction is that the treatment of Jews by Christians and by Christendom over two millennia and culminating in the Holocaust is an indisputable sign of the church's apostasy from authentic Christianity. The wager is that through a sustained grappling with this problem the church may yet secure for itself, if not forgiveness, at least a new sense of its mission before God.

II.   HOLOCAUST THEOLOGY AND THE WITNESS-PEOPLE MYTH

The frequency with which words like "witness" and "sign" are applied to the Jewish people in the writings of Holocaust theologians makes it tempting to subject them to an extensive rhetorical analysis. But there is more to be gained by assuming a broader perspective and highlighting links between the witness-people myth and some of Holocaust theology's formal aspects. The most striking of these formal links involves the symbolic function of Jews in traditional Christian thought and in Holocaust theology. For despite their intention of overturning the tradition they have inherited, the Holocaust theologians actually recapitulate the symbolic structure of the witness-people myth: As superlative symbols of Christian failure, Jewish history, Jewish survival and the Jews themselves are reinvested with the unique signifying function they have so often possessed in the Christian imagination.

A.   Anti-Judaism as a Sign of Apostasy

Over the last thirty years or so many Christian theologians have come to explicitly reject traditional beliefs about Jews, including the notions that Jews are accursed, superseded, or cut off from God, that they were or are dispersed and in exile as a judgment for "rejecting" Jesus Christ, and that as a result of their response to Jesus they have forfeited their role in salvation history. Johann-Baptist Metz has expressed the compulsion in Christian post-Holocaust reflection to avoid conceptions of Jews and Jewish history which have governed the past:

Yet how are we Christians to come to terms with Auschwitz? We will in any case forego the temptation to interpret the suffering of the Jewish people from our standpoint, in terms of saving history. Under no circumstances is it *our* task to mystify this suffering. *We* encounter in this suffering first of all only the riddle of our own lack of feeling, the mystery of our own apathy, not, however the traces of God.[4]

Unfortunately, however, such warnings have not been sufficient to extricate post-Holocaust Christian discourse from the subtle effects of the witness-people myth.

Holocaust theologians have assiduously avoided giving credence to the sort of thinking they believe animates historic anti-Judaism. Most, in fact, would like to extirpate all vestiges of the "teaching of contempt" from Christian faith. But this very desire points to an assumption which is implicit throughout their writings: That Christian anti-Judaism reveals unequivocally the church's failure to live up to its divine calling. Franklin Littell, in one of the key texts of Christian Holocaust Theology, refers to the church's failure *vis-à-vis* the Jews as its "wholesale apostasy."[5] But for Christian anti-Judaism and anti-Semitism to represent a mass apostasy on the part of baptized Christians, the Jew must once again be "the sign that the God who is God yet rules."[6] It is only because the Jew's intimate connection with God is assumed that anti-Semitism among Christians may be confidently condemned as blasphemy.

The Holocaust Theologians' privileging of anti-Judaism as a *topos* in Christianity is an updated version of the witness-people conviction that Jewish fate is extraordinarily relevant for Christians. It is true, of course, that pre-Holocaust theologies regarded the fate of the Jew as *a sign of God's judgment upon Israel for its refusal to embrace the truth manifest in the church*. Holocaust theology, on the other hand, divines in the fate of the Jews *a sign of God's judgment on the church for refusing to recognize the truth manifest in Israel*. Despite this difference in substance, however, there exists an important continuity in form: If the sign to which the attention of the church is directed by Holocaust theology involves Jewish exile, suffering, destruction, resurrection and restoration, and if this is construed as a sign *par excellence* of God's intention for the church, then the writings of the Holocaust theologians can be interpreted as another episode in the life of the witness-people myth.

As we have seen, the ascription of theological import to Jewish life and death has a long history in the Christian mind. In its contention that the church's departure from God's purposes is disclosed in its oppression of the Jew, Christian Holocaust theology reiterates the ancient tenet that God's presence and activity in a fallen and ambiguous world is nevertheless perceived in shifting Jewish fortunes. No matter how vigorously the negative contents of the myth are rejected, the underlying belief that history is the arena of God's judgment – a notion long relied upon by Christian thinkers to explain or justify Jewish misfortune – has not been disavowed. While the rhetoric of Holocaust theology proclaims a repudiation of mythology, the reality is that Holocaust theologians continue to regard the Jewish people *mythically*, which is to say, through the lens of Christian faith.

Recovery from the apostasy to which Christian Holocaust theologians refer requires true *metanoia*. But it is difficult to determine what a Christianity that had experienced true metanoia *vis-à-vis* Jews would look like. For instance, Roy Eckardt responds to The Second Vatican Council's admission of Christian responsibility for Jewish suffering by asking:

> Could there be any more damning judgment upon the church of our century than this one – that not until after the day of Auschwitz did Christians see fit to fabricate a correction of the record?[7]

Some Holocaust theologians have sought to make the Christian posture toward the State of Israel the basis of a new Jewish test for apostasy. In this case too, attitudes toward Jews are thought to provide an infallible diagnostic tool for determining the health of Christianity.

For contemporary Christian Holocaust theologians, then, as for Christian thinkers like Martin Luther and Johannes Pfefferkorn in the Reformation era and Karl Barth in the first half of this century, the church encounters its true reflection only in the "Jewish mirror." Even the titles of books in the Holocaust theology genre – titles like *The Crime of Christendom*, *The Crucifixion of the Jews*, *The Anguish of the Jews*, *The Jews: A Chronicle for Christian Conscience* and *Anti-Semitism and the Christian Mind* – resonate with the notion that Jewish suffering has an unparalleled power to reveal the haggard spiritual condition of Christianity.

B.   The Holocaust as Revelation

A second dimension of Holocaust theology's unconscious recapitulation of the witness-people myth pertains to its interpretation of the Holocaust. If Christianity's historic anti-Judaism is an infallible sign of the church's apostasy, the Holocaust comprises a word from God which may qualify as contemporary revelation. The first step toward establishing the Holocaust's revelatory credentials is an assertion of its import for Christian people. This is fundamental, since the *Shoah* cannot be as a sign or message for the church until it is acknowledged as a *Christian* problem. A useful tool in the task of presenting it as such has been Holocaust theology's "rhetoric of continuity." The rhetoric of continuity is used to imply connections between Christian Jew-hatred and Nazi anti-Semitism.

A prominent example of continuity rhetoric is Franklin Littell's oft-cited assertion that "the cornerstone of Christian Antisemitism is the superseding or displacement myth ... [which] already rings with a genocidal note."[8] Roy Eckardt's writings contain equally powerful examples of this rhetoric, including his claim of a "fateful causal relation between the Christian message and the death camps of Europe," his contention that "the Holocaust shows the final logic ... of Christian anti-Semitism ...," and his allegation that the Nazi Final Solution "comprises an ultimate incarnation" of the church's teaching of contempt for Jews.[9] Harry James Cargas concurs in substance with Littell and Eckardt: "the mistaken emphasis on law over love in Christian teaching, whether it be official or unofficial, is in large part both cause and effect of the Holocaust."[10] And Rosemary Ruether implies something very similar when she asks: "Is it possible to say 'Jesus is Messiah' without, implicitly or explicitly, saying at the same time 'and the Jews be damned'?"[11]

These American Holocaust theologians echo the sentiments of their esteemed predecessor, the British scholar James Parkes, who wrote that "more than six million deliberate murders are the consequence of the teachings about Jews for which the Christian church is ultimately responsible."[12] How does Parkes attempt to demonstrate this responsibility? Not surprisingly, via the rhetoric of continuity:

> there is no break in the line which leads from the beginning of the denigration of Judaism in the formative period of Christian history, from the exclusion of Jews from civic equality in the period of the church's first triumph in the fourth century, through the

horrors of the Middle Ages, to the Death Camps of Hitler in our own day.[13]

An assumption underlying each of these statements is that genocide is intrinsic to the traditional Christian understanding of the Jewish people. While no doubt powerful on an emotional level, this assumption is dubious historically. But of course continuity rhetoric is not careful argumentation. It is a literary method of establishing a point of contact between the Holocaust and the Christian reader.

A second way Holocaust theologians suggest the *Shoah*'s revelatory qualities is by utilizing what might be called the "terminology of disruption." As was noted above words like "break," "rupture," "endpoint," "crisis," "interruption" and *"metanoia"* are frequently used to intimate the *Shoah*'s stature as a watershed in world history. Roy Eckardt speaks of the Holocaust's "transcending uniqueness," of its singular ability to falsify the claims of Christianity, and of its ability to split humankind into two distinct parties (those who take the *Shoah* with "absolute seriousness" and those who do not), and sacred history into two epochs ("BS"– before Shoah – and "AS" – the age of *Shoah* and its aftermath).[14]

Other Holocaust theologians allude to the Holocaust's revelatory character by stressing its theological salience. Franklin Littell avers that the Holocaust and a restored Israel are the most important Christian events in centuries – "alpine events" that Christians must interpret in "mythical (meta-historical) terms" since they comprise "basic events in Christian history."[15] Monika Hellwig encourages Christians to "ask what there is to learn from God in Israel's experience today" with the same reverence accorded traditional revelatory sources like the Bible and the experience of the church.[16] Occasionally, Holocaust theologians refer explicitly to the revelatory quality of the Holocaust:

> The Holocaust is an altogether singular manifestation of evil, with proportions beyond imagination, revealing the demonic possibilities of our civilization. In this sense, the Awful Event is revelatory. It makes known the hidden.
> …
> [T]he Holocaust reveals to the church the dark power of its own symbols. Or more precisely, the Awful Event discloses to the Christian community that contained in its own tradition are destructive ideologies.[17]

The Holocaust is a revelatory event that took place in our time. To Christians it discloses, among other things, the demonic results and malevolent possibilities that reside in our tradition of anti-Jewish preaching and teaching.

The crucifixion of the Jews has been a whirlwind of destruction unmatched in history. Out of that whirlwind, like Job of old, we can hear a voice calling to us. We can hear it, but we may not. It is not only necessary, but imperative, that we do hear it![18]

The meaning of the *Shoah* is unfathomable, but it shows us con-clusively that God is the "hidden" God (cf. Isaiah 45:15), who does not reveal himself, whose judgments are "unsearchable" and "ways past tracing out," whose "counsellor" was no mortal.[19]

In the Holocaust and its lessons God has put before Christians a choice between life and death, between salvation and damnation, as directly as long ago God confronted another people on Mount Carmel.[20]

Yet only one Holocaust theologian has paused to consider how elevating the Holocaust to the level of divine revelation might affect and be affected by other dimensions of Christian confession. In *Discerning the Way* Paul van Buren explores the meaning of revelation in the Jewish and Christian traditions and delineates the conditions under which the Holocaust might be considered revelatory. In "Step Eight: The Course of the Way: History as Revelation," van Buren defines revelation as an acknowledged reinterpretation of tradition in response to Jewish history. Scripture, in turn, is a reinterpretation of Jewish tradition in response to reorienting events. These definitions open the way to perceiving new revelation in the midst of contemporary history.

Van Buren argues that the revelational "pattern" emerges when historical events *reorient* an individual, and through that individual a community. According to van Buren,

The more firmly tradition became established, the more clearly the impact of historical events in Israel's social and political his-tory emerged as the occasion of revelation. Revelation has to do with what is going on in Israel's history ... in the sense that the history itself is seen to be revelatory.[21]

Van Buren claims to have rediscovered the pattern of reinterpretation under the pressure of reorienting events in Israel's history after eighteen centuries of dormancy. But this pattern of revelation has asserted itself within the church, in the "radical reversal" of Christian teaching on the Jews since 1965 which has been prompted by recent events in Jewish history – notably the Holocaust and the founding of the State of Israel. If the reorientation represented by the statements of church authorities leads eventually to a general reorientation of the Christian community, then, van Buren believes, Christians will be able to speak confidently of the Holocaust and the rebirth of Israel as "revelatory."

C. Israel as Message

It will come as no surprise that Christian Holocaust theologians recognize in the State of Israel insurance that a holocaust of the Jewish people will never recur. Like Jewish Holocaust theologians, they have taken to heart a sobering lesson of the *Shoah*: The Jewish people will survive only if they can do so independent of others' goodwill. But the Jewish state is more than a hedge against future catastrophes. While Christian Holocaust theologians rarely refer to the State of Israel in the kind of unequivocally redemptive terms common among religious Jews and fundamentalist Christians (some of Paul van Buren's writings, which are influenced by the mystical Zionism of Abraham Kook are an exception), they nevertheless view the empowerment of Jews in their ancient homeland as a providential event.[22]

As such, the State of Israel not only indicates God's continuing care for Jews, but signals God's reentry into human history following an inexplicable exile during the Holocaust. The Holocaust theologians stress that there is a lesson for Christians in this divine "return to history." Specifically, post-Holocaust Christianity must abandon once and for all the realm of theological abstraction. While thinkers like Dietrich Bonhoeffer – and the Holocaust theologians themselves – may serve as guides in this task, the rebirth of the Jewish state is the example from which every Christian can learn. It is the supreme object-lesson in the difficult process of Christian reeducation on the religious significance of the historical.

But the significance of the State of Israel for Holocaust theologians is not exhausted in its role as a foil to Christian spiritualizing tendencies. In fact, as a theological datum the Jewish state is a seemingly limitless source of knowledge about God, the world and the church. For the restoration of Israel is a challenge and crisis for contemporary Christian theology, a"miraculous" event that tells the church that the Jewish people will not disappear or be subsumed by Christian categories.[23] It is a rainbow set again in the clouds, a sign of hope for oppressed peoples everywhere.[24] "The crucifixion and resurrection of the Jewish people is a sign" that God will uplift the lowly in the end.[25] The rebirth of Israel is an "echo of eternity" which reverses the second-century events that authenticated the church's view of itself as the "New Israel."[26] The return of Israel to its land can be read as a divine comedy, as an instance of "the laughter of God" at those who invented the notion that Jews were doomed to dispersion and exile.[27] Israel aids the Christian imagination in recovering a sense of the "firm relationship that has endured in Jewish thought between people and land."[28] It functions generally as "the crisis of Christianity."[29] As an entity "at once theological and political," Israel calls the church to acknowledge the theological significance of political power.[30] It "open(s) Christian eyes" to the fact that ambiguity has always characterized God's dealings with the world.[31] It "witnesses" to the church concerning how to take responsibility for the covenant without waiting for some "mighty act of God."[32]

These perceptions of Israel's religious meaning, culled from the writings of several Christian Holocaust theologians, suggest the Jewish state's richness and multivalence as an object of theological reflection. In all these versions of Israel's message for Christians, the state operates as a sign of God's presence, power and intention in the world, just as in pre-Holocaust Christian theology Jewish existence in exile was assumed to be a sign of the divine plan. There are even explicit connections with the Restorationist tradition that crested in seventeenth-century Europe. For even when they assiduously avoid speaking of the Jewish state in an explicitly religious manner, the language of the Holocaust Theologians is fraught with the theological import of Israel's restoration to its land.

Of course, the restoration alluded to is not the restoration of Jews to the "Holy Land" in anticipation of the conversion of a representative remnant and Christ's return. Rather, it is a restoration of Jewish life and culture following the European catastrophe; a restoration of the land of Israel after centuries of misuse and decay; a restoration of Jewish political empowerment after centuries of powerlessness; and a restoration of positive significance for Jewish history. While most Holocaust theologians refrain from accentuating the eschatological significance of Jews' return to the land, many instinctively revert to the Christian language of redemption. In fact, the twentieth-century Jewish saga of near-death and rebirth is often consciously framed by the church's story of Jesus: According to Franklin Littell, "the *Christian* importance of the Holocaust and restoration of Israel" may be comprehended only within the symbols of crucifixion and resurrection.[33]

In a few cases, Holocaust theologians have even invested the State of Israel with meanings surrendered by traditional symbols whose signifying power is diminished in the wake of the Holocaust. For example, Franklin Littell writes that evangelistic initiatives like the "atavism called 'Key '73'" is a theological anachronism in the post-Holocaust world. Considering the money and personnel churches typically devote to evangelistic causes, Littell reasons, "putting that money and effort into building up the land and people of Israel would be more appropriate, in the shadow of recent history, yes – more Christian."[34] The migration of theological signification is even more striking in the work of A. Roy Eckardt. In the Holocaust, Eckardt contends, Christian belief in the Resurrection became inextricably linked with Jewish victimization and the murder of Jewish children. In fact, Eckardt denies it is possible to escape the murderous implications of Christian supersessionism as long as one affirms the Resurrection as a "divine event."[35] However, Eckardt wonders, if resurrection faith is not possible in the post-Holocaust world, is there a "historical word from God" capable of rescuing the church from its victimization of Jews and from its own plunge into guilty despair? Eckardt's answer is revealing, if not surprising:

> If there is such an accepting event, and if that event is constituted by the reemerging commonwealth of Israel, we are given a sign and a witness that God continues to accept human beings totally apart from the resurrection of Jesus.[36]

Here Eckardt has experimentally substituted the State of Israel for the Resurrection as harbinger of redemption and reconciliation in the post-Auschwitz world. Curiously, Eckardt insists he is offering only a "theological interpretation of historical events," not a religious justification for the State of Israel. However, it is precisely as a theological interpretation of historical events that Christian mythical thinking about Jews and their fate originally took root in the Christian mind.

Among Christian Holocaust theologians, then, the rebirth of the Jewish state is variously interpreted as a sign of God's return to history after an apparent retreat, a foil to the dispersion as judgment motif in the Christian teaching of contempt, a sign, message and challenge to the church, and even a foreshadowing of redemption. Holocaust theologians do not claim that the Jewish state represents a fulfillment of "Old Testament" prophecy (as many conservative Christians argue), or that it is a sign of the days of the Messiah (as some religious Jews believe). Nor is Israel's founding to be regarded as the commencement of a timetable leading to Christ's Second Coming. Yet the state does possesses a unique capacity to command the attention and support of Christians. If traditional eschatology is absent in the writings of the Holocaust theologians, their renderings of the movement from *Shoah* to Israel are nevertheless enveloped in mythical language.

At the least, Christian Holocaust theologians assume that the State of Israel contains a sign or message directed at the church by its Lord. Different theologians perceive slightly different messages, as we have seen. But that a message is to be discerned in Israel is not disputed. This fact is sometimes obscured by their conscious attempts to demythologize the dialectic of Jewish reprobation and preservation, which they regard as a component of the Christian teaching of contempt. But even when Holocaust theologians claim to understand the state as a secular political solution to the nightmare of Jewish history among the nations, traces of the witness-people myth are present. In particular, the perennial Christian fascination with God's plan for Jewish restoration in the land of Israel resonates in its discourse. More generally, Holocaust theologians' perceptions of the Jewish state show that they have once again placed "Israel" at the center of Christian reflection.

D.   Survival and Preservation

A reflection of the witness-people myth is also discernible in the great consequence assigned by Holocaust theologians to the very survival of Jews. Like pre-Holocaust Christian theologians, they evince awe at the phenomenon of Jewish persistence in the face of tremendous difficulties. More importantly, one also perceives in

Christian Holocaust theology the preservationist impulse that emerges from the positive side of the witness-people myth.

To be sure, Holocaust theologians do not argue that Jews should be "kept alive" in order to fulfill their divinely appointed role at the end of the age. But their writings do resound with the preservationist strain when they announce that insuring Jewish survival and security has become an imperative for Christians following the Holocaust. This imperative is sometimes expressed in a theological idiom, as when Paul van Buren delineates the church's proper mission or "service" to Israel. This service is necessary because the continuing survival of the Jewish people is the only guarantee that the God of Israel will remain present in our world.[37] Instead of the theologically "incoherent" notion of a proselytizing mission to the Jews, van Buren speaks of a Christian duty to preserve, protect and encourage Israel. Van Buren's discussion of the church's role in assisting the post-Holocaust survival of the Jewish people may not be preservationist in the classical sense, but it does exhibit formal similarities with the witness-people tradition.

E.   Continuity, Covenant and Election

Another dimension of Christian Holocaust theology in which links to the witness-people myth are indicated is its assumption of a fundamental connection between Judaism and Christianity. For most Holocaust theologians, this connection is unique and the church's relationship with Israel is *sui generis*.

At times the momentous importance of Jewish existence for Christian identity (and even Christian survival[38]) is established by reminding believers of the implications of Jesus' Jewishness. Roy Eckardt writes that Jesus was

> someone who, had he by some miracle been living in the "right" time and place, would have been dispatched to a Nazi gas chamber or crematorium. And, in all probability, his execution would have been brought off by men who were themselves Christians, and who were thus related to the very one whom they would have been destroying.... "Jesus was a Jew" – in these four short words is established forever the bond between Christianity and the Holocaust of the Jews (as also the Third Jewish Commonwealth). These events become "alpine events" for Christians in a most elementary way: by the mere facts of the Jewish-ness of

these events and, more importantly, by the very nature of Christian historical identity and destiny.[39]

Retrieving the Jewishness of Paul has been another task of Christian post-Holocaust research. Often, attempts to recover the "Judaic base of early Christianity" as a foundation for Christian self-renewal and improved Jewish–Christian relations look to Paul's discussion of the election of Jews and engraftment of Gentiles in Romans 9–11.[40] Peter von der Osten-Sacken describes the importance of this passage for Christian theology after Auschwitz:

> Romans 9–11 has the same constitutive function for the question about the relationship between Christians and Jews as the words of institution have for the interpretation of the Lord's Supper. These chapters are therefore the source providing guidelines for a theology in Christian–Jewish dialogue.[41]

In hopes of elucidating the Jewish roots of Christianity, post-Holocaust theologians extend the hermeneutics of retrieval even beyond Jesus and Paul:

> The Christian God is none other than the God of Israel, the God of Abraham, Isaac and Jacob. Our Christ is none other than Jesus the Jew of Nazareth. Our sacred texts are none other than the Hebrew Scriptures, which also serve as our Old Testament, and the apostolic writings – the apostolic writings of the early Jewish Christians, which we call the New Testament.[42]

Yet even in a theological environment which has fostered such fresh reconsiderations of Christianity's Jewish roots, the writings of the Holocaust Theologians are set apart by their radical emphasis on Jewish–Christian continuity. First, as we have seen, Holocaust theologians fashion a rhetoric of continuity designed to establish historical and emotional connections between Christian and Nazi Jew-hatred. Second, these thinkers surpass others who stress that Christian faith must recover its essential Jewishness by elucidating the "historical-phenomenological link between the Jewish people and the Creator of the world."[43] Thus, the Holocaust theologians say, it is not only appropriate but also necessary that Christians recall God's special history with the Jewish people. For Christians' knowledge of God must derive from God's self-revelation in Israel's story, which is the larger context for the story of Jesus.

To speak of God, then, is to speak directly or indirectly of the religious experience of the Jewish people. And because they are convinced that God *continues* to be uniquely revealed in Jewish existence, Holocaust theologians' Christian affirmations are often qualified by their awareness of contemporary Jewish life: Jesus' death loses absolute significance before the unique godforsakenness of suffering Jewish children; anti-Semitism is a unique phenomenon, "the singularity of the devil [being] manifest in his tie with the world's one uniquely unique evil"; and the Holocaust is the final act of a uniquely unique drama in which "the singularity of the event is tied to the identity of the victims."[44]

The important links shared by Jews and Christians are elaborated even more carefully in the Holocaust theologians' discussions of election and covenant. Much has been written regarding the meaning of "covenant" in the post-Holocaust environment, and there is anything but agreement among theologians concerning whether Christians should speak of their relationship to Judaism in terms of one covenant, two covenants or a "dual" covenant. Yet the Holocaust theologians do agree that Israel's covenant relationship with God is inviolate and that Christians should never think of it as superseded or abrogated. In order to subvert these negative images Holocaust theologians insist that the foundation of the church's own covenant with God is Israel. For instance, Paul van Buren, John Pawlikowski and Johann-Baptist Metz each emphasize the church's theological *dependence* upon Israel and its covenant relationship with God.

The Jews' own eternal covenant is understood to be rooted in the irrevocable nature of their divine election. Israel's election is so significant for Holocaust theology that it is construed as a "landmark event in both faith and history."[45] In turn, the influence of Holocaust theology on the church at large is reflected most clearly in the latter's renewed focus on Israel's continuing place in God's favor. This focus has been especially apparent in official church statements appearing over the last two decades. But the fact that Holocaust theology has so affected the broader church on this issue of the importance of Israel's covenant and election makes it imperative to detect any inadvertent connections with the witness-people myth.

Clearly, the Holocaust theologians have trained their sights on the origins of Christianity in order to discover some new or previously obscured foundation for a positive apprehension of Jews. Their work has uncovered resources for a Christian apprehension of Judaism as a legitimate expression of divine worship, and Jews as something other than theological anachronisms. Yet similarities with the witness-people tradition are present. While affirmation of the Jewish covenant's continuing salvific efficacy may be a new way of thinking for Christians, the underlying belief that Jews remain God's people throughout history is not. And none of the affirmations which grow out of this conviction – that Jews of today are living descendants of biblical Hebrews, that Jews and Christians have been called by the same God who is the author of their Scriptures, that Jews and Christians await the same Kingdom of God – is qualitatively new. Each is a familiar part of the witness-people theology conceived by Augustine and handed down over the centuries.

Indeed, with their convictions that Jewish history is the primary arena for God's interaction with human beings and that Christians and Jews are inextricably linked through covenant and election, the Holocaust theologians implicitly reestablish the witness-people tradition. As in previous eras of church history, this myth is nurtured by the assumptions that the Jews retain a role in salvation history even after the time of Christ and are the objects of God's free choice and the conduits for divine revelation. That Holocaust theology rehabilitates this theology in a way that evinces respect for the integrity of Judaism apart from Christianity is an important consideration. But this cannot disguise its deep connections with the witness-people myth.

F.   A Secular Holocaust Theology?

Ironically, a few Holocaust theologians have given high priority to extricating Christian theology from every vestige of mythical thinking about Jews. For example, James F. Moore has decried mythical Christian views of the State of Israel which must be repudiated, especially views in which Christian guilt is projected on Israelis, or in which the State of Israel is the centerpiece in an apocalyptic scenario.[46] In the post-*Shoah* age, Moore claims, the correct starting point and focus for Christian theology is not mythology, but "Jewish life."

However, because Moore's debt to the witness-people myth has not been acknowledged, his claim to have dismissed mythical visions of Israel is a pretense. Moore insightfully recognizes that at times Christians project on the State of Israel their guilt and discomfort with the exercise of political power. But Moore is unaware of the extent to which his very concern with the connection between Jewish exile, suffering and restoration in the "Shoah-Israel link" is part and parcel of the Christian witness-people tradition. He assumes that the Jewish people, the Holocaust and the State of Israel are all pivotal for Christian reflection, but these assumptions are not critically explored. In the end Moore does nothing to challenge Christian theology's mythical apprehension of the Jewish people. In fact, some mythical aspects of Christian thinking about Jews are only reinforced by Moore's analysis.

A. Roy Eckardt is the Holocaust theologian most committed to demythologizing Christian perceptions of the Jew. Aware that Christians have been incapable of viewing Jews as anything but abnormal people, Eckardt urges the church to embrace a "secular theology of Israel." In this plea he echoes Richard Rubenstein's statement that the only sensible alternative to the unique expectations imposed on Jews by the Christian imagination is a secularization of Christian apprehensions of Jews and the Jewish state. In a penetrating analysis, Eckardt perceives in the theologizing of the political order that is routine among "Christian Zionists" a simple inversion of the traditional game "played by the historicizers of God's judgment."[47] Eckardt notes that if Jews' return to their land is regarded as a special sign of God's mercy, logic requires that Israel's destruction be interpreted as an indication of God's wrath. Eckardt fears that the State of Israel may have replaced the mythical Jew in the Christian mind, and goes so far as saying that to view Israel through a theological lens may qualify as anti-Semitism.[48]

Strong as his rejection of theologizing appears to be, however, Eckardt's dismissal of "Christian Zionism" does not mean his own perceptions of the Jewish people and the State of Israel are disinterested. Actually, Eckardt is far from shy in referring to the State of Israel as a sign and historical witness of the God of Israel. He even argues that the Christian response to the gift of acceptance represented by the State of Israel is "faithful support."[49] Eckardt admits, in fact, that his opposition to Christian Zionism does not exclude "a constitutive link between the will and purposes of God and the Jewish state."[50] His polemic against Christian Zionism notwithstanding, Eckardt's "secular" theology of Israel entails the same call to Christian support for the Jewish state sounded by self-conscious theologizers of Israel like Paul van Buren. Thus,

Christians have a particular duty to support the independence and security of Israel – not alone as a political reality or human achievement, but also within the very frame of reference of the history of the people of God.[51]

Eckardt's desire to desacralize political claims masks the fact that Israel and its "particularity" retain a unique stature in his this-worldly theology.[52] Wittingly or not, Eckardt has allowed to enter through the back door what he had dramatically expelled through the front. Neither his focus on the "human order," nor his observation that Israel is an "increasingly secular reality," can fully obscure Eckardt's identity as a Christian thinker with a deep theological concern for the significance of the Jewish state. His special regard for "Israel" is intimated in explicit statements – the Holocaust, he says, represents the "total effacement of the people of God"[53] – and in occasional double-talk, like his warning that the people of God not be spiritualized. In a curious way, Eckardt's secular theology of Israel theologizes as it secularizes and secularizes as it theologizes. As he himself is forced to admit, "support for a Jewish state would hardly be distinctively Christian were it limited to humanitarian grounds or purely politico-moral justifications."[54]

In considering the possibility of a secular post-Holocaust theology of Israel, it is instructive to note that the writings of Eckardt and other Holocaust theologians are mainly addressed to the church. In communicating the *Shoah*'s lessons, they are intended to preclude another catastrophe by helping Christians to understand, respect and support Jews and the State of Israel. Roy Eckardt in particular has dedicated a good portion of his long career and the majority of his published writings to exposing anti-Jewish bias in Christian belief and behavior. Is it only coincidence that a Christian scholar and clergyman has become concerned so deeply with the history and fate of Jews? Of course not. More important is this question: Is Eckardt capable himself of perceiving Jews as a "normal" people? The very fact of his scholarly preoccupation with Jews, Jewish-Christian relations and the correct Christian view of Israel suggest that for Eckardt, as for other Holocaust theologians, the "people of God" are a people *sui generis*.

A more realistic appraisal of post-Holocaust theology's task comes from the pen of Franklin Littell. He claims that "old myths can only be cast out by new myths," by "a more powerful mythical or meta-historical symbolism."[55] For Littell, the church's historical mythology of the Jew must be replaced by a newer, more positive mythical interpretation of the facts of history. For his part, Paul van Buren does not suppress his conviction that Jews are a people set apart for all time by God. The assumption that Jews were and are God's elect people is beginning, middle and end in van Buren's theology. While repudiating the Christian "teaching of contempt" as vociferously as Eckardt or Littell, van Buren explicitly denies the possibility of a normal existence for the people Israel.

A recent exploration of the "the ritual dimension of public Holocaust discourse" by Martin S. Jaffee suggests that Littell and van Buren come much closer than Eckardt to recognizing the actual nature of Christian Holocaust theology. Jaffee claims that this discourse reveals the "fundamental self-conceptions" of the participants, who assume "a set of very clear roles."[56] He describes how the Christian partner in Holocaust discourse typically takes on "a spiritual self-annihilation, a confessing of one's guilt that mirrors in subtle ways themes of classical Christian theology." At the same time, the Jew becomes not only the audience for Christian confessional prayer, but "like God in Christ, provides gracious forgiveness."[57]

In Holocaust discourse, in other words, the Jew reenacts the Judaic theme of repentance and atonement while the Christian is allowed to relive a profound moment in the Christian redemptive drama. What is striking is that from any perspective one aspect of the drama remains constant: "the Jew stands symbolically in God's place."[58] Jaffee's incisive interpretation of the mythic dimensions in Holocaust discourse elucidates Christian Holocaust theology from another perspective. Newly illumined is the fact that the very structure of Holocaust discourse between Christians and Jews, whether or not the medium is religious language, determines that the role of the Jew is subtly assimilated to the role of God.

We have surveyed much evidence for the view that Christian Holocaust theologians, whether self-proclaimed "secularizers" like Eckardt or "re-mythologizers" like Littell, invariably participate in the ancient witness-people myth. Ultimately, the Holocaust theologians' unwitting but routine remythologization of Jewish existence manifests the same compulsion that has characterized Christian reflection on Israel since at least the time of Augustine – the compulsion to cast Jews as a witness-people whose suffering exile, preservation, restoration and ultimate salvation are the components in a language of natural revelation.

CONCLUSION

Herman and Rosemary Ruether have responded to the recent theological writings of Paul van Buren by calling him "an anti-Semite turned inside out."[59] Although the Ruethers are predisposed by their political commitments to dissent from van Buren's strong support for the State of Israel, their description of van Buren as an anti-Semite turned inside out is an instructive metaphor for Christian Holocaust theology as a whole: While seeking to stem the tide of Christian anti-Semitism and reverse centuries of religious hatred and stereotyping, the Holocaust theologians have not felt obliged to reinvent the bases of Christian theology. Rather, they have focused on resources within the tradition which in their judgment can form the basis for a positive apprehension of the Jewish people. As we have seen, however, these resources are implicated in the witness-people myth, and the Holocaust theologians have not transformed the Christian tradition so much as inverted it. Because this tradition is distinguished by a deep ambivalence toward Jews, it is quite amenable to inversion without the promise of fundamental and lasting change.

7

Dispensational Premillennialism: The Jew as Key to the Kingdom

You can bring almost every nation here and in fifty years they will become extinct, merged into another; but bring a Jew here and in fifty years, a hundred years, or a thousand years, he is still a Jew. When I meet a Jew I can't help having a profound respect for them, for they are God's people.

Dwight L. Moody, *To All People*

Israel today is a living testimony to the words of the Old Testament prophets, and a portent of the triumphant return of Christ. The rebirth of the State of Israel by United Nations decree on November 29, 1947, is by far the greatest biblical event that has taken place during the twentieth century.

Advertisement for the Billy Graham film *His Land*

If I were asked to furnish proof of the world's conversion, of evidence that God will one day bring this whole planet in subjection to himself, and fill it with his glory, as he has promised, I should unhesitatingly point to Israel, the chosen people, the center for blessing for the whole world.

William J. Moorehead, speaking at International Prophecy Conference, 1901

All prophetic truth revolves around the Jews.

Jack van Impe and Roger F. Campbell, *Israel's Final Holocaust*

In a recent study of American fundamentalist attitudes toward Jews and Zionism, Yaakov Ariel observes that since the seventeenth century American Christians have possessed a mixed attitude toward

141

Jews.[1] In fact, Ariel's conclusion about American hopes for the restoration of Zion is that colonial millennial thinkers, nineteenth-century sectarians and modern prophecy teachers all have shared a marked ambivalence toward the Jewish people. Before discussing this ambivalence and its relationship to the witness-people tradition, this chapter will offer a brief survey of the rise of modern dispensational premillennialism among conservative Christians.

In this chapter the common but often misapplied terms "fundamentalism," "evangelicalism," "dispensational," and "premillennialism," will be used. Although some writers have used them almost interchangeably, these terms possess distinct meanings which the reader should keep in mind. The term fundamentalism may be applied historically – to refer to a twentieth-century movement within American Protestantism that opposes "modernism" and its various manifestations in the church and wider culture; or substantively – to denote a broader conservative religious impulse that is expressed in the belief in biblical inerrancy, in hostility to modern theology and critical study of the Bible, and in the conviction that only those sharing fundamentalist views are true Christians.[2] The word "evangelical" may refer to conservative Protestant Christianity in nineteenth-century America before the rise of fundamentalism proper, or describe contemporary Christian conservatives who stress adherence to a variety of orthodox views, but who are more open than fundamentalists to modern thought-currents and critical study of the Bible.[3]

"Dispensational" is employed to denote a school of biblical hermeneutics, a philosophy of history and an eschatological theory that arose in Britain in the mid-nineteenth century.[4] Its chief trait is the conviction that God deals with human beings differently in each dispensation, or "period of time during which man is tested in respect to his obedience to some specific revelation of the will of God."[5] Seven dispensations, including a final age known as the Kingdom or Millennium, are distinguished by dispensationalists. "Premillennialism" is the view that Christ's coming will precede the Millennium, that the physical return of Jesus, that is, will take place before the thousand year period mentioned in Revelation 20:4. Premillennialists emphasize the discontinuities between the present age, which will terminate in judgment and catastrophe, and the coming Millennium.[6]

Thus, the premillennialist outlook is a pessimistic one, especially relative to the "postmillennial" hope in which the return of Christ follows an earthly millennial age brought about partly through human agency. Christians who do not look for a a literal fulfillment of the millennial age alluded to in Revelation are sometimes called "amillennialists."[7] "Dispensational premillennialism," the eschatological perspective which is the focus of this chapter, is the theological outlook of many conservative Christians. These believers insist that "Israel" will be the focus of God's activity both in the millennial era and in "the tribulation" which immediately precedes it.

As was suggested in Chapter 3, the character of Christian millenarian hope has varied significantly throughout church history. Millenarianism in Reformation England and Puritan North America was generally more optimistic than catastrophic. Optimism held sway among those who yearned for the Kingdom even in the eighteenth and early nineteenth centuries,[8] but it was displaced in mid-nineteenth-century popular culture by the dispensational premillennialism of which contemporary "prophecy teachers" are representatives. Typically, millenarian thinking has been accompanied by interest in the mystery of the Jewish people. But dispensational premillennialists merit special attention due to the heightened emphases they place on the fulfillment of God's promises to "national Israel," on Jewish dispersion and exile as God-ordained, and on the Jews' restoration as a sign of providence.

Scholarly advocates of this eschatological outlook who are associated with academic institutions like Dallas Theological Seminary sometimes dismiss the popular versions of dispensational premillennialism that are under consideration here as unauthentic.[9] Nevertheless, the works of Hal Lindsey and other popular writers are useful for understanding the Christian imagination precisely because they are perennial best-sellers which both influence and reflect popular hopes and fears. In fact, it is Lindsey and other popularizers of dispensational premillennialism who are to be credited or blamed for the eschatological views of two recent U.S. Presidents. On the campaign trail in 1976 Jimmy Carter asserted that "the establishment of the modern state of Israel is the fulfillment of biblical prophecy,"[10] while in 1983 Ronald Reagan told the Executive Director of the American-Israel Public Affairs Committee:

> You know, I turn back to your ancient prophecies in the Old Testament and the signs foretelling Armageddon and I find myself wondering if we're the generation that is going to see that come

about. I don't know if you've noted any of those prophecies lately, but, believe me, they certainly describe the times we're going through.[11]

The wide-reaching influence of premillennial eschatology, and the obsession of writers like Lindsey and his epigones with Israel and Jews, make these popularizers natural objects for analysis in this study of contemporary manifestations of the witness-people myth.

I.   DISPENSATIONAL PREMILLENNIALISM AND THE RISE OF FUNDAMENTALISM

Interest in the restoration of Jews to their ancient homeland in anticipation of the "last days" was not intense among American Christians until the last quarter of the nineteenth century.[12] Postmillennial and premillennial eschatologies could be found among New England's Puritans in the seventeenth century, but advocates of both perspectives looked for the Jews' conversion and restoration in the future. Between the Revolution and the Civil War, the postmillennial eschatology – explicitly articulated by Jonathan Edwards and etched on the colonial soul by the Great Awakening of the 1740s[13] – took hold. Edwards's *The History of Redemption* was read throughout the nineteenth century, and the hopeful postmillennial vision described there informed the great systematic theologies of evangelical Protestantism,[14] motivated activism among many Christians, and animated popular views of America's destiny in the world.

However, despite Edwards's own interest in the Jews' future, the conversion and restoration of the Jews did not play a significant role in eschatological thought during this period of American history.[15] It was in Britain, in fact, that premillennial interest in the Jewish people first appeared in the nineteenth century. The early 1800s in Britain were a period of evangelical fervor toward the Jew, a fervor symbolized by special missionary societies like the London Society for Promoting Christianity Among the Jews. In the 1830s, a new premillennial view that came to be known as dispensationalism was developed by the British cleric John Nelson Darby and a group known as the "Plymouth Brethren." The novel eschatological theory produced by Darby and eventually adopted by American dispensationalists was primitivist in intent: In both its eschatological outlook and its fervor for the return of Jesus it sought to emulate the apostolic church.[16]

Yet despite claims for its antiquity, the Darbyite view of the last days was an innovation inasmuch as it departed from traditional, historicist premillennialism and embraced a futurist and strictly literal exegesis of key prophetic texts. Darby's "futurist" pre-millennialism did not attempt to pinpoint the time of the end by determining what predicted events had already taken place. Rather, Darby expected all of the pivotal eschatological developments – beginning with the secret pretribulational rapture of the church (a Darbyite innovation) – to occur in the future. More importantly, because it regarded "Israel" as the crux of biblical prophecy, Darby's version of premillennial thinking placed the Jewish people at the center of the eschatological drama.

To say the least, Darby's ideas found fertile soil among American evangelicals.[17] In fact, by the middle of the twentieth century dispensational premillennialism was the dominant eschatology among conservative Christians in America.[18] The reasons for its success are complex. Darbyism certainly fit the nineteenth-century evangelical temper, but it also arrived at the very moment evangelical leaders were anxious to make adjustments to their theology. In distress over the intractable problems facing American society – including industrialization, urbanization and the influx of immigrants – and the arrival of such modern scourges as Darwinism and "higher criticism," evangelicals began to regard as misplaced their meliorism and their hopes of ushering in the millennium through reformism. Thus, Darbyism was a felicitous discovery because it taught that this world could not be reclaimed for Christ as many evangelicals had previously hoped. Rather, the earth was ripe for judgment and would only be saved by God's intervention at the close of history. Partly under the influence of Darby's personal visit to the United States in 1862, dispensationalism made great inroads into American evangelicalism in the 1860s and 70s.[19]

From its beginnings, American dispensationalism was a more stable movement than in Britain, and its influence in American culture was deeper and more permanent. American dispensational premillennialism even possessed a significant credibility among members of mainline Protestant denominations well into the twentieth century. By the end of the nineteenth century conservative leaders within the Protestant denominations had forged an alliance with sectarian millenarians that culminated in the Northfield,

Massachusetts, prophecy conferences, the American Bible League and the publication of *The Fundamentals*.

But dispensationalism was most closely associated with leading evangelical preachers like Reuben A. Torrey, A. J. Gordon, James M. Gray, A. C. Dixon and Dwight L. Moody, and was widely disseminated through the "prophecy conferences" that were organized at the end of the nineteenth century. Moody was an evangelical convert to dispensational theology who was destined to have a seminal effect on American religious life. Partly through Moody's influence, in fact, dispensational premillennialism has continued to be an essential component in twentieth-century evangelistic movements. Like other prominent dispensationalists, Moody developed a special attraction to the Jewish people. Despite having few personal encounters with Jews, Moody taught that every Jew was "a monument of God's word."[20] This sentiment characterized much nineteenth-century evangelicalism. Addressing Moody's Northfield Bible Conference in 1894, George C. Needham told his audience that "ten men shall take hold of ... a Jew and say 'We shall go with you; for we have heard that God is with you.'"[21]

In the twentieth century, dispensational premillennialism was strengthened among conservative Protestants in America by the publication of *The Fundamentals* beginning in 1910. While this series of landmark pamphlets did not emphasize eschatology, *The Fundamentals'* editors were premillennialists, and the series had the effect of promoting like-minded persons into positions of leadership in the burgeoning fundamentalist movement.[22] But perhaps the most important single vehicle in the spread of dispensationalism was the *Scofield Reference Bible*, first published in 1909 by Cyrus I. Scofield. Though it has been replaced on the shelves of many dispensationalist Christians by the *Ryrie Study Bible*, the Scofield Bible remains a recognized authority in evangelical circles. Scofieldism, which may be thought of as the scholastic form of dispensationalism, eventually found expression as a systematic theology in the work of Lewis S. Chafer.[23]

The influence of dispensational premillennialism upon American Christianity, then, has been a profound one. While there probably never has been a time when all conservative Christians were dispensationalist, the influence of dispensational premillennialism on American Christianity is indisputable. In fact, one scholarly interpretation of American fundamentalism locates its roots not in the fundamentalist-modernist controversy of the 1920s, but in the nineteenth-century revival of millenarian thinking in the form of dispensational premillennialism. According to this view, it was millenarianism that gave life and shape to the fundamentalist movement, and fundamentalism is rightly understood as a chapter in the history of millenarianism.[24]

By the late nineteenth century millenarianism had created a church within the church which offered an implicit corrective to denominationalism. Its mass appeal lay in its ability to cultivate visible expressions of Christian unity and its advocacy of a non-partisan and "scientific" method of inductive Bible study.[25] Furthermore:

> the support of Zionism and the state of Israel on the basis of eschatological beliefs has been deeply implanted in American fundamentalism, and although premillennialists by no means make up the entire evangelical-conservative camp in American Protestantism, their influence in shaping the political standpoint of this segment of American society has been so strong that conservative Protestants have, by and large, adopted a pro-Zionist line.[26]

The influence of dispensational premillennialism on the Christian Zionism of conservative Protestants stems from two deeply-held beliefs: the conviction that ancient biblical prophecies of restoration in Israel (e.g., Ezekiel 37:21) must be literally fulfilled as a prelude to the end, and the expectation of a pretribulation rapture in which believers will be removed from the earth so that God may focus once again on Israel, cleansing her in the tribulation and pouring out blessings upon her during the Millennium. William E. Blackstone was only one of the many Christian leaders who regarded the Zionist movement at the end of the nineteenth century as a sign that the Jewish people were once again assuming a major role in history. Similarly, millenarian thinking gained tremendous momentum as events of the early twentieth century – in particular the First World War, the British victory in Palestine, the Balfour Declaration, and Zionist settlements in the land of Israel – fanned the flames of prophetic zeal. If the British capture of Jerusalem at the end of World War I was recognized by dispensationalists as a "pivot in prophecy,"[27] is it any wonder that for the current generation the establishment of the State of Israel in 1948 is considered the "key to the prophetic puzzle"?[28]

II.   CHRISTIAN FUNDAMENTALISM IN SCHOLARLY PERSPECTIVE

Before beginning my analysis of contemporary dispensational premillennialism and its relationship with the witness-people myth, I wish to distance my approach from that of liberal scholars who consciously portray fundamentalist Christianity as a dangerous societal force that is incorrigibly anti-Jewish and which has fascist political tendencies. Because dispensational premillennialism is a thread that runs through the entire tapestry of Christian fundamentalism, scholars have posited a "fundamentalist" view of the Jews and Israel. But the visible increase in conservative Christians' support for the Jewish state following the Six Day War of 1967 has caused discomfort among many liberal scholars.

In 1977 James Barr cited interest in the Jews and Zionism as a central aspect of the fundamentalist's posture toward contemporary society.[29] Barr noted that for fundamentalists "the Jews" comprise a uniform collectivity in God's plan for the present and future, that the return of the Jews to Palestine and the fortunes of the State of Israel are of special concern for fundamentalists, and that both the Jews and Israel commonly assume "cosmic religious importance." Barr concluded that these attitudes and beliefs result in an uncritical admiration for the Jewish state which makes conservative Christianity a "main source of pro-Israel feeling in the modern world."[30] While Barr was implicitly critical of this aspect of the fundamentalist outlook, he is a paragon of restraint compared with the authors who over the last decade have responded to fundamentalist Christianity's love affair with Israel with considerably less equanimity.

This acute reaction is evident in the work of liberal theologians, political scientists and journalists who in the 1980s sought to unmask what they suspected was a secret and insidious alliance between the State of Israel and the American "Religious Right." Citing written and broadcast statements by American televangelists, these authors investigated the techniques of conservative political activists and the covert activities of religious groups who support right-wing "militarist national security states." In their books, special censure is generally reserved for what they call the fundamentalist "cult of Israel" and its "Armageddon theology."[31]

Along with charges of questionable political strategies and affiliations, fundamentalists have met increasingly of late with claims that they are deeply anti-Semitic. Purveyors of this view do not deny that fundamentalists typically display a keen interest in and unwavering support for the State of Israel. But this phenomenon is interpreted as one half of a paradoxical expression of anti-Jewish bias – a superficial enthusiasm that barely conceals a profound anti-Jewish prejudice. Some authors claim explicitly that Christian anti-Semitism is positively correlated with religious fundamentalism. Others take for granted that conservative theology is the source of anti-Judaism and anti-Semitism within Christianity.

It must be acknowledged that evidence for these views can be found in the anti-Jewish stereotypes expressed by leading nineteenth-century dispensationalist thinkers, in the warm reception with which some of them greeted the American publication of *The Protocols of the Elders of Zion*,[32] and in the portrayal of Jews by some fundamentalists following World War I as members of a grand conspiracy to overthrow Christian civilization.[33] The association of conservativism and anti-Semitism also is encouraged by the comments of fundamentalist leaders, including the well-known American preacher who warns his congregation: "Don't ever bargain with Jesus. He's a Jew."[34] Finally, the perception that anti-Judaism is a function of conservative theology is given currency when Holocaust revisionist groups place their stamp of approval on the writings of fundamentalist Christian authors.[35]

However, the belief that Christian contempt for Jews is a correlate of theological conservatism rests largely on the basis of stereotype and anecdotal evidence. Apparently, nothing more significant is required to convince large segments of the public of its truth. Recently this view has been invested with renewed scholarly respectability by a number of Jewish and Christian commentators, including Rabbi Alexander M. Schindler, Rabbi Abraham Hecht, Irving Kristol and Rabbi Arthur Herzberg, Jack R. Fischel, the National Jewish Community Relations Advisory Council, and on the Christian side by scholars Tom F. Driver and Martin E. Marty.[36] In Driver's strikingly unnuanced account, Jerry Falwell and his ilk on the Christian right are "deeply anti-Semitic,"as well as being anti-Jew, anti-black, anti-feminist, anti-Communist and anti-Third World.[37]

But, of course, the assumption that conservative Christians are anti-Semitic is itself a stereotype, and one that dies hard. Conservative apologists have mounted passionate attacks against it. In two books – *Zionism within Early American Fundamentalism, 1878–1918* and *Fundamentalist-Evangelicals and Anti-Semitism* – David

Rausch has laid down the gauntlet before the more smug representatives of liberal Christianity.[38] In *Zionism within Early American Fundamentalism* Rausch devotes an entire chapter to demonstrating that the notion of fundamentalist anti-Semitism popularized by Martin Marty and other liberals is "totally inaccurate." In fact, he turns this canard back upon the liberals, arguing that fundamentalists are "ardent supporters of Israel and the Jewish heritage" who are more pro-Semitic than their liberal counterparts.[39] According to Rausch, this can be substantiated on three counts: fundamentalists interpret biblical prophecies literally, while liberals spiritualize them; fundamentalists give equal treatment to the Old and New Testaments, while liberals privilege the New Testament and see in the church a New Israel; and fundamentalists accept "Israel" in its unconverted state as part of God's plan for the future, while liberals do not. Specifically, liberals recognize the Jews as God's Chosen People even in their "unbelief," while the latter succumb to the temptation to think of the church as the new Chosen People. Unfortunately however, Rausch fails to offer any convincing proof for his argument, which in any case does not apply to Holocaust theology.

Whether liberal or conservative Christians are more pro-Jewish is a complex question that cannot be adjudicated here. It seems to be the case that liberals are apt to be more pro-Jewish than pro-Israel, while conservatives are likely to be more pro-Israel than pro-Jewish. But even this generalization is problematized by the example of a fundamentalist like Rausch who is extremely sensitive to the nuances of Christian anti-Judaism and has demonstrated the philosemitic dimensions of fundamentalist culture. Nevertheless, the generalization is given credence by the host of fundamentalist and evangelical preachers who are staunch supporters of the State of Israel, but who transmit stereotypes of Jews and Judaism that are implicated in the Christian teaching of contempt.[40] Spokespersons for liberal Protestantism – most of whom are familiar with the etiquette of interfaith engagement – generally show more sensitivity to the presence of Christian anti-Judaism and cultural anti-Semitism and take pains to disavow both. Whether this means they are less prone than conservatives to anti-Jewish bias is difficult to say. In any case, an appreciation of dispensational premillennialism's attitude toward "Israel" will require an open mind and a sensitivity to fundamentalist self-understanding.

III.   KEYS TO THE KINGDOM: THE DISPENSATIONAL PREMILLENNIALIST SCENARIO(S)

In 1982 Gabriel Fackre noted that "the Religious Right is continually scrutinizing events in Jewish history."[41] Indeed, conservative Christians – and especially dispensational premillennialists – are intensely interested in correlating Jewish history with the events predicted in Holy Scripture. Since the nineteenth century dispensationalists have advocated a common sense approach to Scripture that is literal and scientific – even "Baconian"[42] – and which is aimed at establishing the plain meaning of prophetic texts. While disagreement concerning what "events" are actually predicted in the Bible is common, distinct patterns can be identified in the myriad versions of futurist premillennialism that have achieved popularity since the middle of the nineteenth century.

According to the governing dispensational paradigm, God's program for humankind is revealed in several prophetic sections of the Bible, primarily the vision of "seventy weeks" described in Daniel 9.[43] Daniel's weeks are interpreted as referring to a period of 490 years in which God's plan for Israel will unfold. The first 483 years (or 69 prophetic "weeks") correspond to the period between the rebuilding of Jerusalem under Ezra and Nehemiah and the first advent of Jesus Christ. Although just one prophetic week (or seven-year period) remained unfulfilled after Christ's coming, dispensationalists teach that an extended "church age" has intervened between the sixty-ninth and seventieth weeks. Thus, in an ingenious interpretive move that is a hallmark of the dispensational system, the period between Pentecost and the church's "rapture" (the moment in which all true believers are caught up to meet Christ in the air) is viewed as a historical parenthesis. Since neither the "age of the Gentiles" nor the church were predicted in the "Old Testament" or anticipated in the ministry of Jesus,[44] the current dispensation is merely an interruption in which God's predicted program for Israel is placed in temporary suspension.

When the church is "raptured,"[45] the beginning of the end will have arrived and God's attention once again will turn to Israel. The "tribulation," a seven-year period when the earth will be purged and those not taken up in the rapture are subjected to terrible suffering, will have begun. Thus, in the church's absence, "Israel" will experience the "time of Jacob's trouble" (Jeremiah 30:7) when God's wrath will scourge the world. Antichrist will rise to prominence –

probably as the head of a European confederacy – and bring remarkable peace and stability to the world. During the second half of the tribulation, however, conditions on earth will deteriorate. After he has succeeded in bringing peace to the Middle East, Antichrist's identity as a demonic figure who secretly wishes to destroy Israel will be disclosed. The tribulation will consummate in the "Battle of Armageddon" in the northern part of Israel, where the armies of the world will collide and human history will effectively end, perhaps in a nuclear conflagration.

Through these cataclysmic events God will be preparing the Jewish people to meet their Messiah upon his Second Advent. Although most Jews will perish in the tribulation, toward its end a remnant of Israel – the 144,000 Israelites consisting of 12,000 from each of the twelve tribes as mentioned in Revelation 7:3–8 – will acknowledge Jesus as Messiah. These "servants of God" will then missionize the remaining Gentiles, and with phenomenal results. Christ's bodily return will occur at the climax of the last battle when he descends to earth to establish his millennial kingdom. During this millennial reign – the promised restoration of the Davidic Kingdom – Christ will ascend a throne in Jerusalem to rule over those who have survived the judgment of living Gentiles (Matthew 25:31–46) and the judgment on Israel (Ezekiel 20:33–38). In this kingdom Jews will be exalted over Gentiles and Israel will enjoy preeminence among the nations. For many dispensationalists, this will include the rebuilding of the Jerusalem temple.

The emerging Zionist movement and the Balfour Declaration tempted early dispensational premillennialists to compromise their futurist eschatology and interpret these historical events as "signs of the times" pointing to the imminent consummation of the age. Since Israel's declaration of independence in 1948, and especially since the Six Day War of 1967, dispensationalist writers have shown even less hesitation in announcing the arrival of the last days. This is more than a reflection of the apocalyptic ethos that invariably accompanies the end of a millennium. Inspired by Jesus' teaching that the "generation" witnessing the Jews' restoration to their land would not pass away until his return, dispensationalists are confident that the seventieth prophetic week must commence before the end of this century. Dispensationalists who interpret "generation" as referring to a literal forty-year span predicted Christ's return by the late 1980s. Some recently have retreated from this prediction, claiming that the final generation was not inaugurated until the reunification of Jerusalem in 1967. Others have been more prudent about date-setting. In every case, however, contemporary dispensationalists share with their nineteenth-century predecessors a keen interest in the political future of the State of Israel, and like them find in con-temporary forces and events confirmation of Jesus' imminent return.

Thus, for the dispensationalist the Jews' rejection and crucifixion of Jesus has not ended Israel's pivotal role in salvation history. Jewish unbelief has only caused the prophetic clock to stop, as it were, until the exiled people Israel could be reborn as a nation. Jewish restoration is the infallible sign, dispensationalists teach, that God has begun dealing with Israel again. As such, it is also a warn-ing to the church to prepare for its rapture. While the prophetic scenario elaborated above may sound exceedingly fanciful, the founding of the State of Israel in May 1948 is the indisputable fact which makes it compelling for believers. With the Jewish state as tangible evidence of God's unfolding plan, all who have eyes to see know that the time of fulfillment is at hand. For examples of the way the dispensational premillennialist outlook is expressed by influen-tial Christian leaders, we briefly examine the views of Jerry Falwell and Hal Lindsey.

A.   *Jerry Falwell and the Jews*

Although Jerry Falwell has not been a seminal dispensational thinker, his long standing credibility within conservative Christian-ity makes it fruitful to consider his views on the Jews and the State of Israel. Moreover, Falwell's public career demonstrates the polit-ical benefits that can accrue when the traditional dispensational outlook – in which Israel and Jews function as signs and objects of God's final dealings with the world – is combined with a fundamentalist activism.

Jerry Falwell's shifting attitudes toward Israel and the Jews mirror those of many conservative Christians of his generation. Prior to 1967, Falwell shied from mixing religion and politics and rarely if ever spoke of the modern State of Israel.[46] But Israel's vic-tory in the Six Day War left a tremendous impression on Falwell, as it did on many Americans who were living through the era of Viet-nam, hippies and the civil rights movement with a sense of helpless-ness. By the end of the 1970s, Falwell was visiting occupied Palestine as the guest of Israeli Prime Minister Menachem Begin and was declaring that God had shown kindness to America as a result of America's kindness to the Jew.[47] Eventually Falwell was to become the first Gentile recipient of the Jabotinsky Award, which Begin bestowed on him in 1981. To Falwell's critics this honor is a compelling symbol of his political naiveté. But Falwell himself speaks proudly of the award, which in his autobiography he describes as "the highest honor an Israeli prime minister can bestow on friends of Israel for their friendship and service to that land."[48]

During the 1980s, Falwell repaid the State of Israel by lending it his unflagging support. In *Listen, America!*, a book that signaled the emergence of the American Religious Right, Falwell devoted an entire chapter to "That Miracle Called Israel." For Falwell, no word other than "miracle" is able to capture the enduring wonder of the Jewish people and the state they created. The Jews' persistence as a people is a "miracle of God," as is the State of Israel's record of military victories: "There is no way that the tiny nation of Israel could have stood against the Arabs in a miraculous six-day war had it not been for the intervention of God Almighty."[49] Clearly, religious and political considerations merge in Falwell's descriptions of the Jewish state. He does not exaggerate when he affirms that his "political support for Israel is unconditional."[50]

Like an earlier generation of dispensationalists who believed America had inherited a special responsibility to insure the restoration of the Jewish people to Palestine,[51] Falwell sees a crucial role for Americans in supporting the Jewish state. Falwell summons U.S. citizens and their government to aid and protect this tiny country that is so crucial to the interests and destiny of America. Falwell emphasizes a stipulation of the Abrahamic covenant which he believes American Christians must not forget: "God deals with nations in relation to how nations deal with Israel."[52] America's future, then, is dependent on its posture toward Israel as the guarantor of Jews' security. Not surprisingly, Falwell portrays Israel and the United States as natural political allies who fight on a common front for democracy and freedom in the Middle East. Both oppose the Arab nations which are undemocratic, totalitarian and bent on Israel's destruction. Again not surprisingly, Falwell believes that the only solution to the so-called Palestinian problem lies in the Arab nations' obligation to make a home for Palestinians within their borders.

The most concentrated and revealing collections of Falwell's perceptions of Israel and Jews is to be found in a book of interviews entitled *Jerry Falwell and the Jews*. In the interviews published in this volume, Falwell articulates his belief that contemporary Jews stand in unbroken descent from the patriarchs of the Old Testament: "Beginning with Abraham ... Israel was front and center on the stage of God's program for man. The Jew was the repository of God's Divine revelation (the Bible) and an example of how God dealt with nations."[53] In the Old Testament the role of the Jews was one of witnessing, according to Falwell; but today Jews are called to wait for the consummation of the age. Falwell avers that the very existence of Jews today is accounted for only by divine intervention. These theological perspectives on the Jewish people have practical results that should not be underestimated. According to the literature of the the organization Falwell founded in 1979, "no anti-Semitic influence is allowed in Moral Majority, Inc." Falwell himself has boasted that one cannot belong to the Moral Majority without being Zionist.[54]

Not surprisingly, Falwell warns against viewing Israel as one nation-state among others. He is convinced that "the miracle of statehood in 1948 was providential in every sense of the word ... [t]he State of Israel remains the focal point in history." To convince Christians of this fact Falwell notes that the land which this nation inhabits is sacred. In fact, Israel controls the very area promised to Abraham by God in Genesis 15:18, and thus thus has every right to the land between the Euphrates and the "river of Egypt." The conclusion Falwell draws from his maximalist interpretation of Scripture is predictable: Judea and Samaria are "the eternal possession of the Jewish people" and the Golan Heights should be an integral part of the State of Israel.[55]

For Falwell, the State of Israel is a sign without parallel in the midst of the contemporary world. He is confident that every Bible-believer will acknowledge the unbreakable link between Christianity and the State of Israel. For the Christian, "the Jewish people represent the sovereignty, the grace, and the love of God"; "the Jewish people are the key to God's plans and purposes for this world ... the glue that has held the Jewish people together has been nothing but the sovereign purpose of God."[56] Quite apart from their usefulness in documenting Falwell's staunch Christian Zionism and his territorial maximalism, these interviews reveal the presence of the witness-people myth behind Falwell's fundamentalist dispensationalism. Reflections of the myth proliferate Falwell's apprehensions of the State of Israel and his convictions regarding the survival and significance of Jews.

B.   Hal Lindsey

Hal Lindsey is the purveyor of dispensational premillennialist theology who is best known outside fundamentalist circles. Lindsey is the author of several works that attempt to bring together biblical prophecy and current events, but his book *The Late Great Planet Earth* (1970) has achieved a unique popularity. It was the best-selling nonfiction book of any kind in the 1970s, and estimates of world sales approach forty million. While Lindsey's initial predictions about the end of human history and the return of Christ have required significant adjustment over the last two decades (for instance, he has been forced to shift the commencement point for the last "generation" from 1948 to 1967),[57] he continues to offer confident prognostications about the last days and remains a leading popularizer of the dispensational outlook.

Lindsey can be distinguished from other dispensational premillennialist authors by his ability to write for an audience of some historical and theological sophistication.[58] But his position as acknowledged leader of fundamentalist "prophecy teachers" rests not on his intellectual prowess but on his claim to be a life-long "student of biblical prophecy." This self-description is important to note because it indicates that for those who are disposed to take it seriously, the "Armageddon theology" proffered by Lindsey and others is virtually beyond falsification. Lindsey's sympathetic readers assume that the events he predicts are clearly described in Scripture. Furthermore, Lindsey's readers know they are living in the final days of human history – partly because the world is in such a sorry state and partly because the Jews have been restored to their land in a miraculous way and have enjoyed the obvious protection of God in their history as a nation. Like other popular prophecy teachers, Lindsey reminds us that only very recently has biblical prophecy coincided with international politics in such a promising way.

Hal Lindsey exemplifies the ambivalence with regard to the Jewish people that has characterized every generation of dispensational thinkers. Typically, the unique position occupied by Jews in Lindsey's prophetic outlook is qualified by a deep distrust of Judaism and the Jewish character. On one hand, Jews are the sign *par excellence* of God's activity in these last days. Thus, in *The Late Great Planet Earth* Lindsey claims to have located in the founding of the State of Israel "the key to the prophetic puzzle." The Jews' return to the land of Israel following thousands of years of dispersion makes "the Jew ... the most important sign of this generation."[59] The preservation of the Jews is a "miracle of history" and their restoration has set the stage for Christ's return. In his most recent book, *The Road to Holocaust*, Lindsey expatiates further on the Jew as the object of God's special love and as the focus of an unfolding divine plan. Lindsey is adamant that the Jew continues to occupy center stage in the drama of history, and explicitly denies that the church either "existed in the Old Testament" or is the "new Israel."

At the same time, however, Lindsey's descriptions of Judaism and the Jewish people are steeped in the anti-Jewishness of historic Christianity. Explaining why most Jews did not recognize Jesus as their Messiah, Lindsey remarks in *The Late Great Planet Earth* that "the Jews ... had degenerated in their own religious convictions to the point where they didn't believe they were sinful." The Judaism of Jesus' time, Lindsey continues, had become "merely an external thing." This conception of Judaism is also operative in *The Road to Holocaust*. In chapter 7, "Israel in the Present: Rejected," Lindsey manifests a familiar Christian antipathy for Jewish "legalism" when he repeats a pernicious cliché: "the Israelites sought to establish their own righteousness through keeping the Law."[60] Thus, affirmations about the centrality of the Jews in history exist in uneasy tension with Lindsey's dismissal of Jewish religion and ignorance of Jewish self-understanding. This deep ambivalence concerning things Jewish is suggestive of the continuity between dispensational premillennialism and the witness-people tradition.

C.   Other Figures

There are many high profile American fundamentalist preachers who perceive the State of Israel as a direct sign of God's intervention in history. Kenneth Copeland, whose television programs reached nearly five million American households in 1989, is a dispensationalist teacher with growing appeal. According to Copeland, "God has raised up Israel ... We're watching Him move in behalf of Israel ... What an excellent time to begin to support our government as it supports Israel."[61]

Among the popularizers of prophetic scenarios, Pat Robertson deserves mention as well – for his preeminence among so-called television evangelists, for his candidacy for U.S. President in 1988, and for the consistent popularity of his television show "The 700 Club." In 1985 Robertson's show led all such broadcasts, entering 16 million American households. In the wake of sex scandals involving televangelists Jimmy Swaggert and Jim Bakker, Robertson emerged as America's most popular TV preacher by the end of the 1980s. Like Falwell and Lindsey, Robertson is a staunch supporter of the State of Israel. Robertson views the return of Jews to the land of Israel to build a nation as an "incredible miracle." He anticipates the coming "time of Jacob's trouble" from which the Jews will be rescued by the direct intervention of God, and sees increasing anti-Semitism as a harbinger of the final days. Robertson claims biblical support for the unification of Jerusalem under Jewish rule and concurs with Falwell that America will suffer divine judgment if it turns its back on Israel.[62] Although Robertson has spoken critically of America's "liberal Jews" and is more likely than his co-religionists to question Israeli policies, he shares their theological estimation of Israel's reemergence: "It is my considered judgment that there is a firm Biblical mandate in both the Old and New Testament for the establishment of the Nation of Israel in the Holy Land," he has written.[63]

IV.   FUNDAMENTALIST CHRISTIANITY AND THE WITNESS-PEOPLE MYTH

In many ways conservative American Christianity continues to bear the stamp of nineteenth-century dispensational premillennialism and its obsession with the fulfillment of God's plan for "Israel." As the statements of Jerry Falwell, Hal Lindsey, Pat Robertson and other popular figures demonstrate, dispensational assumptions inform the eschatological and political views of the most visible fundamentalist leaders. But their statements also imply that the contemporary representatives of dispensational premillennialism stand squarely in the witness-people tradition.

Occasionally connections with witness-people theology are explicit, for instance in Hal Lindsey's recapitulation of the Augustinian notion that the Jews are preserved as bearers of sacred books.[64] But prophecy teachers transmit the witness-people myth in a variety of more subtle ways. They do so in their profound ambivalence toward all things Jewish, in their adoption of the dialectic of dispersion and restoration to interpret Jewish history, in their unflagging Christian Zionism, and in their conviction that God's purposes for the world are nowhere revealed more clearly than in the story of the Jews. These standard aspects of witness-people thinking are accompanied by one that is unique to fundamentalist Christianity: the belief in the demonic nature of anti-Semitism.

A. Ambivalence in Dispensational Eschatology

In his definitive study of American dispensationalism's historical origins, Yaakov Ariel notes the "striking ambivalence" which animates dispensational views of the Jewish people and their dual role in history:

> [A]lthough dispensationalists have recognized the Jews to be God's chosen nation and have anticipated a great future for that nation, they have also expressed a certain amount of bitterness concerning the Jewish refusal to accept Jesus, which caused the delay in the advancement of the ages and the materialization of the kingdom.[65]

Ambivalence toward the Jew was always evident in the International Prophetic Conferences which began in America in 1878. Conference addresses typically affirmed the centrality of the Jewish people and expressed hope for their restoration and conversion, while also proclaiming God's judgment upon the Jews' unbelief and hard-heartedness:

> On the one hand they are God's chosen nation to whom the biblical prophecies refer. They will be restored to their ancient status and serve as the central nation in the millennial kingdom. On the other hand, as they have refused to recognize Jesus as their Messiah, their character reflects obnoxiousness and rebellion. Their road to glory is paved with suffering and destruction.[66]

This two-sided apprehension of Israel is unmistakable in the sentiments of William E. Blackstone and Arno C. Gaebelein, the two great figures of American dispensationalism whom Ariel treats in detail. Ariel is struck by the persistent anti-Jewish strains in these men's pronouncements, despite remarkable philosemitic characteristics such as Blackstone's strong opposition to anti-Semitism and friendship with leading Jews, and Gaebelein's impressive knowledge of Judaism. What Ariel calls a "twofold perception of the fate of the Jews" is evident in every generation of the dispensational movement, and this ambivalence represents one aspect of continuity between contemporary fundamentalism and the witness-people tradition.

B.   The Jew in Sacred History: Election/Dispersion/Preservation/ Restoration/Destruction

Since dispensational premillennialists are keen to anchor their convictions in the plain meaning of the Bible, we might expect the biblical cycle of covenant, infidelity, punishment and restoration to figure largely in their writings. And indeed it does. While promises of election, land and special divine favor are understood to be at the heart of the "Old Testament," predictions of dispersion from and future return to the land of Israel also are seen as a biblical leitmotif. And between the Jews' providential dispersion and promised homecoming, their miraculous preservation becomes a compelling datum of natural theology. According to John Wesley White,

> History knows of no other instance of a people which, while separated from the country of its national origin for some nineteen centuries, not only retained its ethnic and theological identity but also, at the end of those two millennia, returned from far and near to its ancient homeland.[67]

In Jewish preservation "between the times" dispensational prophecy teachers find extra-biblical confirmation that God is still directing Israel's destiny. But preservation also means God-ordained suffering, so that the interim between the biblical and eschatological phases of God's dealings with the Jew, otherwise known as the "church age," is a period of "chastening" for elect Israel. Thus, the insistence that "God is not through with Israel" is riddled with ambivalence, implying as it does both survival and unremitting suffering as the result of unbelief:

> In the past Israel suffered under the Babylonians, Medo-Persians, Greeks and Romans. They suffered after the Roman era at the hands of Crusaders and various European leaders, culminating with Adolf Hitler. They have suffered since that time. All that suffering has served as God's disciplining rod. Their sufferings are

designed to purge their rebellion and rejection, leading them to turn back to God in faith.[68]

Naturally, the watershed in the Jews' history of disobedience is their refusal to acknowledge Jesus: "Since the rejection and crucifixion of their Messiah, the story of the Jews has been one of misery."[69]

In the mind of dispensational Christianity, then, Jewish chosenness and Jewish suffering are two sides of the same coin. The cycle of Jewish election, punishment and dispersion which figures prominently in Christian theology from Augustine to Barth is retained by dispensational prophecy teachers, who add to this a grand dialectic of restoration and destruction: The ingathering of Jews in the land of Zion is only a prelude to Armageddon, where the majority of the Jewish people will perish. According to the most optimistic of dispensational blueprints, only one third of all Jews will remain alive following the glorious ingathering of the exiles which precedes the Second Coming and Millennium. What is more, this one third who survive the disasters associated with the tribulation and Armageddon will be recent converts to faith in Christ.

It is paradoxical – but typical of the sort of dualistic thinking about Jews that distinguishes the Christian imagination in every age – that the very same Bible expositors who exult in the rebirth of Israel as a national entity calmly go on to describe Israel's final destruction as a catastrophe "beyond any it has previously experienced."[70] Despite the surviving Jewish converts' exalted identity as "Brahmins of the millennial commonwealth,"[71] Jewish religion and civilization as it is currently known will cease to exist. In a very literal sense the Israel which dispensationalists regard as a fulfillment of prophecy is born to die. Thus, it is not without warrant that traditional references to "the time of Jacob's trouble" have been replaced in descriptions of Israel's prophetic destiny with phrases like "the coming holocaust" and the "holocaust of tribulation." Armageddon is now the "final holocaust," and the Antichrist who will lead Israel down the primrose path of destruction is "the future Führer."[72]

The preservationist element in dispensational premillennialism certainly is qualified by its vision of ultimate conversion and destruction. Yet the dispensational conception of the Jewish people retains – and actually highlights and intensifies – the curious paradox which is a hallmark of the witness-people myth. On one hand, the Jews occupy center stage in the eschatological drama which begins in the rapture of the saints and culminates in Armageddon. Jews are not displaced from this position even during the Millennium, in which Jerusalem is capital not only of a restored national Israel, but of the entire earth. On the other hand, however, the period of "great tribulation" between the two phases of Jesus' Second Coming is portrayed by dispensationalists as a time of horrific suffering and destruction for the Jewish people. Dispensational thought follows orthodox Christian theology to the extent that the biblical dialectic of election and dispersion has the effect of normalizing Jewish exile and suffering; it goes beyond traditional orthodoxy inasmuch as it conceives of Israel's final salvation explicitly and exclusively in terms of annihilation and conversion.

C.   Christian Zionism and the Land of Israel

In the nineteenth and early twentieth centuries support for Zionism among dispensational premillennialists was largely passive: "They derived enormous encouragement from Zionism, but contributed very little to it."[73] This passive phase gradually came to an end in the 1960s and 1970s, however. Although conservative Christians responded in a variety of ways to the Israeli victory in the Six Day War, after 1967 dispensationalists began to exercise their clout within American fundamentalism and by the late 1970s the issue of Israel's security was high on the agenda of the burgeoning Religious Right. The growth of militant conservatism in Israel during the same period ultimately led to the forging of a remarkable alliance between the Israeli government and the American Religious Right.[74]

In 1990 the number of Christian Zionists in the United States was estimated at 40 million; this at a time when the world Jewish population numbered just 18 million.[75] These numbers suggest the extent of Zionist sentiment and potential activism among fundamentalist Christians. But this is not entirely a movement of the 1970s and 80s. These numbers should not obscure the fact that for over a century Zionist immigration to Palestine has been interpreted in the light of biblical prophecy, and that since 1948 conservative Christians have invested Israel and its military victories with eschatological significance.

David Hocking's *What the Bible Says about Israel and its Land*[76] briefly and conveniently summarizes the enduring foundations of conservative Christian Zionism. Hocking elaborates twelve facts that comprise the biblical foundation for a Christian view of "the land of Israel": 1. The land belongs to God. 2. The land was given by God to the descendants of Abraham. 3. The gift of this land to Abraham and his descendants was based on an unconditional covenant from God. 4. The land was not given to the descendants of Ishmael, but rather to the descendants of Isaac. 5. This land was not given to the other sons of Abraham, but only to Isaac. 6. The land was not given to the descendants of Esau, but only to Jacob. 7. God continued to remind the children of Israel of this covenant during their bondage in Egypt and wilderness wanderings. 8. God told Israel to conquer the land He had given to them. 9. Israel's sin and captivity did not change their divine right to this land. 10. God's promise to Israel is as certain as the existence and order of the universe. 11. The name of this land is not "Palestine," but "Israel." 12. The full restoration of Israel to its land with complete peace and security will require the coming of Messiah.

Underlying these "facts," of course, are some crucial assumptions – that contemporary Jews are direct descendants of the biblical patriarchs and matriarchs; that the modern State of Israel is heir to the land and the divine command to conquer it; and that the land promise includes all the territory between the "river of Egypt" and the Euphrates, as stipulated in Genesis 15:18. It is when these assumptions are illuminated that the connection between the witness-people myth and the dominant fundamentalist view of Israel comes into focus: Like the existence and survival of the Jew in many Christian theologies of the patristic, medieval, Reformation and modern periods, the State of Israel in the land of Israel is the prime locus of God's involvement with the world. Thus, "nowhere can we see the hand of God more clearly than in Israel." This "sign of the nation Israel," which in 1948 initiated the countdown to Armageddon, is the key for understanding all end-time prophecy. The State of Israel is "the center of the entire prophetic forecast." With Israel's declaration of independence, the "prophetic countdown began."[77]

D.   Jews as Keys to the Kingdom

Contemporary Christians influenced by dispensational premillennialism see Jewish restoration in the land of Israel as a sign and precondition of the millennial Kingdom's imminence. Nevertheless, in dispensational theology significance is not limited to the land of Israel or to Jews living there, but is projected onto every

Jewish individual in the world. Dispensationalists are impervious to the ebb and flow of Zionist sentiment among Jews in the Diaspora. Even when Jews adamantly deny that they wish to return to Zion, dispensationalist Restorationism is not diminished.

Evidence for this observation can be found in two incidents separated by nearly a century. At the "Christian–Jewish Conference" organized by William E. Blackstone in 1890, Reform Rabbi Emil G. Hirsch pleaded with his Christian auditors to recognize that "we modern Jews do not wish to be restored to Palestine." However, in the "Memorial" Blackstone submitted to President Harrison the following year, he referred to contemporary Jews as "sojourners ... [waiting to] return to Palestine and till their own land."[78] Similarly, at the first Christian Zionist Conference sponsored by the International Christian Embassy in Jerusalem in the early 1980s, a resolution proposing annexation of the West Bank was met with the observation that a significant segment of the Israeli population favored trading territory for peace. In response, a Christian leader is reported to have shouted: "We don't care what the Israelis vote! We care what God says! And God gave the land to the Jews."[79]

These incidents reveal that conservative Christians influenced by the ethos of dispensationalism are typically unconcerned with the nuances of Jewish self-understanding. Jews are viewed as part of a monolithic theological entity known as "God's People." Ironically, attention to Jewish history only encourages this perception. The survival of the Jews in such unfavorable historical circumstances serves as proof that they are a unique, perpetual and indivisible group. According to one popular prophecy book, "the ability of the Jews to remain a people apart while scattered throughout the world is another evidence of the divine plan."[80] A dispensationalist expositor remarks that "Israel" has been preserved against all odds because God is on their side, refers to the Jews as "this impossible-to-extinguish nation," and does not find it unusual that the 144,000 Jewish evangelists of Revelation 7:4 will be virtually immortal.[81]

It is the Jew, then, who is the key to Christ's millennial Kingdom in dispensational thought, while the Jewish state fulfills this function only indirectly. The Jew's central place is described unambiguously by two leading proponents of the dispensational gospel who claim to begin with the Jew because he is God's timepiece and the key that unlocks every door into prophecy.[82] In addition to being God's timepiece and a symbol of God's kept promises, the Jew also serves as God's standard for determining the righteousness of the nations. A claim routinely made by the authors of prophecy books and pamphlets is that God's disposition toward any nation is determined by that nation's disposition toward the Jew. The basis for this claim is Genesis 12:3: "I will bless those who bless you, and the one who curses you I will curse." In fact, if he had attended to the logic of this scriptural warning, the greatest of all Jew-haters might have realized political success:

> Had Hitler loved the Israelites instead of hating them, he might have averted the greatest of all wars, the greatest of all destruction programs, and engendered the admiration of the world instead of its hatred.[83]

Because "the righteous" alone will enjoy God's millennial reign, and because love for God's people is a primary requirement for righteousness, the Jew is a reluctant gatekeeper in Christ's Kingdom.

E.   The Devil and the Jews

It is necessary to distinguish contemporary dispensational premillennialism from the medieval mindset to which it is sometimes mistakenly compared. In contrast to popular Christian fantasies of the Middle Ages, fundamentalists maintain that the anti-Semite, not the Jew, is an agent of Satan. Anti-Semitism, dispensational prophecy teachers argue, is a thinly-veiled demonic conspiracy to destroy the Chosen People of God. Hal Lindsey unmasks the spiritual force orchestrating this plot:

> Satan hates Israel with an undying passion because she is the instrument through which the Messiah, His conqueror, was born. Satan also hates Israel because God's reality and veracity are proven by the way He has kept the many prophecies and promises He made to Israel, even though she hasn't deserved it. These amazing fulfillments are recorded in history for all honest inquirers to see.[84]

Jerry Falwell concurs: Anti-Semitism is simply a consequence of Satan's desire to thwart God's purposes for the world. It is "produced by Satan himself as an antithesis to the God of Heaven who selected and ordained the Jewish people as His own chosen family."[85]

The logic animating this interpretation of anti-Semitism appears sound enough: Satan is continually plotting to frustrate or undermine God's intentions; the Jew is the plainest representation in the human realm of God's redemptive purposes; thus, the irrational hatred for the Jew which recurs throughout history must have its ultimate source in the Devil himself. The association of the Jew and the Devil that was a distinguishing feature of medieval anti-Judaism was based on a similar logic: The Jew, who is on principle an enemy of Christ, must be in league with that arch-enemy of God who seeks the destruction of Christendom. In contemporary fundamentalism, however, this medieval logic has been inverted by a philosemitic interest in the Jews as God's Chosen.

Ironically, the conviction that anti-Semitism is actually a Satanic plot to destroy God's people encourages some dispensational prophecy teachers to exhibit a certain quiescence before it. After all, outbreaks of anti-Semitism must be expected if they only manifest the suffering that God predicted would befall Jews when they violated the covenant.[86] Even when dispensationalists oppose anti-Semitism, they are aware that it can not be overcome on the human plane, since it is essentially a spiritual plague. Thus, prophecy teachers retain little hope that Arab–Israel enmity will ever be mitigated, since the Middle East conflict represents a collision of cosmic forces. These are

> [o]n the one hand, the grace of God working toward Israel's restoration; and on the other hand, the deceitful strategies of Satan, who is opposing this process by every means in his power.[87]

Thus, affirmations of the inexorable nature of anti-Semitism qualify dispensationalists' claims of philosemitism in the same way their supposed love for Israel is called into question by their teaching that a "final holocaust" will befall the Jews during the second half of the tribulation.

Its internal tensions notwithstanding, the dispensational analysis of anti-Semitism as demonically-inspired answers a question that has perplexed some of the twentieth century's most incisive minds, including Karl Barth, Nicholas Berdyaev and Jean-Paul Sartre. All have asked why there should be such hatred directed against Jews. In addition, dispensational prophecy teachers offer a direct explanation for the phenomenon of Nazism: Hitler and his henchmen were instruments of the Devil. Some dispensationalists have even sought to document Hitler's occult and satanic activities.[88] Thus, contrary to a popular stereotype that assumes a close connection between Holocaust revisionism and religious fundamentalism, the alleged demonic nature of anti-Semitism prompts prophecy teachers to regard the Holocaust as an event of transcendent evil which was orchestrated by Satan himself and which is only dimly illumined by the study of history and politics.

According to one recent best-selling prophecy book, the Antichrist will be Hitler *redivivus*, although the true identity of the resurrected Nazi leader will remain hidden until his power is solidified.[89] It is not surprising that in the Christian imagination a figure as menacing and mysterious as Antichrist has from time to time been associated with the Jews. According to popular legend and some ecclesiastical teaching in the Middle Ages Antichrist was to *be* a Jew. Contemporary dispensationalists, however, envision a mirror image of this medieval Antichrist. He is now a treacherous anti-Semite whose demonic task is to destroy the Jews in a "covenant of death."

The dispensational interpretation of anti-Semitism as a Satanic plot and Antichrist as an anti-Semite *par excellence* comprises a unique manifestation of the witness-people myth.[90] But this novel interpretation of Jewish suffering is nevertheless unmistakable evidence of the Christian imagination at work: Because the fate of the Jew is inseparable from divine providence, hatred of the Jew is not simple prejudice, but possesses a unique, spiritual character. Since it is God's will for the Jew to prosper, Jewish travail must reflect the antithetical intentions of the Devil.

F. The Infallible Sign

The prophecy teachers discussed in this chapter all insist that Israel's national rebirth in 1948 should be construed as an infallible sign of the faithfulness of God, of the reliability of Scripture, and of the fact that the last days are under way. According to Tim Lahaye, "the existence of the Jewish people ... can be attributed only to the supernatural power and special purpose of God. This phenomenon should convince doubting individuals that God keeps his promises."[91] Most importantly for the dispensationalists, the reorganization of the nation of Israel is "irrefutable proof" of Christ's return.[92]

In fact, the recent reemergence of Israel on the world stage following millennia of Jewish wanderings would provide a compelling proof of God's very existence, were such a proof required. As Dave Hunt puts it, "for those who are willing to face the facts, the very existence of Israel today proves the existence of her God."[93] Hal Lindsey concurs, offering his own version of a familiar story:

The story is told of Napoleon that one of his generals asked him what he believed to be the greatest miracle of all time. Without hesitation Napoleon answered, "The Jews." There's no question that [the State of] Israel is one of the greatest phenomena that history has witnessed. What God has done *to* that nation, *for* that nation, and *through* that nation has done more to make men aware of a personal God and how to have a relationship with him than any other factor in human history.[94]

The conviction underlying the statements of Hunt and Lindsey – that the Jew is an eternally reliable symbol of the comings and goings of God – is also the lifeblood of witness-people theology. We can only conclude that dispensational premillennialism's apprehension of Jews as reluctant witnesses of Christian truth is but one more contemporary manifestation of the witness-people myth.

EPILOGUE: PARALLELS BETWEEN DISPENSATIONALISM AND HOLOCAUST THEOLOGY

Since Holocaust theologians and dispensational premillennialists react from opposite ends of the theological spectrum to the ambivalence and hostility *vis-à-vis* the Jewish state which characterizes the Christian mainstream, they evince a curious set of similarities.

Dispensationalists and Holocaust theologians share an insistence – aimed at the displacement theology of much Christian orthodoxy – that the church has not replaced Israel in salvation history. In opposing supersessionism, both groups remind Christians of the debt which the church owes to Israel for its own covenant with God. Both Holocaust theologians and dispensationalists lament the "spiritualization" of Christian thinking through the ages: Dispensationalists view allegorical interpretation of Bible prophecy as the root of anti-Semitism in the church, and Holocaust theologians claim that the church's flight into theological abstractions is behind its failure to appreciate the meaning of the Holocaust and a reborn Israel. Conservative prophecy teachers proclaim a principle derived from Genesis 12:1–3 – whoever blesses the Jew will be blessed by God, while those who curse the Jew will be cursed by God. While Holocaust theologians rarely find their theological bearings in literal interpretations of Scripture, their charge that the church's apostasy is made visible in its failure to understand and protect the Jew communicates a similar idea.

On political matters, both Holocaust theologians and dis-pensational premillennialists embrace and defend what some his-torians have come to call the "myths" surrounding the State of Israel's birth.[95] Both commonly meet criticism of Israeli policies with the "double standard" charge, arguing that the Jewish state is saddled with a unique set of moral expectations. Both groups assume that opposition to Zionism typically (and even necessarily) stems from anti-Semitism, with liberals finding an explanation in the anti-Jewish Christian psyche and conservatives in the inspira-tion of Satan himself. Both suspect that anti-Zionism/anti-Semitism is present wherever there is serious criticism of the State of Israel or its policies. Both have portrayed the PLO as an extremist organ-ization composed of terrorists, and the Palestinians (when they are considered at all) as anonymous Arab refugees who are victims of the Arab nations' refusal to assimilate them. When asked to assess the prospects for a "Palestinian state," representatives of both theo-logical movements are likely to respond that such a state already exists – in Jordan. As Paul van Buren and Jerry Falwell assert inde-pendently, the so-called "Palestinian problem" does not reflect Israel's shortcomings, but the intransigence and hostility of the Arab nations. Both men speak to Christians of their religious duty to support and defend the Jewish state. Finally, Holocaust theologians and dispensationalists each typically deny that for Christians Jews can be "just another people" or Israel "just another state," and both describe authentic Christianity as that which is philo- rather than anti-Semitic.

The uncommon unification of liberals and conservatives which "Israel" can create was symbolized in a two-page advertisement which appeared in the *New Republic* on June 15, 1992. Affixed to the ad sponsored by "The American Jewish Committee" and titled "Christians Speak Out: We support democracy. We support Israel," are the signatures of a broad array of liberal and conservative Chris-tian pastors, religious, laypersons and theologians. Among the names included were those of Catholic and Protestant liberals like Franklin Littell, Alice and Roy Eckardt, Harry James Cargas, Edward Flannery, Michael McGarry and Robert Everett, and conservatives like Jerry Falwell and Marvin Wilson. A similar advertisement, sponsored by the "National Christian Leadership Conference for Israel" and boasting the support of liberal and conservative Christians, appeared ten years earlier in the midst of Israel's campaign to remove the PLO from southern Lebanon.[96]

Such an enduring theological alliance across what are nearly impervious boundaries is unusual indeed. This remarkable cohesion between liberals and fundamentalists requires an object of concern that has a singular power to compel Christians of nearly every theological stripe. Given what has been said in preceding chapters about the Christian imagination and its perennial myth of the witness-people, it should not be surprising that the basis for this rare display of ecumenical solidarity has the name "Israel." In the final chapter, further evidence for the efficacy of the witness-people myth in contemporary Christianity will be considered, and some conclusions to this study will be offered.

8

Conclusions

If ... mutual comprehension is indispensable for dialogue between Christians and Jews, reflection on the mystery of Israel is also indispensable for Christianity to define itself, both as to its origins and in its nature as people of God.

The Vatican's '69 Working Document'

The existence of the Jewish witness to God is essential to the Christian belief, if it is to proclaim the living God. And if after Auschwitz there is really to be a task for theology, then it is to consider what we lack in God if we have lost Israel.

Fr.-W. Marquardt, *Von Elend und Heimsuchung der Theologie –*
Prologemena zur Dogmatik

It may be impossible for Christians to remain Christians without regarding Jews in mythic, magic and theological categories. Jews alone of all the people in the world are regarded as actors and participants in the drama of sin and innocence, guilt and salvation, perdition and redemption...

Richard Rubenstein, *After Auschwitz*

In this final chapter, further reflections of the witness-people myth in post-Holocaust Christian thought will be noted. Overviews of church statements on Jewish–Christian relations and of post-Holocaust theologies that have not received attention to this point will be followed by a brief exploration of the witness-people myth's relationship to Jewish self-understanding. Finally, some implications of this study will be outlined.

I. THE WITNESS-PEOPLE MYTH IN POST-HOLOCAUST CHRISTIAN DISCOURSE

A. Church Statements

In statements on Jewish–Christian relations published by church bodies over the last three decades one discovers a rich collection of contemporary expressions of the witness-people myth. From a variety of approaches these statements attempt to define the normative Christian attitude toward Jews, Judaism, anti-Semitism and the State of Israel.[1] Despite a reluctance to address some issues – the church's complicity in the "Final Solution," for instance – and ambivalence regarding the religious significance of the Jewish state, a few themes run through all these documents. Among the leitmotifs are an affirmation of the validity of the Jewish people's election and covenant, a condemnation of anti-Semitism and a repudiation of the theological notion that the Jews relinquished their role in salvation history with the advent of Christ.

The so-called supersessionist doctrine, according to which the church is depicted as the "New Israel," is categorically denied by nearly every mainstream Christian document on Jewish – Christian relations since the end of World War II.[2] Post-Holocaust church documents offer various descriptions of the continuing relevance of the Jewish people for authentic Christian faith, but each declares unambiguously the continuing salience of "Israel" as a datum for theological reflection. God "has chosen his people Israel and he stands by the election."[3] Thus, the Jews are "the people of the Bible living in our midst."[4] And since "the promises which the God of Abraham, Isaac, and Jacob has made to the Jewish people have never been revoked by their God," renewed attention must be paid to "the actual place of the Jewish people in the history of salvation…"[5] The perpetual existence of God's people reminds the church of its "duty to be concerned with this people."[6] These and other examples of the documents' language help to locate the church's post-Holocaust affirmation of Israel within the context of the witness-people tradition.

One church statement in which witness-people theology is particularly visible resulted from the Bristol meeting of the World Council of Churches Commission on Faith and Order in 1967. At Bristol a report of the Committee on the Church and the Jewish People was accepted and commended for theological study. Its authors declared that "it was God's own will and decision which made this one distinct people [Israel] with its special place in history." Chosen by God to be the "bearer of a particular promise and to act as his covenant-partner and special instrument," as well as a "perpetual reminder that God's purpose and promise are not yet realized," the Jewish people are to be a *"living revelation* to others." The authors of this report reject the notion that Jewish suffering might be proof of some unique Jewish guilt; yet they affirm that in their very survival the Jews reveal that God has not abandoned them. Thus it is by virtue of their miraculous persistence that Jews become a *"living and visible sign* of God's faithfulness to men..."[7]

Another church document which indicates the pervasive influence of the witness-people tradition in Christian meditation upon the Jewish people is "Israel: People, Land and State," a paper adopted in 1970 by the Netherlands Reformed Church. This Dutch statement emphasizes that Israel is "a people unlike all other peoples," a people with a "unique destiny," whose irrevocable election as God's covenant-people places upon it a "visible mark," and whose very existence constitutes a *"visible sign* of [God's] electing faithfulness." The Old Testament, according to "Israel: People, Land and State, is both a *"sign* of Israel's identity" and a *"sign* of Israel's vocation to be a blessing to all nations," while Israel's faithlessness "mirrors our own alienation from God." The return of the Jews to their land reminds the church of the "special significance of this people in the midst of the nations," and is "a *sign* for us." Christians, the authors conclude, cannot be silent about Israel, in whose history they are "somehow indirectly dealing with God."[8]

A Roman Catholic document in which witness-people thinking is apparent is the "Statement by the French Bishop's Committee for Relations with Jews" (1973). The bishops speak of the Jewish people's "permanent vocation," stress that the second covenant does not imply an invalidation of the first, note the dependence of the church on the Jewish scriptural and Pharisaic traditions, and contend that anti-Jewish teaching does not conform to the spirit of Christ. A key to discerning the theological foundation on which the bishops erect these positive pictures of the Jewish people appears in the opening section of the statement, "Jewish existence as a problem addressed to the conscience of Christians":

> The present existence of the Jewish people, its often precarious fate in the course of history, its hopes, the tragic trials it has known in the past and particularly in modern times, and its partial gathering in the land of the Bible; all these realities can enlighten the life of Christians and add to a more profound understanding of their own faith. The continuity through the ages of this people that has survived other civilizations, its presence as a rigorous and exacting partner of Christendom, are facts of great importance that we must not treat with ignorance or contempt.

The Church, speaking in the name of Jesus Christ and, through Him, linked to the Jewish people since her beginnings and for all time, *perceives in the uninterrupted existence of this people through the centuries a sign that she would wish fully to comprehend.*[9]

Another statement suggestive of the witness-people myth's power to inform the language of church reflection on "Israel" was published by the Synod of the Protestant Church of the Rhineland in 1980.[10] The authors of this German document proclaim the "permanent election of the Jewish people," disavow supersessionism, and wish to establish the "unbreakable connection of the New Testament with the Old Testament in a new way." They illuminate the Jewish roots of Christianity by highlighting the church's use of Hebrew Scripture and Jesus' identity as the Jewish Messiah. They also commend a one-covenant model for understanding the relationship of church and Israel.[11] This document, too, provides insight into the authors' deepest yearnings to understand the Jew. The Synod, they claim, is brought to its task in part by

the insight that the continuing existence of the Jewish people, its return to the Land of Promise, and also the creation of the State of Israel, *are signs of the faithfulness of God toward his people.*[12]

Two conclusions emerge from this review of ecclesiastical documents which address the church-Israel relationship in the shadow of the Holocaust. First, these statements utilize witness-people terminology and conceptions in a remarkably consistent way.[13] Second, despite continual references to the "turning point" in Christian thinking about Jews and Judaism that is supposedly represented by documents like "Nostra aetate" and the dozens of official pronouncements that have followed it, the theological grid through which Christian theologians view the Jewish people has not been shattered by the Holocaust and the birth of the State of Israel. These documents are distinguished by ubiquitous references to "Israel" in terms of salvation history, covenant, election, uniqueness, and divine calling; and they repeatedly affirm the mystery of Jewish existence, Jewish suffering, Jewish survival and Jewish restoration. All this demonstrates that the church's interpretation of God's way with the Jew is once again being animated at the deepest levels by the witness-people myth.

Without doubt the tone of these pronouncements is more uniformly positive than has been typical in previous eras of church history. But it is strikingly clear that, for the church's official theologians at least, the Jew continues to constitute a unique witness and sign of God's purpose and presence in the world. The witness-people myth, in other words, continues to inform Christian thought and action affecting the Jewish people. As a scholar associated for twenty years with the WCC Consultation on the Church and the Jewish People recently has suggested, "the image of Israel held by the World Council ... reinforces and perpetuates the ambivalency toward Jews, Judaism and Israel which already prevails in the secular political culture."[14]

B. Theological Reflection

One finds myriad attempts to comprehend "Israel" and its significance for Christianity in post-Holocaust academic theology as well. What is remarkable about these exercises of the theological imagination is the recurrent influence of the witness-people myth precisely where the pernicious consequences of Christian theologizing about Jews are confronted. A striking but by no means atypical example of this phenomenon appears in Charles Journet's "The Mysterious Destinies of Israel" (1956).[15]

Journet's article represents the thinking of a Christian philosemite – one who cherishes Israel because Israel is God's first love. But despite all his moving language about the unique place of Israel in the heart of God, despite his talk of Israel's unique capacity to unveil the mysteries of God's presence in the mundane, Journet remains convinced that Israel will ultimately recognize the Messiah it has rejected. In this way the "Israel of exile" will someday be metamorphosed into the "Israel of reintegration." As Barth, Bonhoeffer, and Niemöller did in the 1930s, and Christian fundamentalists continue to do in the 1990s, Journet proffers a version of Israel's nature and destiny consciously designed to combat Christian anti-Judaism. But because it is so steeped in the language and concepts of the witness-people myth, Journet's attempt to speak anew of Israel is doomed from the outset.

Surprisingly perhaps, more recent Christian post-Holocaust reflection has only rarely departed from the familiar territory of witness-people theology. As we have seen, in 1961 Heinrich Grüber amazed and bewildered Richard Rubenstein by insisting that the Jews' suffering at the hands of the Nazis must be inter-preted according to the "for thy sake" of Psalm 44. But thirty years later, Franz Mussner, a theologian renowned for his contributions to the post-Holocaust relationship of Christianity and Judaism, invokes the very same rationale. This is the concluding paragraph in Mussner's article "Theology After Auschwitz" (1991):

> Finally, the terrible events of the *Shoah* cannot be comprehended without taking into account the 'for thy sake' of the Psalm [44]. And that means: by God's will! The six million Jews who perished in the places of the *Shoah*, as in Auschwitz, were 'for thy sake ... killed all the day long' and 'counted as sheep for the slaughter.' If the Jews were not God's chosen people, then they would not be those unique people who are out of place among the Goyim, and for which the Gentiles cannot forgive them. Herein, up to the present day, lies the true roots of antisemitism. If anything can be said for the 'meaning' of the *Shoah*, then only this 'for thy sake.' "Suffering befalls the community because it belongs to God." And "Here the *signa crucis* already lie upon God's people of the Old Testament." But the Cross rises in the dark mystery of the deity; its mystery is inexplicable, seen in a theology after Auschwitz.[16]

That these words could be penned in the 1990s in the German lan-guage by a theologian explicitly concerned with the *Shoah* and its relevance for Christian theology gives us much to consider. But Franz Mussner is not an anomaly. The following statements, selected from books and articles published over the last 15 years by Christian scholars recognized for their contributions to Jewish–Christian rapprochement, demonstrate this. In its own way, each statement reflects the sway of the witness-people myth on its author:

> Empirical Israel, embodied in the Jews and Judaism of our day, is a concrete *sign* of God's presence with us.[17]

> The Jews are truly the key.[18]

> The Jews have the continuing task of reminding us of the first commandment.[19]

> We see the fidelity of the people of Israel over the centuries of Christian history – fidelity frequently under conditions of brutal

persecution, heroically giving *witness* to the nations of the absolute claims of the One God, and of the loving fidelity of that God.... It comes to us with all the force of the Burning Bush – as a *living revelation* of the creative fidelity of God, which it reflects in human history. This *sign* cannot well be read as the testimony of an arbitrary God setting aside a people who on their side remain faithful.[20]

The riddle of the 'obduracy' of Israel reveals that it is according to God's will that the Jews *post Christum* must submit; as the *lasting witness* to the tangibility of the doctrine of salvation, as the lasting 'root' of the Church and its God-willed companion throughout history to the end of time, as the *living witness* to the unfathomable ways of God, as the ultimate and eschatological *witness* to the predominance of mercy.[21]

The fundamental dependence of the Christian church and theology on Judaism after Auschwitz is based on Judaism
as *witness* to the remembrance
as *witness* to the Messianic expectation
as *witness* of God and the experience of God in and after Auschwitz
as *witness* of the one people of God and
as *witness* of the universal service to suffering humanity in the Messianic perspective of a righteous world society.[22]

The Jewish *witness* to God arising out of the Shoa causes me to encounter my Jewish brothers and sisters ... with the costly openness of faith in a God who calls on his Suffering Servant Israel to be the *sign* once again of God's Mastery and Compassion to all the nations, including the Christian community.[23]

These texts' substantive and terminological links with the ancient theory of the Jews as a witness-people are truly arresting. Conspicuous in several of the selections are the words "sign" and "witness," terms employed without regard for their prominence in the church's traditional theology of Israel. For these reasons it is perhaps necessary to remind ourselves that each of these statements was published in books or scholarly journals between 1979 and 1992 by American and European Christian scholars dedicated to the task post-Holocaust theological reconstruction.

II. ALTERNATIVES?

Are we to conclude that mystifying and mythicizing are necessary concomitants of Christian reflection about Jews? Is it simply the case that Christianity "must insist on the separate and special character of the Jewish people in order that its claims concerning the significance of Jesus may gain credence"?[24] Or is it not legitimate to insist that in its endeavor to render truth in the post-Holocaust era, Christian discourse assume greater responsibility for demythicizing "Israel"? If so, must not Christians actively pursue what Roy Eckardt has called a "secular theology of Israel"? Eckardt's suggestion seems a natural alternative to the tendency of contemporary Christian thought across the theological spectrum to conceive of Israel in mythic terms. But as we concluded in Chapter 6, successfully secularizing theology is difficult indeed when the object of reflection is the Jewish people. Is it simply impossible, then, for Christians to think of Jews and the Jewish state in utterly normal terms? And what are the sacrifices required to achieve such normalization?

An answer to this last question was suggested by a sociological study of American Christians' attitudes toward Jews and other groups which was published in 1963.[25] In order to test the correlation between prejudice and religious belief, Bernhard E. Olson and his colleagues undertook an extensive analysis of the curricula produced for internal use by American Protestant churches during the 1950s. The study distinguished four groups, which the researchers labeled "fundamentalist," "conservative," "neo-orthodox" and "liberal."[26] It is instructive to recall some aspects of the "liberal" curriculum, since it seems to represent a secular understanding of "Israel" designed to appeal to persons in the pew.

Happily, such traditional notions as the deicide charge and Jewish exile and dispersion as punishment are entirely absent from this curriculum. But while the "liberals'" enlightened view of the Bible as a human document tended to downplay the idea of Jewish chosenness, it also gave rise to portrayals of the Old Testament as the record of a primitive religion.[27] Furthermore, while "liberals" refrained from imposing restorationist hopes on the modern State of Israel, these were substituted by strong anti-Zionist sentiments.[28] Are the only alternatives for Christian reflection on Israel, then, a traditional Christianity that conceives of Jews in terms that are implicated in historic anti-Judaism, and a liberal Christianity whose secular approach to Israel is fertile ground for the seeds of "enlightened" anti-Semitism?

III. JEWISH VOICES

Before hazarding an answer to this troubling question, it will behove us to recognize a potentially serious obstacle facing any plan to restrict the play of the witness-people myth upon the Christian imagination. This obstacle was identified in the 1960s by Richard Rubenstein, but since that time few Christian scholars have given it due consideration. Following his fateful meeting with Dean Grüber, Rubenstein was led to wonder whether Christian mythologizing of the Jewish people in fact receives inadvertent substantiation from Jews. "Can we really blame the Christian community for viewing us through the prism of a mythology of history," Rubenstein asked, "when we were the first to assert this history of ourselves?"[29] In 1966, Rubenstein perceived in the Reconstructionist movement within Judaism a way to escape this dilemma. But today it appears unlikely that Reconstructionism will displace more traditional Jewish self-understandings.

In fact, those who would substitute a cultural for a religious definition of Jewishness are at most a vocal minority within the Jewish community. Meanwhile, there are many Jewish spokespersons whose descriptions of what it means to be a Jew continue to lend credence to the sort of Christian thinking Rubenstein encountered in Grüber's study. Perhaps it is no exaggeration to say that in the post-Holocaust environment Jewish writers are as likely as their Christian counterparts to speak of chosenness, to exult in the miraculous nature of Jewish survival and the redemptive aspects of Jewish restoration in Israel, and to assign theological meaning to the persistence of anti-Semitism.[30] This mood in contemporary Jewish thought may be elucidated with a few passages from the texts of well-known thinkers:

> Theologically speaking, the decision to kill every last Jew was an attempt to kill God, the covenantal partner known to humanity through the Jewish people's life and covenant.... Thus the physical presence of the Jewish people – and that existence is made possible by secular Israelis as well as religious Jews – is the best testimony to the Divine.... The great Biblical sign of the ongoing validity of

the covenant – the affirmation of God and hope – is the restoration of Jewry to Israel.... The re-creation of the state [of Israel] is the strongest suggestion that God's promises are still valid and reliable.[31]

Hitler knew, as we know, that not every Jew is just, merciful and truthful. But Hitler also knew that the Jew, historically and existentially, even without any choice, stands for justice, mercy and truth ... Doing nothing, the Jew created by his mere existence a situation in which Germany was visible as a land of Baal ... [The Jews] proved to be what others, what millions were not: they were chosen. In the apocalyptic hour of modern mankind the Jews did not bow before the Moloch. God did not let them. They were his people. Their election was still valid.[32]

Jews are the conscience of Western civilization and the Holocaust was the inevitable and desperate conclusion of that fact.[33]

The only enduring witness to God's ultimate control over the course of things is the Jewish people.... God's manifest reality in the world is necessarily linked to the fate of the Jewish people.[34]

The fate of Israel is of central concern because Israel is the elect people of God through whom God's redemptive work is done in the world. However tragic human suffering is on the human plane, what happens to Israel is directly tied to its role as that nation to which God attaches His name and through which He will redeem man. He who strikes Israel, therefore, engages himself in battle with God and it is for this reason that the history of Israel is the fulcrum of human history. The suffering of others must, therefore, be seen in the light of Israel's suffering. The travail of man is not abandoned, precisely because Israel suffers and, thereby God's presence is drawn into human history and redemption enters the horizon of human existence.[35]

... Judaism produced a summons to perfection and sought to impose it on the current and currency of Western life. Deep loathing built up in the social subconscious, murderous resentments. The mechanism is simple but primordial. We hate most those who hold out to us a goal, an ideal, a visionary promise which, even though we have stretched our muscles to the utmost, we cannot reach, which slips, again and again, just out of range of our racked fingers – yet, and this is crucial, which remains profoundly desirable, which we cannot reject because we fully acknowledge its supreme value. In his exasperating "strangeness," in his acceptance of suffering as part of a covenant with the absolute, the Jew became, as it were, the "bad conscience" of Western history.[36]

Without Jews there is no Jewish God.
If we leave this world
The light will go out in your tent.[37]

These selections from the writings of Jewish theologians, poets, and cultural critics reveal the religious and mythical elements that are retained and even intensified in post-Holocaust Jewish discourse. Even in the writings of Jewish thinkers who wish to undermine the mythical apprehensions of Christians, one is likely to discover mixed messages:

And the Jew who stands before the church in this world is no longer the cathedral image of the blindfolded synagogue, its staff broken, renouncing this world. His testimony is to the world and in this world: Israel is *not* a meta-historical people. Through the teachings of men like Leo Baeck, we see Israel performing the ancient task of God's witness and prophet.[38]

This admittedly superficial evaluation of contemporary Jewish thought at least demonstrates the continuing salience of Rubenstein's quandary: Is it realistic to demand that Christians refrain from speaking and thinking of the Jews as possessing a unique divine mission and signifying capacity as long as both secular and religious Jews encourage them to do so?

This dilemma illuminates the difficulties inherent in any consideration of Christian theologizing about "Israel." Stinging criticisms continue to be leveled at "pre-Holocaust" Christianity's proclivity for defining Jews and Judaism without sufficient attention to Jewish self-understanding, and indeed ignorance of Jewish thinking remains a critical failure of Christian discourse. But because influential Jewish writers articulate Jewishness in ways that are so accommodating to the witness-people myth, Christian appreciation of Jewish self-understanding cannot in itself be regarded as a foil to mythical influences in theology.[39]

IV. CONCLUSION

Unlike many works concerned with the Jewish–Christian encounter, this one is essentially a study in intellectual history. In these chapters I have attempted to track a single imaginative construct through various territories of the Christian mind. Along the way, I have sought to verify the presence of the witness-people myth wherever it appears, my primary intention being to understand rather than judge. In this sense, I have proceeded in the spirit of Michel Foucault, whose method was to explore how a particular knowledge functions, rather than whether or not it is "true."

Thus, I have not paid direct attention to the problem of distinguishing appropriate from inappropriate ways for Christians to regard Jews. However, it has been difficult for me to conceal my feeling that the witness-people myth in all its modern and pre-modern versions spells danger for the Jewish people. For, as I think the evidence of the preceding chapters has indicated, Jewish security is threatened whenever real Jews are associated with "the Jew" of the Christian imagination. Thus even apparently positive or philosemitic aspects of Christian thought cannot operate in the interest of Jews as long as they are rooted in mythology. If Jews are assumed to be witnesses and signs – regardless of what it is they are thought to be witnessing to – they are likely also to be objects of unnatural expectations, religious projections, and irrational fantasies.

Many Jews, keenly aware of this dilemma, have seen in Zionism a solution to persistent anti-Semitism and to the alien status that has characterized Jewish life in the West. This perspective was explicit in the Zionist thought of Leo Pinsker, who in *Auto-Emancipation* (1882) wrote that "[Jews] must not admit that we are doomed to play on in the future the hopeless role of the 'Wandering Jew.' This role is truly hopeless; it is enough to drive one to despair."[40] Since Pinsker's day, many Jews have perceived a national existence as the symbol and guarantor of Jewish normalcy, and as an implicit rejection of the theological role assigned to Jews by the Christian imagination. But we have seen that, ironically, the emergence of the Jewish state has only revivified the witness-people tradition among many influential Christians. In fact, then, the witness-people myth has not been undercut by the existence of the State of Israel among the nations, despite repeated claims to this effect by both Jews and Christians.

It appears that the only effective antidote to Christian mystification of the Jew would be an active and ongoing process of demystification, and that attempts to reform Christianity will be inconsequential until anti-Judaism is viewed as one symptom of an underlying theological disease that compels Christians of all kinds to perceive Jews as visible representations of their own hopes and fears. But can such a project of demystification and demythicization succeed?

Personally, I do not believe the witness-people myth can be extirpated from the Christian mind. For even if the myth were to be more widely recognized, formidable obstacles remain: Witness-people thinking has exceedingly deep and extensive roots in every source for Christian reflection. It is entrenched in the Bible, in dogmatic traditions, in theological works from every era of church history, in Christian interpretations of contemporary culture and history and, as we have seen, even in the Jewish thought to which Christians have increasingly looked for intellectual bearings. Furthermore, resistance to the process of demythicization has been exacerbated by recent church statements and by works of post-Holocaust theological reflection which reassert Israel's permanent election and its eternal vocation as a divine witness and sign.

Without great hope for reconstructing the Christian tradition, then, we return once more to the sage views of Roy Eckardt and Franklin Littell, Christian Holocaust theologians who have at least recognized the necessity of such a reconstruction. Despite unwitting links between their own theologies and the witness-people tradition, both men comprehend the dilemma faced by Christians after the Holocaust: On one hand, those who have come to recognize Jewish denigration and suffering as a Christian problem are naturally moved to address this problem by attempting to reform Christianity. Yet theological reform is hindered by the Christian mind's congenital instinct to cast the Jews in mythical categories. But because Eckardt and Littell lean toward different sides of this dilemma, they propose very different solutions, which it will be helpful to recall.

Fearing the mythologizing compulsion in Christian thought, Eckardt is led to conclude that even "a positive Christian theologizing of Jews cannot escape imperialism." Citing as evidence the constructive theological projects of Paul van Buren, Clemens Thoma and Franz Mussner, Eckardt contends that there should be no "Christian theology of Judaism." "The very affirmation ... that

Judaism and the Jewish people comprise the integral foundation of Christianity may itself only aggravate Christian supersessionism," Eckardt cautions us. He warns that "[s]eemingly blessed words have a way of carrying us along the pavement of good intentions toward a woeful destination."[41] In order to avoid this dangerous road, Eckardt effectively bans Christian speculation on the mystery of Israel. But this radical approach to protecting the Jewish people from Christian imperialism and self-interest simply is not a realistic answer to post-Holocaust Christian theology's dilemma. In fact, Eckardt's own inability to abide by his restrictions is sufficient proof that Christian thinkers are, *qua* Christians, incapable of speaking about Jews in a thoroughly normal, non-mythical manner.

Franklin Littell offers a different strategy for reforming post-Holocaust Christian theology. While Eckardt wants to shield Jews from anti-Jewish ideology by "secularizing" Christianity's apprehension of Israel, Littell challenges those on the Christian side of the Jewish–Christian encounter to recognize their authentic roots. He contends that Christian identity cannot be conceived apart from "the role of the Jewish people in meaningful history,"[42] noting that while Jews do not require Christians for comprehending their mission, Christians do need Jews – particularly as a model of peoplehood in history. Littell concludes that "Christians cannot establish a self-identity except in relationship to the Jewish people – past and present, and whenever the Christians have attempted to do so, they have fallen into grievous heresy and sin."[43] Thus Littell chooses to begin the task of post-Holocaust theological reconstruction with the historically-determined necessities of Christian reflection in full view.

In these responses to the dilemma of post-Holocaust Christian theology a dialectic of fear and necessity is perceptible. It appears that Christian reflection on Israel is condemned to operate within this dialectic until a more direct way forward comes into view. In the meantime, it is hoped that this explication of the dangers of the witness-people tradition will assist those Christian thinkers who must approach the task of interpreting anew God's way with Israel.

Notes

CHAPTER 1: INTRODUCTION

1. *Inferno*, 34: 61–3, from *The Divine Comedy of Dante Alighieri*, Vol. 1, tr. John D. Sinclair (New York: Oxford University Press, 1939), 423.
2. Jews are conspicuously absent from Dante's hell. Although Caiaphas makes a brief appearance in canto XXIII, Dante's description of usurers in canto XVII is without explicit references to Jews. This is especially surprising given that "[b]y the twelfth century the terms 'Jew' and 'usurer' were synonymous...." [Jeffrey Richards, *Sex, Dissidence and Damnation: Minority Groups in the Middle Ages* (London: Routledge, 1991), 113.]
3. Hyam Maccoby, *Judas Iscariot and the Myth of Jewish Evil* (New York: The Free Press, 1992), 117.
4. "Jews and Devils: Anti-Semitic Stereotypes of Late Medieval and Renaissance England," *Journal of Literature and Theology* 4:1 (March, 1990), 15–28; 25.
5. See Chapter 5
6. I am concerned that my treatment of Christian Holocaust Theology may lead some readers mistakenly to infer hostility on my part toward radical attempts to reformulate Christian thought in the post-Holocaust environment. I want to say explicitly, therefore, that my critique reflects not disapproval of the task Holocaust Theologians have undertaken, but my opinion that too many Christian responses to anti-Judaism have sought to redress this problem by carelessly reiterating mythical forms.
7. My concern with the phenomenon of ambivalence has forced me to keep the relatively positive aspects of Christian mythical thinking constantly in view. If this is interpreted by some readers as a subtle apologetic for this type of thinking, I can only respond that this is not my intent.
8. From *Le Cru et le cuit*, cited in Terrence Hawkes, *Structuralism and Semiotics* (London: Routledge, 1977), 41. My discussion of Lévi-Strauss and Barthes is indebted to Hawkes' excellent introduction to their work.
9. The Restorationist teaching was not a consistent part of witness-people thinking until the seventeenth century. While Augustine did not believe the Jews would return to their land, many fathers of the church did not rule out such a return. On Restorationist and anti-Restorationist thinking in the first few centuries of church history, especially as it relates to Julian the Apostate's unsuccessful attempt to rebuild the Jerusalem Temple in 363 CE., see Edward H. flannery, "Theological Aspects of the State of Israel," in John Oesterreicher, ed., *The Bridge*, Vol. 3 (New York: Pantheon, 1958), 301–24; 306ff.

10. See "Myth Today" in Roland Barthes' *Mythologies*, tr. Annette Lavers (New York: Hill & Wang, 1972).
11. Ibid., 113.
12. See Ibid., 115.

CHAPTER 2: THE WITNESS-PEOPLE MYTH AND ITS ALTERNATIVES

1. See, for example, Rosemary Ruether, *Faith and Fratricide: The Theological Roots of Anti-Semitism* (Minneapolis: Seabury, 1974), ch. 2.
2. See Gavin I. Langmuir, *History, Religion and Anti-Semitism* (Berkeley: University of California Press, 1990), 282.
3. See Langmuir, *History, Religion and Anti-Semitism*, 282–3; and Ruether, *Faith and Fratricide*.
4. See "Response to Rosemary Ruether," in Eva Fleischner, ed., *Auschwitz: Beginning of a New Era?* (New York: Ktav, 1977), 97–107.
5. See Randolph L. Braham, ed., *The Origins of the Holocaust: Christian Anti-Semitism* (New York: Columbia University Press, 1986).
6. See *Moments of Crisis in Jewish-Christian Relations* (Philadelphia: Trinity Press International, 1989).
7. This is Marc Tanenbaum's term. See Braham, ed. *The Origins of the Holocaust: Christian Anti-Semitism*, 55.
8. See Eugene Fisher, "The Origins of Anti-Semitism in Theology: A Reaction and Critique," in Braham, ed., *The Origins of the Holocaust: Christian Anti-Semitism*, 22.
9. Yerushalmi, "Response to Rosemary Ruether."
10. See Arthur Hertzberg, "Is Anti-Semitism Declining?", *New York Review of Books* (June 24, 1993, 51–7), where the author delineates recent competing trends in understanding the sources of anti-Semitism.
11. John G. Gager, *The Origins of Anti-Semitism: Attitudes toward Judaism in Pagan and Christian Antiquity* (New York: Oxford University Press, 1983), 15.
12. Gager, *Origins*, 16.
13. *The Teaching of Contempt*, tr. Helen Weaver (New York: Holt, Rinehart & Winston, 1964).
14. *The Crucifixion of the Jews: The Failure of Christians to Understand the Jewish Experience*, Rose Reprints (Macon, Ga: Mercer University Press, 1986), 2.
15. "Rethinking Christ," in Alan T. Davies, ed., *Antisemitism and the Foundations of Christianity* (New York: Paulist Press, 1979), 167–87; 168.
16. Trachtenberg writes in a tradition of Jewish historiography of anti-Semitism pioneered by Heinrich Graetz. See also Jacques Danielou's *Dialogue With Israel* [tr. Joan Marie Roth (Baltimore: Helicon, 1968), 92], where the author claims anti-Semitism is a popular phenomenon, bound to the lowest, "inferior" forms of religious sentiment, and thus a product of "religious fanaticism."

17. *The Devil and the Jews,* 3.
18. Ibid, 4.
19. *History, Religion and Antisemitism,* 267.
20. Ibid., 285. For Langmuir, "anti-Judaism is a nonrational reaction to overcome nonrational doubts, while anti-semitism is an irrational reaction to repressed rational doubts", 276.
21. Ibid., 302, 304.
22. Ibid., 305, 346. The apparent continuity here between Christian and Nazi attitudes toward Jews is somewhat misleading. Langmuir notes that "in contrast with Christian antisemitism, Nazis were obsessed with the alleged physical characteristics of Jews ... Nazism was a physiocentric religion, not a psychocentric one, and the difference was lethal," (344–5). See Langmuir's discussion of "physiocentric antisemitism" in ch. 16.
23. See Fred Gladstone Bratton's *The Crime of Christendom* (Boston: Beacon Press, 1969), where the author anticipates Ruether in seeing the root of the problem of anti-Semitism in the body of Christological doctrine which has remained intact since the fourth century.
24. *Faith and Fratricide,* 246.
25. See Gager, *Origins,* 19, 20. For all her pessimism about historical Christianity's anti-Judaism, Ruether believes that this could be overcome if the church returned to its original orientation in the life and message of Jesus the messianic prophet.
26. In addition to Gager's book, see Davies, ed., *Anti-Semitism and the Foundations of Christianity;* and Gregory Baum's introduction to Reuther, *Faith and Fratricide.*
27. Yerushalmi, "Response to Rosemary Ruether," passim; For a more recent critique of Ruether's view of the relationship between Christian anti-Semitism and the Holocaust, see Isabel Wollaston, "Faith and Fratricide: Christianity, Anti-Semitism and the Holocaust in the Work of Rosemary Radford Ruether," *Modern Churchman* 33:1 (1991), 8–14.
28. Yerushalmi, "Response," 103.
29. This discussion of Maccoby's views is based on his "The Origins of Anti-Semitism," in Braham, ed. *The Origins of the Holocaust: Christian Anti-Semitism,* 1-14. See also Maccoby's "Theologian of the Holocaust," *Commentary* (December 1982), 33–7. For a similar view of the centrality of the deicide charge, but with an appreciation for the concomitant ambivalence toward Jews, see J. L. Talmon, "European History – Seedbed of the Holocaust," *Midstream* 19:5 (May 1973), 3–25; 6.
30. He speaks, for example, of the "strange mixture of loathing and awe that characterizes anti-Semitism" ("The Origins of Anti-Semitism," 4). The theme of ambivalence is more prominent in his book *The Sacred Executioner: Human Sacrifice and the Legacy of Guilt* (London, Thames & Hudson, 1982), but even here it is symbolic of Maccoby's undialectical view that his chapter on "The Church and the Jews" includes only one paragraph on Augustine.
31. See also Maccoby's recent book, *Judas Iscariot and the Myth of Jewish Evil.*

32.   Ibid., 8.
33.   Maccoby, "Theologian of the Holocaust," 36.
34.   Ibid., 5.
35.   Ibid., 9. See also Maccoby's book *The Mythmaker: Paul and the Invention of Christianity* (New York: Harper & Row, 1986).
36.   Ibid., 12.
37.   Ibid., 14.
38.   Ibid., 11.
39.   No examples of millenarian sects are given in "The Origins of Anti-Semitism," even though millenarianism is identified there as linking Christian and Nazi Jew-hatred.
40.   Eugene J. Fisher, "The Origins of Anti-Semitism in Theology: A Reaction and Critique," in Braham, ed., *The Origins of the Holocaust*, 17–29; 24–5.
41.   Ibid., 19.
42.   Fisher locates in the development of the Passion Play in the thirteenth century the first occasion in which Judas functioned as the "eponymous representative of the Jewish people" (Ibid., 23).

CHAPTER 3: THE WITNESS-PEOPLE MYTH IN HISTORY

1.   All Scripture quotations are from the New Revised Standard Version unless otherwise noted.
2.   See J. Christiaan Beker, "The New Testament View of Judaism," in James H. Charlesworth, ed., *Jews and Christians: Exploring the Past, Present and Future* (New York: Crossroad, 1990), 60–9; 61.
3.   For a useful survey, see David Rokeah, "The Church Fathers and the Jews in Writings Designed for Internal and External Use," in Shmuel Almog, ed., *Antisemitism through the Ages*, trans. Nathan H. Reisner (Oxford: Pergamon Press, 1988), 39–69.
4.   For the discussion that follows I am indebted to Clark Williamson, *Has God Rejected His People? Anti-Judaism in the Christian Church* (Nashville: Abingdon, 1982), ch. 5.
5.   According to Edward Flannery, Lactantius first adumbrated the witness-people theory. The theory gained no currency, however, until Augustine elaborated it in his writings.
6.   To my knowledge, the only scholar to use the term "witness-people doctrine" with reference to Augustine's theology is Edward Flannery in *The Anguish of the Jews: Twenty-Three Centuries of Antisemitism*. (New York: Atheneum, 1985). In addition to Augustine's works cited in this section, see also *Sermones* 200:2; *Enarrationes in Psalmos* 58:21–2; 59:18–19, and *Tractatus Adversus Judaeos*.
6.   Flannery, *The Anguish of the Jews*, 53.
7.   Ibid.
8.   See Ruether, *Faith and Fratricide*, 124ff. Clark Williamson suggests that Melito of Sardis (late second century) was the originator of the notion of deicide (*Has God Rejected His People?*, 93)

9. "On Psalm 64, 1," in Vernon J. Bourke, *The Essential Augustine* (Indianapolis: Hackett, 1964), 224.

10. *City of God*, 4:34; tr. Henry Bettenson (Harmondsworth: Penguin, 1972).

11. *City of God*, 18:46.

12. *Enarratio in Psalm 40*, cited in A. Lukyn Williams, *Adversus Judaeos* (Cambridge: Cambridge University Press, 1935), 313n2.

13. *City of God*, 18:46.

14. *Tractatus Adversos Judaeos*; cited in Yehuda Bauer, *A History of the Holocaust* (New York: Franklin Watts, 1982), 9.

15. *On Faith in Things Unseen*, 6:9; in Ludwig Schopp, ed. *Writings of Augustine, Volume 2, The Fathers of the Church* (New York: CIMA Publications, 1947).

16. *City of God*, 20:29.

17. Augustine, *Tractatus Adversus Judaeos*, 15; cited in Flannery, *The Anguish of the Jews*, 53.

18. For one of the classic studies of this period, see James Parkes, *The Conflict of the Church and The Synagogue: A Study in the Origins of Antisemitism* (New York: Hermon Press, 1974).

19. See Parkes, *Conflict*, 183: "Certainly, so far as the fourth century is concerned, it was better to be a Jew than a heretic."

20. Parkes, *Conflict*, 184.

21. Justinian Code, Novella 146; in Parkes, *Conflict*, 392–3.

22. Parkes, *Conflict*, 254.

23. Ibid., 248.

24. From *Las Siete Partidas*, translation by Donald Tucker. Cited in Grayzel, *The Church and the Jews in the Thirteenth Century* (New York: Hermon Press, 1966), 12.

25. According to James Parkes, twenty of Gregory's 800 extant letters deal with matters affecting the Jews; for a discussion of Gregory's successors in the seventh and eighth centuries, see *Conflict*, 221ff. Parkes concludes that they "continued the equable tenor of their ways, showing no special favour to the Jews, but allowing them the rights which were theirs by law."

26. Parkes, *Conflict*, 211; 220.

27. Ruether, *Faith and Fratricide*, 200.

28. Jacob R. Marcus, *The Jew in the Medieval World* (New York: Harper & Row, 1965), 111.

29. From Gregory's letter of June, 598 to Victor, Bishop of Palermo; in Marcus, *The Jew in the Medieval World*, 113.

30. Ruether, *Faith and Fratricide*, 197, 199.

31. See *Faith and Fratricide*, 201ff; and Parkes, *Conflict*, ch. 10.

32. Leon Poliakov, *The History of anti-Semitism*, vol. 1., tr. Richard Howard (New York: Vanguard, 1965), 32. Poliakov notes that at this time the reference to "Jews and pagans" in Good Friday prayers for catechumens was changed, and the words "do not genuflect to the Jews" were added.

33. Poliakov, *History*, 33; and Ruether, *Faith and Fratricide*, 204.

34. Poliakov, *History*, 34.

35. Cited in Jeffrey Richards, *Sex, Dissidence and Damnation*, 90.
36. Poliakov, *History*, 31.
37. *Faith and Fratricide*, 205–6.
38. See, e.g., Shlomo Eidelberg, ed., *The Jews and the Crusaders* (Madison: University of Wisconsin Press, 1977).
39. From "The Book of Remembrance" of Rabbi Ephraim of Bonn, cited in Eidelberg, *The Jews and the Crusaders*, 122.
40. Cited in Marc Saperstein, *Moments of Crisis in Jewish–Christian Relations*, 19. See also David Berger "The Attitude of St. Bernard of Clairvaux to the Jews," *PAAJR* 40 (1972), 89–108.
41. Eidelberg, *The Jews and the Crusades*, 8.
42. Letter to the Archbishop of Bordeaux and to the Bishops of Saintes, Angouleme and Poitiers, September 5, 1236. Cited in Grayzel, *The Church and the Jews*, 227.
43. Grayzel, *The Church and the Jews*, 2.
44. See *Faith and Fratricide*, 209.
45. Letter to Count of Nevers, Jan. 17, 1208; in Saperstein, *Moments of Crisis in Jewish–Christian Relations*, 67–23.
46. Grayzel, *The Church and the Jews*, 9; see documents 5, 14; yet see Grayzel, 78, where we learn that Innocent III declared, as a preface to his bull of toleration, that the Jews should not be killed, despite their perfidy, because they are guardians of the Law of God.
47. See the papal letters in Grayzel, *The Church and the Jews*, documents 31, 32, 70, 87, 88, 110, 113–117, 132.
48. See Grayzel, *The Church and the Jews*, documents 5, 110.
49. Ibid., documents 5, 8, 87, 116.
50. Ibid., documents 87, 115, 117.
51. Ibid., documents 14, 70, 110, 113, 117. Grayzel notes that the thirteenth-century conciliar decrees reveal similar reasoning with regard to the Jews. See documents 1, 16 and 31.
52. Grayzel, *The Church and the Jews*, 76ff. See also Jeffrey Richards, *Sex, Dissidence and Damnation*, 93ff.
53. See Jacob Marcus, *The Jews in the Middle Ages*, 151ff.
54. "Letter to the Duchess of Brabant," in A. P. d'Entrèves, ed., *Selected Political Writings*, tr. J. G. Dawson (New York: Macmillan, 1959), 85. In the work of Dante and Shakespeare as well Christian anti-Judaism is moderated by the positive side of witness-people thinking. Cf. Martin D. Yaffe, Moderating Christian anti-Judaism: Usury in Thomas Aquinas' *De Regimine Judaeorum* (1270?) and Shakespeare's *The Merchant of Venice* (1596), paper presented at the American Academy of Religion Annual Meeting, November 1991, Kansas City.
55. See Jeremy Cohen, *The Friars and the Jews* (Ithaca: Cornell University Press, 1982), 25. My discussion is dependent on Cohen's summary of Funkenstein's writings, which have appeared mainly in Hebrew. See also David E. Timmer, "Biblical Exegesis and the Jewish–Christian Controversy in the Early Twelfth Century," *Church History* 58 (Spring, 1989), 309–21; and Marcus, *The Jew in the Medieval World*, 142f, 145f.
56. See Cohen, *The Friars and the Jews*, 28ff.

57. Ibid., 14.
58. Ibid., 15.
59. See Richards, *Sex, Dissidence and Damnation*, 88ff.
60. Ibid., 97–8.
61. Maccoby, *The Sacred Executioner*, 154.
62. Ibid.
63. Ibid
64. *Semites and anti-Semites* (New York: W.W. Norton, 1986), 81. See pages 80–5.
65. In *Faith and Fratricide*, Rosemary Ruether makes the connection between medieval Christian and Nazi Jew-hatred even more explicit. The "laws of purity of blood" in sixteenth-century Spain were "purely racial," and are the "ancestor of the Nazi Nuremberg laws" (203). For a critique of Ruether's view, see Alan Davies, "On Religious Myths and Their Secular Translation: Some Historical Reflections," in Davies, ed., *Antisemitism and the Origins of* Christianity (New York: Paulist Press, 1979), 188–207.
66. In Heiko A. Oberman, *The Origins of anti-Semitism in the Age of Renaissance and Reformation*, tr. James I. Porter (Philadelphia: Fortress, 1984), 15.
67. On Eck, see Oberman, *The Origins of anti-Semitism*, 36, 47, 72ff; on Erasmus, 38–40.
68. Oberman, *The Origins of anti-Semitism*, 71.
69. See Luther, *On the Jews and their Lies*, in *Luther's Works*, tr. Martin H. Bertram and ed. by Franklin Sherman and Helmut T. Lehman (Philadelphia: Fortress Press, 1971) vol. 47, 137–306, especially 268, 272.
70. Luther, *On the Jews and their Lies*, 292.
71. Oberman, *The Origins of anti-Semitism*, 27, 30, 50.
72. Ibid., 28.
73. Ibid., 14.
74. In Saperstein, *Moments of Crisis*, 35.
75. Richard L. Rubenstein and John K. Roth, *Approaches to Auschwitz: The Holocaust and Its Legacy* (Atlanta: John Knox Press, 1987), 57.
76. Cited in Rubenstein and Roth, *Approaches to Auschwitz*, 53.
77. *On the Jews and Their Lies*, 138–9; in Rubenstein and Roth, *Approaches to Auschwitz*, 56.
78. See *On the Jews and their Lies*, 271; This approach is not unique to Luther, however. Precedents can be found in Eusebius of Caesarea and Hilary of Poitiers in the patristic age. See Parkes, *Conflict*, 160ff.
79. Oberman, *The Origins of anti-Semitism*, 104.
80. Ibid.
81. Ibid., 105.
82. Ibid., 108, 109.
83. R. H. Popkin, "Some Aspects of Jewish–Christian Theological Interchanges in Holland and England 1640–1700," in *Jewish–Christian Relations in the Seventeenth Century: Studies and Documents*, ed. J. van den Berg and Ernestine G. E. van der Wall (Dordrecht: Kluwer, 1988), 4.

84. Calvin so firmly rejected the millennial fanaticism of his time that *Revelation* was the only biblical book on which he did not write a commentary. Peter Toon, ed., *Puritans, the Millennium and the Future of Israel: Puritan Eschatology 1600–1660* (London: James Clarke, 1970), 19; and Jonathan Edwards, *Apocalyptic Writings*, ed. Stephen J. Stein (New Haven: Yale University Press, 1977), 3.

85. Especially Theodore Beza and the editors of the *Geneva Bible*. See Toon, *Puritans*, 6, 24; Luther and Calvin had identified Paul's references to "Israel" with the church comprised of Jews and Gentiles.

86. From the late sixteenth century on, Christian Restorationism has developed and adjusted to changing times. It has taken on a variety of organisational forms (For example, the Palestine societies and Bible societies which began in early nineteenth-century Britain) and it assumed an increasingly practical, political orientation in the eighteenth and nineteenth centuries. It is the ideological predecessor of twentieth-century Christian Zionism. See Peter Gardella, "Gentile Zionism," *Midstream* 37:4 (May, 1991), 29–32, where the connection between seventeenth and twentieth century "Zionism" among American Christians is emphasized; and Lawrence J. Epstein, *Zion's Call: Christian Contributions to the Origins and Development of Israel* (Lanham, Md.: University Press of America, 1984). Epstein observes that the most vigorous advocates of "Zionist" aims between the late sixteenth and late nineteenth centuries were Christians.

87. See Stanley J. Grenz, *The Millennial Maze: Sorting Out Evangelical Options* (Downers Grove, Ill.: Inter Varsity Press, 1992), 46ff.

88. Rubenstein and Roth, *Approaches to Auschwitz*, 52.

89. *The Origins of anti-Semitism*, 140.

90. On Jewish–Christian relations in seventeenth-century Europe, especially Holland, see van den Berg and van der Wall, *Jewish–Christian Relations in the Seventeenth Century.*

91. See Epstein, *Zion's Call*, 6f; Thomas Brightman's Restorationist ideas seem to have preceded those of Finch, but were published later.

92. Egal Feldman, *Dual Destinies* (Urbana: University of Illinois Press, 1990), 5.

93. See Epstein, *Zion's Call*, 9–10; and Feldman, *Dual Destinies*, ch. 2.

94. Feldman, *Dual Destinies*, 15.

95. See especially Increase Mather's tract, "The Mystery of Israel's Salvation" (1667). See also Yaakov S. Ariel, *On Behalf of Israel: American Fundamentalist Attitudes toward Jews, Judaism, and Zionism, 1865–1945*, Chicago Studies in the History of American Religion (Brooklyn, NY: Carlson, 1991), 2ff.

96. See Feldman, *Dual Destinies*, 21; and Epstein, *Zion's Call*, 11

97. Feldman stresses the instrumental importance of the American Puritan view of the Jew: "to the New England orthodox mind Jews were mere instruments to be employed for the salvation of the Christian soul" (20)); "Jews served as an indispensable link in the chain that would lead Mather and other Puritans toward the Kingdom of Heaven" (22). It is interesting to compare these instrumental-

ist views with those of contemporary Americans like Hal Lindsey and Jerry Falwell. See Chapter 7.

98. Edwards, "Notes on the Apocalypse," ch. 16, 135 (emphasis added). See also Ariel, *On Behalf of Israel*, 5.

99. Popkin, "Some Aspects," 5.

100. Popkin, "Some Aspects," 4; 22. The Sabbatian movement in particular seems to have had a stimulating influence on many Restorationists. It has also been suggested that Zvi himself was influenced by the English millenarianism of the Fifth Monarchy Men. See Peter Toon, ed., *Puritans, the Millennium and the Future of Israel*, 143.

101. See Popkin, "Some Aspects," 21–2.

102. See Popkin, "Some Aspects," 16–17.

103. "Jews and Devils," 25.

104. See Popkin, "Some Aspects, 17.

105. Count Stanislas de Clermont-Tonnere made this statement on December 22, 1789.

106. Poliakov, *The History of anti-Semitism*, vol. 1, viii.

107. *Semites and anti-Semites*, 87.

108. *The History of anti-Semitism*, vol. 1, viii.

109. Cited in Rosemary R. Ruether and Herman J. Ruether, *The Wrath of Jonah: The Crisis of Religious Nationalism in the Israeli–Palestinian Conflict* (San Francisco: Harper & Row, 1989), 81.

110. Jacob Katz, *From Prejudice to Destruction: anti-Semitism 1700–1933* (Cambridge Mass.: Harvard University Press, 1980), 23. This discussion of Eisenmenger is based on Katz, 20–2.

111. Katz, *From Prejudice to Destruction*, 20–1.

112. See *Warrant for Genocide: The Myth of the Jewish World-Conspiracy and the Protocols of the Elders of Zion* (Chico, Calif.: Scholars Press, 1981.). See also Jacob Katz, *Jews and Freemasons in Europe 1723–1939* (Cambridge, Mass.: 1970).

113. See especially the letters cited in Cohn, *Warrant for Genocide*, 45–6.

114. *The History of anti-Semitism*, vol. 1, vii.

115. In Ariel, *On Behalf of Israel*, 44.

116. *The New Millennium: Ten Trends that will Impact You and Your Family by the Year 2000* (Waco: Word Publishing, 1990), 271–2. In *Listen, America!* (Garden City, NY: Doubleday, 1980), Jerry Falwell also traces the story to Disraeli and Victoria, citing dispensationalist guru Jack van Impe's book *Israel's Final Holocaust* as his source.

117. *"The Time of Jacob's Trouble": An Answer to the Question of a Little Jewish Child – "Tell Me, Father, What Makes Folks Hate Us So?"* (New York: American Board of Mission to the Jews, 1938), Preface to the 4th edn.

118. See Tim Lahaye, *The Beginning of the End* (Wheaton, Ill: Tyndale House, 1972), 43; and Hal Lindsey, *There's a New World Coming* (New York: Bantam, 1973), 158. Jack van Impe and Roger S. Campbell, *Israel's Final Holocaust* (Troy, Mich.: Jack van Impe Ministries, 1979), 57.

119. A striking example of this phenomenon is to be found among the people of the French Huguenot village of Le Chambon-sur-Lignon, whose Reformed pastor led the town's 5000 people in rescuing about 5000 Jews. In the documentary movie "Weapons of the Spirit,"

rescuers from Le Chambon interviewed over forty years later cite their religious understanding of the Jewish people as motivation for their brave efforts.

120. Uriel Tal, "Introduction," in John M. Snoek, *The Grey Book* (New York: Humanities Press, 1970), ii.

121. Quotations are from Hitler's speeches and are taken from Lucy Dawidowicz, *The War Against the Jews 1933–1945* (New York: Bantam, 1986), 19, 164, 21, respectively.

122. See Friedrich Heer, *God's First Love: Christians and Jews Over Two Thousand Years*, tr. Geoffrey Skelton (New York: Weybright & Talley, 1970), 40ff.

123. Tal, "Introduction" in *The Grey Book*, xi.

124. Cited in Ruether, *Faith and Fratricide.*, 203–4.

125. See *Mein Kampf*, tr. Ralph Manheim (Boston: Houghton Mifflin, 1971), ch. 11, "Nation and Race."

126. In Eva Fleischner, ed., *Auschwitz: Beginning of a New Era?*, 7–55. Greenberg stresses that these are only two of "literally hundreds of similar anti-Semitic statements by individual people reported in the Holocaust literature" (12).

127. In Greenberg, "Cloud of Smoke, Pillar of Fire," 11–12.

128. Ibid., 12.

129. Yerushalmi, "Response," 104.

CHAPTER 4: KARL BARTH AND THE GERMAN CHURCH STRUGGLE

1. See Stephen R. Haynes, *Prospects for Post-Holocaust Theology: "Israel" in the Theologies of Karl Barth, Jürgen Moltmann and Paul van Buren*, American Academy of Religion Academy Series, 77 (Atlanta: Scholars Press, 1991), ch. 2. Unless otherwise specified I am using "Israel" to refer to the Jewish people as a historical and theological entity, not the Middle Eastern state of the same name.

2. For recent interpretations of Barth's theology of Israel see Haynes, *Prospects for Post-Holocaust Theology*; Katherine Sonderegger, *That Jesus Christ was Born a Jew: Karl Barth's "Doctrine of Israel"* (University Park, Pa: The Pennsylvania State University Press, 1992); Berthold Klappert, *Israel und die Kirche: Erwagungen zur Israellehre Karl Barths*, Theologische Existenz Heute, 207 (München: Christian Kaiser, 1980); and Friedrich-Wilhelm Marquardt, *Die Entdeckung des Judentums für die Christliche Theologie: Israel im Denkens Karl Barth*, Abhandlung zum Christlich-Judischen Dialog, 1 (München: Christian Kaiser, 1967).

3. Cited in Richard Gutteridge, *The German Evangelical Church and the Jews 1879–1950* (New York: Harper & Row, 1976), 58.

4. Cited in Dieter Kraft, "Israel in der Theologie Karl Barths," *Communio Viatorum* 27:1 (1984), 63.

5. See Gutteridge, *The German Evangelical Church and the Jews*, 125. See also Klaus Scholder, *The Churches and the Third Reich, Volume Two, The*

Year of Disillusionment: 1934: Barmen and Rome (Philadelphia: Fortress, 1989).

6. See, e.g., *The Book of Confessions, Part One of the Constitution of the Presbyterian Church (U.S.A.)* (New York: Office of the General Assembly, 1983), ch. 8.

7. Gutteridge, *The German Evangelical Church and the Jews*, 125. Ironically, Barth had written privately to a friend just a few months before Barmen that "anyone who believes in Christ ... simply cannot be involved in the contempt for Jews and in the ill-treatment of them which is now the order of the day" [Letter to E. Steffens, January 10, 1934, cited in Philip J. Rosato, "The Influence of Karl Barth on Catholic Theology," *Gregorianum* 67:4 (1986), 659–78; 664]. See also Ruether, *Faith and Fratricide*, 224.

8. Jürgen Fangmeier and Heinrich Stoevesandt, eds., *Karl Barth, Letters 1961–68*, tr. Geoffrey W. Bromiley (Edinburgh: T. & T. Clark, 1981), 250. Cf. Barth's statement soon after World War II that "where the Confessing Church was concerned, during the whole period of the church struggle, as much as was humanly possible was done for the persecuted Jews" (Cited in Gutteridge, *The German Evangelical Church and the Jews*, 267).

9. Kraft, "Israel in der Theologie Karl Barths," 63-4. See also Eberhard Busch, *Glaubensheiterkeit Karl Barth: Erfahrungen und Begegnungen* (Vluyn: Neukirchner, 1986).

10. See Kraft, "Israel in der Theologie Karl Barths," 64.

11. Cited in Klappert, *Israel und die Kirche*, 11.

12. See, e.g., the references to Barth's correspondence with Rabbi H.-J. Schoeps in Klappert, *Israel und die Kirche*.

13. Cited in Gutteridge, *The German Evangelical Church and the Jews*, 298.

14. All references are to the Authorised English Translation of Barth's *Kirchliche Dogmatik*, in four volumes, edited by G. W. Bromiley and T. F. Torrance (Edinburgh: T. & T. Clark, 1936–69). Hereafter the English title *Church Dogmatics* will be abbreviated as *CD*, and Volume I, part 1 will be referred to as I:1, etc.

15. See Kraft, "Israel in der Theologie Karl Barths," 65.

16. *CD* I:2, 510.

17. *CD* II:2, 195.

18. Ibid., 198.

19. Ibid., 211.

20. Ibid., 233.

21. Ibid., 259.

22. Ibid., 198.

23. Ibid., 201.

24. Ibid., 205.

25. Ibid., 208; 263.

26. Barth makes this assertion several times; see *CD* II:2, 201, 267, and 279.

27. *CD* II:2, 263.

28. Ibid. II:2, 209.

29. "Israel in itself and as such is the 'vessel of dishonor.' It is the witness to the divine judgment. It embodies human impotence and unworthiness" (*CD* II:2, 245).

30. *CD* II:2, 227.
31. It is from this perspective that Barth can speak of "the pre-existence of the Church in Israel" (212), declare that Israel's mission is "a preparation for the Church" (233), and state that the church is "in fact the first and final determination of Israel" (266).
32. I have borrowed this term, and its application to Barth, from Bertold Klappert's *Israel und did Kirche*.
33. *CD* III:3, 176ff.
34. Ibid., 210ff.
35. *CD* II:2, 209.
36. Ibid., 211.
37. It appears that the founding of the modern State of Israel in the ancient Jewish homeland at first conflicted with Barth's theological conviction that Jews as Jews were not to experience political sovereignty after the destruction of the Temple in 70 CE. But Barth eventually saw this as a sign of God's providence. When Barth writes in 1950 of the founding of the modern State of Israel his words reflect surprise and pleasure (see *CD* III:3, 212); and when he refers to the Israeli victory of 1967 there is near euphoria. [See Eberhard Busch, *Karl Barth, His Life from Letters and Autobiographical Texts* (Philadelphia: Fortress, 1976), 492–3; and Barth's "The Jewish Problem and the Christian Answer" (1949), 196, in *Against the Stream: Shorter Post-War Writings, 1946–52.*, ed. Ronald Gregor Smith (London: SCM, 1954), 195–201].
38. *CD* III:3, 213.
39. Ibid., 215.
40. Ibid., 219.
41. Ibid., 220.
42. Ibid., 221.
43. Ibid.
44. *CD* III:3, 222.
45. Ibid.
46. *CD* III:3, 225.
47. In *Against the Stream*, 195–201. This radio address was delivered while Barth was at work on *Church Dogmatics* III:3 and touches on many of the same themes.
48. Ibid., 197.
49. Ibid., 198.
50. Ibid., 200.
51. Ibid., 199.
52. Ibid., 200.
53. Ibid., 200.
54. Tr. Keith R. Crim (Edinburgh: St Andrews Press, 1969). For what follows, see "Account of the Trip to Rome," 9ff.
55. Ibid., 36–7.
56. See especially *CD* III:3. In 1949 Barth wrote approvingly of the "surprising position of historical permanence" achieved by the Jewish nation in Palestine ("The Jewish Problem and the Christian Answer," 196).

57. Cited in Sonderegger, *That Jesus Christ was Born a Jew*, 159-60.
58. Ibid.
59. *CD* III:3, 212.
60. From a recording of conversation with friends; in Rosato, "The Influence of Karl Barth," 666.
61. Letter to Ernst Wolf, August 18, 1967; in Fangmeier and Stoevesandt, eds., *Letters*, 260, especially n.1.
62. Barth does not call the Jews Christ-killers *per se*, but repeats several times that they "delivered Jesus up" to be crucified. The connection between this language and the deicide charge is all too evident.
63. "The Jewish Problem and the Christian Answer," 196–8, passim.
64. There are possible sources for Barth's idea of the Jew as mirror in the writings of Martin Luther and Johannes Pfefferkorn. See Oberman, *The Roots of Anti-Semitism*, especially 32, 104, 107.
65. *That Jesus Christ was Born a Jew*, 3. See also 7, 10.
66. Indianapolis: Bobbs-Merrill, 1966. See chapter 2, "The Dean and the Chosen People."
67. *After Auschwitz*, 52. Rubenstein's main objection to such thinking is that it yields the "inescapable conclusion" that God willed the Nazi slaughter of six million Jews.
68. Katherine Sonderegger remarks that according to one interpretation of Barth, "in his mature work, the history of Israel and the people of the Jews *put on the weight of reality in their role as chosen people*" (163, italics added). This view, and Sonderegger's reluctance in criticizing it, apparently stem from Christian interpreters' own sympathy with Barth's mythical portrayals of the Jewish people.
69. Barth's debt to "the anti-Semites of the New Romanticism," from whose Jewish caricatures he adapted his association of the Jew and "religion," is discussed in Sonderegger, *That Jesus Christ was Born a Jew*, 170f.
70. See "The Church and the Jewish Question," in *No Rusty Swords: Letters, Lectures and Notes 1928–1936* (New York: Harper & Row, 1965), 221–9.
71. Ibid., 226.
72. Ibid., 226–7.
73. Ibid., 227.
74. See *No Rusty Swords*, 240–2. The witness-people theme, and its double-sided emphasis on God's mercy and judgment, is also evident in a passage from Bonhoeffer's *Ethics*:

> Western history is, by God's will, indissolubly linked with the people of Israel, not only genetically but also in a genuine uninterrupted encounter. The Jew keeps open the question of Christ. He is the sign of the free mercy-choice and of the repudiating wrath of God. [*Ethics*, ed. Eberhard Bethge (New York: Macmillan, 1955), 89].

75. *No Rusty Swords*, 242.
76. Ibid. (emphasis added).
77. Ibid., 241.

78. Ibid., 229.
79. Like Barth's mirror-concept, Bonhoeffer's description of the false church as a Judaistic heresy has roots in the German Reformation. See Heiko Oberman's discussion of Luther's "Jew-detector" and his belief that the Jews "yielded a foolproof identification of the false church" (*The Roots of Anti-Semitism*, 106, 109).
80. See Hubert Locke, ed., *Exile in the Fatherland: Martin Niemöller's Letters from Moabit Prison* (Grand Rapids: Eerdmans, 1986), "Introduction."
81. Sermon excerpt in Gutteridge, *The German Evangelical Church and the Jews*, 103–4.
82. For what follows on Kittel and Althaus, see Robert P. Ericksen, *Theologians Under Hitler* (New Haven: Yale University Press, 1985).
83. See Ericksen, *Theologians under Hitler*, 41–2. Kittel cites Matthew 23:15 and John 8:40–44 as passages that reflect the most "terrible judgment" ever on Judaism.
84. See Ericksen, *Theologians under Hitler*, 32; 56.
85. Kittel even claimed to have risked personal harm in aiding individual Jews (especially Jewish Christians) in 1933 and after. See Ericksen, *Theologians under Hitler*, 39.
86. It is difficult to know whether Kittel means that extermination would be unacceptable on theological/ethical grounds or in conflict with historic preservationist teachings. See Ericksen, *Theologians under Hitler*, 59.
87. Ibid., 104.
88. Ericksen, *Theologians under Hitler*, 108.
89. Ibid., 107.
90. "Introduction" to *The Grey Book*, xxii.
91. *Moments of Crisis in Jewish-Christian Relations*, 41.
92. Frank Talmage, *Disputation and Dialogue* (New York: Ktav, 1975), 38.
93. Rubenstein, *After Auschwitz*, 52.
94. Ibid., 57.
95. Ibid.

CHAPTER 5: WALKER PERCY AND THE WITNESS-PEOPLE

1. For insight on the influence on Percy of his "Uncle Will," see William Alexander Percy, *Lanterns on the Levee: Recollections of A Planter's Son* (Baton Rouge: Louisiana State University, 1990), especially the introduction by Walker Percy. For the definitive biographical work on Percy see Jay Tolson, *Pilgrim in the Ruins: A Life of Walker Percy* (New York: Simon & Schuster, 1992).
2. See Linda Whitney Hobson, *Walker Percy: A Comprehensive Descriptive Bibliography* (New Orleans: Faust Publishing , 1988).
3. "Author's Note," in *The Message in the Bottle: How Queer Man Is, How Queer Language Is, and What One Has to Do With the Other* (New York: Farrar, Straus, & Giroux, 1989 (1975)), viii.
4. Although Percy was uncomfortable with the label "Southern writer," an understanding of the heritage and contradictions of the South in

general and the Mississippi Delta in particular is useful in interpreting his fiction. It is especially instructive to examine William Alexander Percy's lament for the agrarian South in *Lanterns on the Levee*.

5. See *Lanterns on the Levee*, 39f.
6. "Notes For a Novel About the End of the World," in *The Message in the Bottle*, 111.
7. Ibid., 111.
8. See "The Diagnostic Novel: On the Uses of Modern Fiction," *Harper's* (June, 1986), 39–45.
9. Ibid., 45.
10. Not discussed here are *The Last Gentleman* (New York: Farrar, Straus, & Giroux, 1966), *Lancelot* (New York: Farrar, Straus, & Giroux, 1977), and *Love in the Ruins: The Adventures of a Bad Catholic at a Time Near the End of the World* (New York: Farrar, Straus & Giroux, 1971).
11. *The Moviegoer* (New York: Ivy Books, 1988), 76–7.
12. While insurance salesman Binx Bolling is able to detect Jews with the "Geiger counter in his head," psychiatrist Tom Moore in *Love in the Ruins* uses his Qualitative Quantitative Ontological Lapsometer to determine that a character named Ethel is Jewish. More observes that Ethel displays "contradictory Judaism – because [she] believe(s) at one and the same time that the Jews are unique and that they are not. Thus you would be offended if a Jew told you that the Jews were chosen by God, but you would also be offended if a non-Jew told you they were not." When Ethel responds that she will not listen to some bastard tell her she has a Jewish brain, More admits that he "shows the same reading" (46).
13. *The Moviegoer*, 60.
14. See "Accepting the National Book Award for *The Moviegoer*," in Patrick Samway, ed., *Signposts in A Strange Land* (New York: Noonday Press, 1991), 246. For Percy's version of the "Judeo-Christian story," see Percy's "The Delta Factor" in *The Message in the Bottle*, 3–45; and Patricia Lewis Poteat, *Walker Percy and the Old Modern Age: Reflections on Language, Argument, and the Telling of Stories* (Baton Rouge: Louisiana State University Press, 1985), especially 33–7.
15. Cf. Will Barrett in *The Last Gentleman*, who realizes that "he didn't live anywhere and had no address," and Tom More in *Love in the Ruins* whose ancestors sustained a minority existence as Anglo-Saxon Catholics: "Wanderers we became, like Jews in the wilderness." See Mark Johnson, "The Search For Place in Walker Percy's Novels," in J. Donald Crowley and Sue Mitchell Crowley, eds, *Critical Essays on Walker Percy* (Boston: G. K. Hall, 1989), 155; and Martin Luschei, *The Sovereign Wayfarer: Walker Percy's Diagnosis of the Malaise* (Baton Rouge: Louisiana State University Press, 1972), 182.
16. Luschei, *The Sovereign Wayfarer*, 99.
17. Thomas Leclair, "The Eschatological Vision of Walker Percy," in Crowley and Crowley, *Critical Essays*, 132.
18. Gary C. Cuiba, *Walker Percy: Books of Revelations* (Athens: University of Georgia Press, 1991), 69.

19. Other characters who entertain fantastic ideas about Jews include *The Last Gentleman's* Mrs. Vaught, who is troubled by an international conspiracy representing European and Jewish finance that she believes was responsible for selling out the Confederacy, and P. T. Bledsoe, a colorful, but apparently sane character in *Love in the Ruins* who lives in fear of a variety of Communist, Negro and Jewish conspiracies.

20. *The Second Coming* (New York: Washington Square Press, 1980), 12–13. In a later conversation with Episcopal clergyman Jack Curl, Barrett says of his wife: "Marion thought the Jews, the strange history of the Jews, was a sign of God's existence" (158).

21. Ibid., 13.

22. Ibid., 21.

23. On the uses to which modern science and technology may be put, compare Vance Battle's statement later in the novel that "the hydrogen atom may even solve the Jewish question" (348).

24. *The Second Coming*, 154.

25. Cf. also the reference to Buchenwald in *The Second Coming*, mentioned below, and a brief mention of Dachau in *The Moviegoer* ("That poor little boy – he's so hideously thin and yellow, like one of those wrecks lying on a flatcar at Dachau" (209).

26. *The Second Coming*, 155.

27. Ibid., 158.

28. On the other hand, in the letter Barrett sends to his friend Sutter Vaught before entering the cave, Will asks Sutter to continue his "investigation" in the event that the answer to his "little experiment" is negative: "I wish you to monitor the demographic movement of Jews not only from North Carolina but from other states and other countries as well – if, for example there has occurred or should occur a massive exodus of Jews from the U.S. to Israel, I request that you establish an observation post in the village of Megiddo in the narrow waist of Israel–from this point you can monitor any unusual events in the Arab countries to the east, particularly the emergence of a leader of extraordinary abilities – another putative sign of the last days" (225).

29. *The Second Coming*, 221.

30. Ibid., 246.

31. Ibid., 408.

32. Ibid.

33. Ibid., 156.

34. *The Thanatos Syndrome* (New York: Ivy Books, 1987), 217.

35. See Ibid., 47, 52, 65 and 67.

36. Ibid., 131–2.

37. Ibid., 130–5, passim.

38. Ibid., 137. Some believe this cryptic statement has its source in a passage from Flannery O'Connor's "Preface" to *A Memoir of Mary Ann* [*Mystery and Manners*, ed. Sally Fitzgerald (New York: Noonday Press, 1970), 227]. For Percy's debt to O'Connor in his understanding of the Holocaust, see John F. Desmond, "Walker Percy, Flannery

O'Connor and the Holocaust," *Southern Quarterly* 28 (Winter, 1990), 35–42. Whatever its source, the philosophical aphorism Percy places on the lips of Father Smith is faithful to the historical fact that Hitler's euthanasia program, aimed at children and the mentally ill and beginning in 1939, was intended to create an atmosphere of public acceptance for his plans to deport and exterminate Jews.

39. This episode in the novel is directly dependent on Frederic Wertham's *A Sign for Cain: An Exploration of Human Violence* (New York: Macmillan, 1966). See chapter 9, "The Geranium in the Window: The 'Euthanasia' Murders," 153–91, especially 187–8.

40. Ellen provides a foil for the Catholic view when she protests to "the mixing up of body and spirit, Catholic trafficking in bread, wine, oil, salt, water, body, blood, spit – things" (353).

41. In an interview with Phil McCombs, Percy comments on Smith's talk of the Jews' refusal to be subsumed by saying "So I guess I have to agree with Father Smith." ["Century of Thanatos: Walker Percy and His 'Subversive Message'," *The Southern Review* 24 (1988), 809–24; 810].

42. *The Thanatos Syndrome*, 133–4.

43. "The Delta Factor," in *The Message in the Bottle*, 3–45; 6.

44. See Lewis A. Lawson and Victor A. Kramer, eds, *Conversations with Walker Percy* (Oxford: University of Mississippi Press, 1985), especially 11, 15, 29.

45. Review of Walter M. Miller's *A Canticle for Leibowitz*, in Samway, *Signposts in a Strange Land*, 227–33; 230.

46. Percy is indebted to Eric Voegelin for this observation on the two distinct conceptions of time. See Lawson and Kramer, *Conversations with Walker Percy*, 13.

47. "Why Are You a Catholic?", in Samway, *Signposts in A Strange Land*, 304–15; 314.

48. "Why Are You a Catholic?", 314. Here Percy suggests that the church, to the extent that it is "Jewish," can also be a sign. See also "Culture, the Church, and Evangelization," in *Signposts in a Strange Land*, 303.

49. "A 'Cranky Novelist' Reflects on the Church," in Samway, *Signposts in a Strange Land*, 316–25; 319-20.

50. An even more celebratory Jewish response to Percy's writing appeared in an article by Joseph Cohen entitled "What a Friend We Have in Walker Percy," (*The Jewish Times* [New Orleans] (September 9, 1983), 10). Cohen writes that "the pro-Semitic position Percy takes is predicated upon his belief that the election of the Jews, that is, their Chosenness is, indeed, part of God's master plan in providing for salvation and redemption achieved through Judeo-Christian history." "Southern Jewry," Cohen concludes, "indeed, all Jewry, has been fortunate to have Percy's Southern Jewish voice. It's high time somebody said so." Cohen's article is the closest thing to a "Jewish response" to Percy's work I am aware of.

51. *Walker Percy* (New York: Chelsea House, 1986), 5–7.

52. *Walker Percy: Books of Revelations*, 273.

53. Ibid., 274.

54. Desmond, "Walker Percy, Flannery O'Connor and the Holocaust," 37.

55. Ibid., 40.

56. Ibid., 39–40.

57. Ibid., 41.

58. See also Patricia Lewis Poteat, "Pilgrim's Progress; or, A Few Night Thoughts on Tenderness and the Will to Power," in Jan Nordby Gretlund and Karl-Heinz Westarp, eds, *Walker Percy: Novelist and Philosopher* (Jackson: University Press of Mississippi, 1991), 210–24, where the author enthusiastically reiterates Percy's understanding of the Jews in *The Thanatos Syndrome* – they are the "one inescapable sign of the action of God in history," etc. – while at the same time unconsciously utilizing terms like "the mark of Cain" and "the Wandering Jew" which reveal an insensitivity to Jewish suffering.

59. *Renascence* 40 (1988), 67–76.

60. She cites the following reviews: Robert Royal, "Death in the Ruins," *National Review* 39 (May 22, 1987), 50-52; Sven Berkits, "The Plot Sickens," *The New Republic* 196 (April 13, 1987), 31-33; Patrick Samway, "The Thanatos Syndrome," *America* 156 (April 11, 1987), 308–11; and Joseph Schwartz, "The Thanatos Syndrome," *Crisis* 5:3 (September, 1987), 19–21. According to Scullin-Esser, "Schwartz alone gives the theme prominence, devoting a full paragraph" to the connection between the Jews and humanitarian murder (76).

61. Scullin-Esser, "Connecting the Self With What is Outside the Self in *The Thanatos Syndrome*," 73.

62. Ibid., 75.

63. Ibid., 69.

64. Luschei, *The Sovereign Wayfarer*, 77.

65. Percy, "The Diagnostic Novel," 41. See John F. Zeugner, ""Walker Percy and Gabriel Marcel: The Castaway and the Wayfarer," *Mississippi Quarterly* 28 (1975), 21–53.

66. Unpublished manuscript graciously shared with the author. Citations are from page 12 in the manuscript.

67. Wood's own view of the Jews' religious significance resonates with Barthian tones: "What offends every epoch and culture, medieval Christendom no less than modern totalitarianism, is Jewish *faith*. The Jews are a scandal precisely insofar as they are a people animated by the faith that not the state, not humanity, not even life itself, but God alone rules human existence" (17).

68. See Tolson, *Pilgrim in the Ruins*, 56, 74, 80, 84, 127, 482.

69. For the most complete account of Percy's trip see Tolson, *Pilgrim in the Ruins*, 115ff.

70. See Patrick H. Samway, "Some Thoughts...," 38.

71. Jan Nordby Gretlund, "Laying the Ghost of Marcus Aurelius," 208.

72. Phil McCombs, "Century of Thanatos," 810.

73. Tolson, *Pilgrim in the Ruins*, 118.

74. This is the description of Percy's friend Shelby Foote. (Cited in Tolson, *Pilgrim in the Ruins*, 115).

75. Lucy Dawidowicz relates that Hitler remembered and recorded his first encounter with an actual Jew in Vienna (*The War against the Jews*,

8). This story provides an intriguing parallel to Binx Bolling's comments in *The Moviegoer* about first becoming "acutely aware of Jews."
76. *The Second Coming*, 21.
77. Ibid., 135.

CHAPTER 6: CHRISTIAN HOLOCAUST THEOLOGY AND THE WITNESS-PEOPLE MYTH

1. As far as I know, none of the thinkers whose work I am analyzing uses the term "Holocaust theology" to describe his or her own work. Paul van Buren has protested against its use, commenting that he is concerned with live, not dead Jews. "Holocaust theology" is a term of convenience, then, a piece of shorthand for identifying the assumptions and conclusions shared by an ecclesiastically diverse collection of thinkers.
2. A. Roy Eckardt has ventured such a critique in some of his writings, but it is not a developed one. See, e.g., *Jews and Christians: The Contemporary Meeting* (Bloomington: Indiana University Press, 1986), 142ff.
3. The first statement is from Johann-Baptist Metz, "Facing the Jews: Christian Theology after Auschwitz," in David Tracy and Elisabeth Schüssler Fiorenza, ed., *The Holocaust as Interruption, Concilium* 175 (Edinburgh: T. & T. Clark, 1984), 26–42, 30; the second from Metz's "Christians and Jews after Auschwitz," in *The Emergent Church: The Future of Christianity in a Postbourgeois World*, tr. Peter Mann (New York: Crossroad, 1981), 22; the third from Darrell Fasching, *Narrative Theology after Auschwitz: From Alienation to Ethics* (Minneapolis: Fortress, 1992), 15. Fasching has found inspiration in Irving Greenberg's warning that "no statement, theological or otherwise, should be made that would not be credible in the presence of burning children."
4. "Christians and Jews After Auschwitz," in *The Emergent Church*, 19.
5. *The Crucifixion of the Jews*, 1.
6. Ibid., 79. See also 65.
7. Cited by Egal Feldman, "American Protestant Theologians," in David A. Gerber, ed., *Anti-Semitism in American History* (Urbana: University of Illinois Press, 1987), 374.
8. *The Crucifixion of the Jews*, 2. On the previous page, Littell speaks of "the red thread that ties a Justin Martyr or a Chrysostom to Auschwitz and Treblinka..." On page 30 he describes the "final solution" as a "logical extension" of Christian supersessionism.
9. See "Salient Christian-Jewish Issues of Today," in Charlesworth, ed., *Jews and Christians: Exploring the Past, Present and Future*, 163 and 184; and Alice L. and A. Roy Eckardt, *Long Night's Journey into Day: A Revised Retrospective on the Holocaust* (Detroit: Wayne State University Press, 1982), 127.
10. *Reflections of a Post-Auschwitz Christian* (Detroit: Wayne State University Press, 1989), 64.

11. *Faith and Fratricide*, 246.

12. Cited in Saperstein, *Moments of Crisis in Jewish-Christian Relations*, 74n2.

13. James Parkes, *Antisemitism* (Chicago: Quadrangle, 1963), 60.

14. See Feldman, "American Protestant Theologies," 375; and Eckardt, "Contemporary Christian Theology and A Protestant Witness for the Shoah," *Shoah* 2:1 (1980), 10–13; 12.

15. Littell, "Christendom, Holocaust and Israel: The Importance for Christians of Recent Major Events in Jewish History," *Journal of Ecumenical Studies* 10 (1973), 483–97; 493, 496; See *Crucifixion of the Jews*, 2, 6, 96, 114, et passim.

16. "Christian Theology and the Covenant of Israel," *Journal of Ecumenical Studies* 7 (1970), 37–51; 51.

17. Gregory Baum, *Christian Theology after Auschwitz* (London: Council of Christians and Jews, 1977), 7; 12. See also Eberhard Bethge, "The Holocaust as Turning Point," where the author cautions that "If [the Holocaust is] revelation, then [it is] one of suffering and death, of a terrifying horror and the reverse of any evangelical affirmation" [*Christian–Jewish Relations* 22:3, 4 (1989), 55–67; 65].

18. Williamson, *Has God Rejected His People?*, 142; 138.

19. Franz Mussner, "Theology After Auschwitz," *Christian–Jewish Relations* 24:1, 2 (1991), 46–53; 51.

20. Franklin Littell, cited in A. Roy Eckardt, *Jews and Christians: The Contemporary Meeting*, 67.

21. *A Theology of the Jewish–Christian Reality, Volume One: Discerning the Way* (San Francisco: Harper & Row, 1980), 170.

22. Robert Willis is one of the few Christian Holocaust theologians who actually uses the term providence in relation to Israel, although it is implicit throughout the writings of others: "In that respect [in counteracting the image of the Jews as a homeless and wandering people] the emergence of the Zionist movement at the end of the nineteenth century can be viewed theologically, as providential" ("Christian Theology After Auschwitz," *Journal of Ecumenical Studies* 12 (Fall, 1975), 493–519; 516.

23. Franklin H. Littell, "Christendom, Holocaust and Israel," 497; and *The Crucifixion of the Jews*, 2.

24. Eckardts, *Long Night's Journey into Day*, 161. Paul van Buren has even suggested that Zionism could serve as a guide for leaders of the African-American community.

25. Littell, *The Crucifixion of the Jews*, cited in James F. Moore, "A Spectrum of Views: Traditional Christian Responses to the Holocaust," *Journal of Ecumenical Studies* 15:2 (Spring, 1988), 212–224; 222.

26. See Peter Schneider, *The Christian Debate on Israel* (Birmingham: Centre for the Study of Judaism and Jewish–Christian Relations, 1985), 17. The term "echo of eternity" is borrowed from Abraham Joshua Heschel.

27. Roy Eckardt, *Jews and Christians: The Contemporary Meeting*, 80, 154.

28. Robert Willis, "Christian Theology After Auschwitz," 516.

29. This is the subtitle of chapter 5 in Littell's *The Crucifixion of the Jews*.

30. Paul van Buren, "*Ecclesia Semper Reformanda*: The Challenge of Israel," in *Faith and Freedom: Essays in Honor of Franklin Littell* (Oxford: Pergamon, 1987), 120. Ruether and Ruether, note the same message in the Eckardt's theology: "this unification of the religious and the political, which they [the Eckardts] see as a central Jewish insight that Christians need to learn from Jewish 'elder brothers,' also has implications for a Christian support for Israel as a Jewish state" (*Wrath of Jonah*, 208).

31. Ibid., 122.

32. Ibid., 124.

33. "Christendom, Holocaust and Israel," 496 (italics in the original). See also 489: "The way from Auschwitz to a united Jerusalem is the way from death to resurrection."

34. Ibid. See also 497: "In the long haul, it is the restoration of Israel upon which the wicked will break their teeth, through which the believing will be purged of their false teachings and turned toward the meaning of God in history."

35. "Salient Christian-Jewish Issues of Today, " in Charlesworth, *Jews and Christians*, 179; See also the dialogue on 178–184.

36. Ibid., 167. The Resurrection-Israel connection is also made in Eckardt's "Contemporary Christian Theology and a Protestant Witness for the Shoah, 12.": "In the *Shoah* ... the Resurrection of Jesus is denied and transubstantiated into the anti-triumphalist, coming resurrection of all the people of God (with its first fruits in the re-creation of the State of Israel)."

37. See *A Theology of the Jewish–Christian Reality, Volume Two, A Christian Theology of the People Israel* (San Francisco: Harper & Row, 1985), chapter 11, "the Church's Service to Israel," 320ff.

38. According to Roy Eckardt, "in the aftermath of the Holocaust, the moral question that is posed concerns Christian survival" (*Jews and Christians: The Contemporary Meeting*, 65.)

39. "Christians and Jews: Along a Theological Frontier," in Richard W. Rousseau, S. J., ed., *Christianity and Judaism: The Deepening Dialogue* (Ridge Row Press, 1983), 32. The same point is made in the recent documentary film "Shadow on the Cross."

40. See John T. Pawlikowski, *What are They Saying about Christian–Jewish Relations?* (New York: Paulist Press, 1980), 63. See also Stephen R. Haynes, "'Recovering the Real Paul': Theology and Exegesis in Romans 9–11," *Ex Auditu* 4 (1988), 70–84. For a critical review of the influential work of scholars like Lloyd Gaston, John Gager and Krister Stendahl, see Hyam Maccoby, *Paul and Hellenism* (Philadelphia: Trinity Press International, 1991), especially chapter 6.

41. *Christian–Jewish Dialogue: Theological Foundations*, trans. Margaret Kohl (Philadelphia: Fortress, 1986), 162.

42. David Tracy, "Religious Values After the Holocaust: A Catholic View," in Abraham J. Peck, ed., *Jews and Christians after the Holocaust* (Philadelphia: Fortress, 1982), 96.

43. Eckardts, *Long Night's Journey into Day*, 56. This link is especially emphasized in the writings of Paul van Buren.

44. Eckardts, *Long Night's Journey into Day*, 56, 62, 67, 135. See also 61.
45. Littell, *Crucifixion of the Jews*, 38.
46. "The Shoah-Israel Link: Christian Theology Facing Up in the Post-Shoah Age," paper presented at the "International Scholars' Conference on the Holocaust and the Church Struggle," University of Washington, Seattle, March 2, 1992.
47. "Toward a Secular Theology of Israel," *Religion in Life* 48:4 (Winter, 1979), 462–73; 466.
48. See Egal Feldman, "American Protestant Theologians," 377.
49. *Jews and Christians: The Contemporary Meeting*, 156.
50. Ibid., 79. As Eckardt himself recognizes, "the religious orientation among pro-Israel Christian reformers emphasizes the link between the divine will and purpose and the Jewish state" (Ibid.).
51. *Long Night's Journey into Day*, 101.
52. "Toward a Secular Theology of Israel," 468.
53. "Contemporary Christian Theology and the Protestant Witness for the Shoah," 12.
54. Ibid., 470.
55. See "Christendom, Holocaust and Israel," 490, 492.
56. "The Victim-Community in Myth and History: Holocaust Ritual, The Question of Palestine, and the Rhetoric of Christian Witness," *Journal of Ecumenical Studies* 28:2 (Spring, 1991), 223–38.
57. Ibid., 227.
58. Jaffee's contentions about the manner in which Holocaust discourse recapitulates the ritual enactments of religious myth underlie a challenge to Jews: Relinquish their privileged role in the drama for the sake of less privileged victims; and to Christians: Take the initiative in carving out a new discourse in which Jew and Palestinian can address one other.
59. The Ruethers' actual words are useful to recall, since they aid in establishing the inadvertent connection with the witness-people myth in Holocaust Theology: "...van Buren's theology seems to exhibit a peculiar flip side of the Christian relationship to Judaism, in the form of a self-abnegating philo-Semitism. This is expressed in an over-compensatory identification with Jews that, finally, is unable to allow Jews to be ordinary human beings." See *The Wrath of Jonah*, 215.

CHAPTER 7: DISPENSATIONAL PREMILLENNIALISM

1. Ariel, *On Behalf of Israel*, 3–4.
2. See James Barr, *Fundamentalism* (Philadelphia: Westminster, 1977), 1.
3. For an in-depth treatment of these matters, see George M. Marsden, *Understanding Fundamentalism and Evangelicalism* (Grand Rapids, Mich.: Eerdmans, 1991). For an entertaining and faithful description of conservative Christianity in America, see Randall Balmer, *Mine Eyes Have Seen the Glory: A Journey Into the Evangelical Subculture in America* (New York: Oxford University Press, 1989). Because the atti-

tudes of evangelicals toward Jews are not discussed here, it is important to note that contemporary evangelicalism is increasingly sensitive to the presence of anti-Judaism in its midst. Furthermore, so-called liberal evangelicals have dissented vociferously from the Christian Zionism that characterizes conservative American Christianity.

4. See Ariel, *On Behalf of Israel*. The notion that salvation history can be divided into seven ages reaches back to Augustine. Given Augustine's profound amillennialism, it is ironic that he may have been the first Christian "dispensationalist." And given the fact that premillennialists recapitulate much of his understanding of the Jews, it is ironic that they view him as a major root of error in the church's eschatological doctrine.

5. This definition is from *The New Scofield Bible* of 1967, cited by Anthony A. Hoekema, *The Bible and the Future* (Grand Rapids, Mich.: Eerdmans, 1979), 188.

6. See Grenz, *The Millennial Maze*, 25–6.

7. See Hoekema, *The Bible and the Future*, ch. 14, "Major Millennial Views." It should be noted that although the amillennialist and postmillennialist views will not be discussed here, versions of both emphasize the promised conversion of Israel as an event associated with the Second Coming. See Hoekema, 174–5 and 139ff.

8. Ernest Sandeen points out that the history of millenarianism in Western thought is actually discontinuous, and that the modern revival of millenarian thought stems from the period of the French Revolution. See *The Roots of Fundamentalism: British and American Millenarianism 1800–1930* (Chicago: University of Chicago Press, 1970), xviii.

9. See, for instance, Craig A. Blaising and Darrell L. Bock, eds., *Dispensationalism, Israel and the Church: The Search for Definition* (Grand Rapids, Mich.: Zondervan, 1992). While popular writers are distinguished by the confidence with which they posit their detailed end time scenarios, they share with progressive dispensationalists the classical focus on the future restored nation of Israel (See Grenz, *The Millennial Maze*, 117).

10. Wes Michaelson, "Evangelical Zionism," *Sojourners* (March 1977), 3–5.

11. Cited in Grenz, *The Millennial Maze*, 19–20.

12. Ibid., 5. This discussion follows Ariel, chs. 1 and 2.

13. Grenz, *The Millennial Maze*, 56.

14. Ibid., 69.

15. It is true that in the early nineteenth century Joseph Smith, the founder of an indigenous religious movement known as Mormonism, taught that the Jews would experience both conversion and restoration to their home in Jerusalem. But in the first popular premillennialist movement in America – which revolved around William Miller's prediction that Jesus would return on October 22, 1844, and out of which the movement known as Seventh-Day Adventism grew – the Jews did not occupy a special place.

16 . According to Darby, "the careful reading of Acts afforded me a practical picture of the early church, which made me feel deeply the contrast with its actual present state" (cited in Ariel, *On Behalf of Israel*, 12).

17. This discussion is dependent on Balmer, *Mine Eyes Have Seen the Glory,* 32ff.
18. Grenz, *The Millennial Maze,* 63.
19. See Ariel, *On Behalf of Israel,* 25. The following discussion is indebted to Ariel, ch. 3.
20. Ariel, *On Behalf of Israel,* 34.
21. Ibid, 36.
22. Ibid, 49f.
23. Blaising, *Israel, Dispensationalism and the Church,* "Introduction," 23.
24. See Sandeen, *The Roots of Fundamentalism,* "Introduction." James Barr likewise stresses the importance of millennial thinking in the origins of American fundamentalism, adding that historically the two share a deep hostility toward modern critical study of the Bible (*Fundamentalism,* 118f).
25. Blaising and Bock, *Israel, Dispensationalism and the Church,* "Introduction," 17ff.
26. Ariel, *On Behalf of Israel,* 50.
27. So Albert E. Thompson. See Ariel, *On Behalf of Israel,* 46.
28. Hal Lindsey, *The Late Great Planet Earth* (Grand Rapids, Mich.: Zondervan, 1970), 42.
29. Barr, *Fundamentalism,* 118f.
30. Ibid., 119.
31. See especially Grace Halsell, *Prophecy and Politics: The Secret Alliance between Israel and the U.S. Christian Right* (Chicago: Lawrence Hill Books, 1989); Sara Diamond, *Spiritual Warfare: The Politics of the Christian Right* (Boston: South End Press, 1989); and A. G. Mojtabai, *Blessed Assurance: At Home with the Bomb in Amarillo, Texas* (Boston: Houghton Mifflin, 1986). For explicitly theological responses to the Religious Right and its politics, see Gabriel Fackre, *The Religious Right and Christian Faith* (Grand Rapids, Mich.: Eerdmans, 1982); and Rosemary R. Ruether, "Standing Up to State Theology: The Global Reach of Christian Zionism," *Sojourners* (January 30, 1990), 30–2.
32. See Ariel, 112ff.
33. See Marsden, *Fundamentalism and American Culture,* 210.
34 . John MacArthur, cited in Richard Pierard, "Anti-Jewish Sentiments in an Unexpected Context: Evangelical Bible Expositor John Mac-Arthur," *Covenant Quarterly* XLV:4 (November, 1987), 179–97; 179. See also *Thinking the Unthinkable,* where author John Wesley White makes the remarkable claim that the media in much of the Western world is "masterminded by Jewish interests" (Lake Mary, Fla: Creation House, 1992, 131).
35. See, for example, the introduction to David Rausch's recent edition of Arno C. Gaebelein's *The Conflict of the Ages* (Neptune, NJ: Loizeaux Brothers, 1983). Gaebelein's anti-communism seems to be an attractive feature for right-wing groups who do not share his love for "Israel."
36. For Fischel's comments, see "The Fundamentalist Perception of Jews," *Midstream* (December, 1982), 30–1, and the angry reactions to his article in an exchange entitled "Fundamentalists and Jews," in

Midstream (November, 1983), 45–50. For references to Schindler, the NJCRAC and Marty, see *Zionism Within Early American Fundamentalism*, 1–2. For references to Driver, Hecht, Kristol and Hertzberg, see Ronald R. Stockton, "Christian Zionism: Prophecy and Public Opinion," *Middle East Journal* 41:2 (Spring, 1987), 235–3; 240–2.

37. Tom F. Driver, "Hating Jews for Jesus' Sake," *Christianity and Crisis* (November 24, 1980), 325ff.

38. *Zionism within Early American Fundamentalism, 1878–1918: A Convergence of Two Traditions* (New York: Edwin Mellen Press, 1979); and *Fundamentalist-Evangelicals and Anti-Semitism* (Philadelphia: Trinity Press International, 1992). See also Rausch's *Communities in Conflict: Evangelicals and Jews* (Philadelphia: Trinity Press International, 1991), 41ff; 84ff. See also William F. Buckley, *In Search of Anti-Semitism* (New York: Continuum, 1992).

39. The term "liberal" suffers from a lack of clarity in Rausch's analysis. Without saying so, Rausch has defined "fundamentalist" as premillennialist and "liberal" as amillennialist or postmillennialist. Oddly, Rausch cites no primary source which might qualify as a liberal Protestant view of Israel, Judaism or the Jewish people. He is too reliant on the interpretation of liberal Protestantism by Hertzel Fishman.

40. See, e.g., my review-essay of Hal Lindsey's *The Road to Holocaust* in *Fides et Historia* XXIV:3 (Fall, 1993), 111–28; and Pierard, "Anti-Jewish Sentiments in an Unexpected Context."

41. *The Religious Right and Christian Faith*, 59.

42. See Blaising, *Israel, Dispensationalism and the Church*, "Introduction", 18–19; and Marsden, *Fundamentalism and American Culture*, 55ff.

43. This discussion is dependent on Hoekema, *The Bible and the Future*, and Marsden, *Fundamentalism and American Culture*.

44. This was at least the view of early dispensationalists. See Marsden, *Fundamentalism and American Culture*, 52.

45. Most dispensational scenarios call for a "pretribulation" rapture in which true Christians are removed from the earth before the tribulation begins. A few teach that the rapture will be "posttribulation," "midtribulation" or "pre-wrath" (midway through the second half of the tribulation).

46. See Halsell, *Prophecy and Politics*, 72.

47. Ibid., 73f.

48. *Strength for the Journey: An Autobiography* (New York: Simon & Schuster, 1987), 376. See Halsell, *Prophecy and Politics*, 74-5, for a discussion of Falwell's "Jabotinsky Christ."

49. Garden City, NY: Doubleday, 1980, 112.

50. Merrill Simon, ed., *Jerry Falwell and the Jews* (Middle Village, NY: Jonathan David Publishers, 1988), 64.

51. Ariel, *On Behalf of Israel*, 93.

52. Ibid., 99.

53.. *Jerry Falwell and the Jews*, 40.

54. Epstein, *Zion's Call*, 130–1.

55. *Jerry Falwell and the Jews*, 83, 85.

56.   Ibid., 25, 38.
57.   See the quotation from Lindsey's radio program cited in Sara Diamond, *Spiritual Warfare*, 134.
58.   See especially *The Road to Holocaust* (New York: Bantam, 1989).
59.   *The Late Great Planet Earth*, page opposite title page.
60.   *The Road to Holocaust*, 149. See also 173.
61.   Halsell, *Prophecy and Politics*, 16.
62.   See Pat Robertson, *The New Millennium: Ten Trends that will Impact You and Your Family by the Year 2000* (Dallas: Word Publishing, 1990), ch. 11, "The Rise of Anti-Semitism."
63.   Cited in Epstein, *Zion's Call*, 133.
64.   See *There's a New World Coming*, 98f.
65.   Ariel, *On Behalf of Israel*, 17.
66.   Ibid., 40.
67.   *Thinking the Unthinkable*, 127. See also Derek Prince, *Prophetic Destinies* (Lake Mary, Fla: Creation House, 1992).
68.   John MacArthur, *The Future of Israel: Daniel 9:20–12:13* (Chicago: Moody Bible Institute, 1991), 116. See also Prince, *Prophetic Destinies*, ch. 4.
69.   Van Impe and Campbell, *Israel's Final Holocaust*, 55.
70.   MacArthur, *The Future of Israel*, 45.
71.   Ariel, *On Behalf of Israel*, 22.
72.   See Jerry Johnston, *The Last Days of Planet Earth* (Eugene, Oreg: Harvest House, 1991), 90; Hal Lindsey, *The Late Great Planet Earth*; and Jack van Impe, *Israel's Final Holocaust*, 147. Robert van Kampen identifies the Third Reich under the "demonic dictatorship" of Adolf Hitler as the "seventh beast empire" mentioned in Rev. 17 [*The Sign*, (Wheaton, Ill.: Crossway Books, 1992), 107.] Book titles are also instructive here. See Lindsey's *The Road to Holocaust*, Dave Hunt's *Peace, Prosperity and the Coming Holocaust*, and van Impe and Campbell's *Israel's Final Holocaust*.
73.   Ariel, *On Behalf of Israel*, 120.
74.   See especially Halsell, *Prophecy and Politics*.
75.   Kermit Zarley, *Palestine is Coming: The Revival of Ancient Philistia* (Hannibal, Mo.: Hannibal Books, 1990), 145.
76.   Portland, Oreg.: Multnomah Press, 1983.
77.   These three quotations are taken from Jerry Johnston, *The Last Days of Planet Earth*, 83; the title of chapter 1 in Jack van Impe's pamphlet, *America, Israel and World War III* (Troy, Mich.: Jack van Impe Ministries, 1984); and Hal Lindsey, *The 1980s: Countdown to Armageddon* (New York: Bantam, 1980), 11, 12.
78.   In Ariel, *On Behalf of Israel*, 70–71.
79.   Halsell, *Prophecy and Politics* 11.
80.   Van Impe and Campbell, *Israel's Final Holocaust*, 59.
81.   Jerry Johnston, *The Last Days of Planet Earth*, 79, 89.
82.   See van Impe and Campbell, *Israel's Final Holocaust*.
83.   Cited in van Impe and Campbell, *Israel's Final Holocaust*, 85.
84.   *The Road to Holocaust*, 5.
85.   *Jerry Falwell and the Jews*, 25.

86. See John Ankerberg and John Weldon, *One World: Biblical Prophecy and the New World Order* (Chicago: Moody Press, 1991), 30f.

87. Prince, *Prophetic Destinies*, 114.

88. See especially Robert van Kampen, *The Sign*; and Dave Hunt, *Peace, Prosperity and the Coming Holocaust* (Eugene, Oreg: Harvest House Publishers, 1983), ch. 11, "Hitler: The Almost Antichrist." .

89. Van Kampen, *The Sign*, 208.

90. There would appear to be a parallel in Alice and Roy Eckardt's offering of "the devil" as an explanation for anti-Semitism and the Holocaust. But, unlike the fundamentalist Christians we are considering, the Devil does not really figure into the Eckardts' world view. They utilize what they call "the concept of 'the Devil'" in their attempt to explain the "totally unique evil" of anti-Semitism and the "unique uniquness" of the Holocaust. See, e.g., *Long Night's Journey into Day*, 59ff.

91. *The Beginning of the End*, 43.

92. Johnston, *The Last Days of Planet Earth*, 43. Johnson writes that "no area of Bible prophecy substantiates the return of the Lord Jesus Christ more dramatically and is more mentally stimulating than the topic of the nation of Israel" (79).

93. *Peace, Prosperity and The Coming Holocaust*, 229.

94. *There's a New World Coming*, 158.

95. See Simha Flapan, *The Birth of Israel* (London and New York, 1987).

96. See David Allen Lewis, *Magog 1982 Cancelled* (Harrison, Ark.: New Leaf Press, 1982), ch. 5.

CHAPTER 8: CONCLUSIONS

1. Vatican II's "Nostra aetate" (1965) is generally seen as a starting point and turning point for post-Holocaust Christian-Jewish relations. Here I am focusing on statements which follow "Nostra aetate" and which take its affirmations for granted.

2. Even "Nostra aetate," which has been criticized for calling the church "the new people of God," also proclaims that "the Jews should not be presented as rejected or accursed by God." See Helga Croner, ed., *Stepping Stones to Further Jewish–Christian Relations: An Unabridged Collection of Christian Documents* (New York: Paulist/Stimulus, 1977), 2.

3. In Helga Croner, ed., *More Stepping Stones to Jewish–Christian Relations: An Unabridged Collection of Christian Documents 1975-1983* (New York: Paulist/Stimulus, 1985), 218.

4. In *Stepping Stones*, 6.

5. In *More Stepping Stones*, 211; and *Stepping Stones*, 6.

6. In *More Stepping Stones*, 199.

7. In *The Theology of the Churches and the Jewish People: Statements by the World Council of Churches and its Member Churches*, ed., Allan Brock-

way, Paul van Buren, Rolf Rendtorff, and Simon Schoon (Geneva: WCC Publications, 1988), 17ff. (emphasis added).

8. Ibid., 51–60. In 1951 the Netherlands Reformed Church referred to "Israel" in its constitution as the "Chosen People" (emphasis added).

9. In *Stepping Stones*, 60 (emphasis added).

10. "Toward Renovation of the Relationship of Christians and Jews," in *More Stepping Stones*, 207–9.

11. "We ... realize that through Jesus Christ the church is taken into the covenant of God with His people" (*More Stepping Stones*, 208).

12. Ibid., 207, emphasis added.

13. See also the 1988 WCC statement adopted by the Consultation on the Church and the Jewish People at Sigtuna, Sweden, entitled "The Churches and the Jewish People: Towards a New Understanding." Affirmation 5 reads, "We rejoice in the continuing existence and vocation of the Jewish people, despite attempts to eradicate them, as a sign of God's love and faithfulness towards them."

14. Schneider, *The Christian Debate on Israel*, 28.

15. In *The Bridge*, vol. 2, ed. John M. Oesterreicher (New York: Pantheon, 1956), 35–90.

16. Mussner, "Theology After Auschwitz," 53.

17. John Koenig, *Jews and Christians in Dialogue: New Testament Foundations* (Philadelphia: Westminster, 1979), 156 (emphasis added).

18. Helmut Gollwitzer, interview with Victoria Barnett (Nov. 6, 1980), cited in *For the Soul of the People: Protestant Protest Against Hitler* (New York: Oxford University Press, 1992), 132.

19. Eberhard Bethge, interview with Victoria Barnett (November 12, 1985), cited in Barnett, *For the Soul of the People*, 131.

20. Monika Hellwig, "From the Jesus of Story to the Christ of Dogma," in Davies, ed., *Antisemitism and the Foundations of Christianity*, 118–36; 121 (emphasis added).

21. Mussner, "Theology After Auschwitz," 49 (emphasis added).

22. Berthold Klappert, cited in Mussner, "Theology After Auschwitz," 49 (emphasis added).

23. Joep van Beeck, in Eugene Borowitz and Joep van Beeck, "The Holocaust and Meaning: An Exchange," *Cross Currents* (Fall, 1992), 417–24; 421 (emphasis added).

24. Rubenstein, *After Auschwitz*, 56.

25. Bernhard E. Olson, *Faith and Prejudice: Problems in Protestant Curricula* (New Haven: Yale University Press, 1963).

26. These labels were assigned to curricula published by Scripture Press, the Lutheran Church "Missouri Synod", the United Presbyterian Church, and The Council of Liberal (Unitarian-Universalist) Churches, respectively.

27. Olson, *Faith and Prejudice*, 36.

28. Ibid., 107.

29. Rubenstein, *After Auschwitz*, 58.

30. A recent and popular example of this tendency is Dennis Prager and Joseph Telushkin, *Why the Jews?: The Reason for Antisemitism* (New York: Touchstone, 1983). Prager and Telushkin decry the "dejudaiza-

tion of Jew-hatred" as they reassert what they call the "traditional Jewish" explanation for the existence of anti-Semitism – that it is a response to Judaism.

31. Irving Greenberg, "The Third Great Cycle of Jewish History" (1981), *CLAL Perspectives* (New York: The National Jewish Center for Learning and Leadership, nd.), 8, 10; and "Cloud of Smoke, Pillar of Fire: Judaism, Christianity and Modernity After the Holocaust," 50.
32. Ignaz Maybaum, cited in Steven Katz, *Post-Holocaust Dialogues: Critical Studies in Modern Jewish Thought* (New York: New York University Press, 1985), 157.
33. Stanley Rosenbaum, comment made during a panel discussion entitled "After Auschwitz: Twenty-five Years Later," American Academy of Religion Annual Meeting, New Orleans, November 1990.
34. Eliezer Berkovits, cited in Katz, *Post-Holocaust Dialogues*, 166–7.
35. Michael Wyschogrod, "Faith After the Holocaust," *Judaism* 29:3 (Summer, 1971), 299.
36. George Steiner, "A Season in Hell," *In Bluebeard's Castle: Notes on a Post-Culture* (New Haven: Yale University Press, 1971), 45.
37. Jacob Glatstein, "Without Jews," in Charles Fishman, ed., *Blood to Remember: American Poets on the Holocaust* (Texas Tech University Press, 1991), 139.
38. Albert H. Friedlander, cited in Willis, "Christian Theology After Auschwitz," 518.
39. Paul van Buren's three-volume *A Theology of the Jewish–Christian Reality* provides an excellent case in point. The Jewish voices to which van Buren pays most heed as he constructs his "Christian theology of the people Israel" emanate from Orthodox and Zionist quarters of the Jewish community. This means that while van Buren's theology is a milestone in Christian appropriation of Jewish self-understanding, it focuses on Israel's election and redemption in ways that recapitulate much of the witness-people tradition described in these pages.
40. Cited in Arthur Hertzberg, ed., *The Zionist Idea: A Historical Analysis and Reader* (New York: Atheneum, 1984), 191.
41. *Jews and Christians: The Contemporary Meeting*, 146, 143.
42. Littell, *The Crucifixion of the Jews*, 4.
43. Ibid., 66.

Bibliography

John Ankerberg and John Weldon, *One World: Biblical Prophecy and the New World Order* (Chicago: Moody Press, 1991).

Yaakov S. Ariel, *On Behalf of Israel: American Fundamentalist Attitudes toward Jews, Judaism, and Zionism, 1865–1945*, Chicago Studies in the History of American Religion (Brooklyn, NY: Carlson, 1991).

Radall Balmer, *Mine Eyes Have Seen the Glory: A Journey into the Evangelical Subculture in America* (New York: Oxford University Press, 1989).

Victoria Barnett, *For the Soul of the People: Protestant Protest Against Hitler* (New York: Oxford University Press, 1992).

James Barr, *Fundamentalism* (Philadelphia: Westminster, 1977).

Karl Barth, *Against the Stream: Shorter Post-War Writings, 1946–52* ed. Ronald Gregor Smith (London: SCM, 1954).

Karl Barth, *Church Dogmatics*, 4 vols., ed. G. W. Bromiley and T. F. Torrance (Edinburgh: T. & T. Clark, 1936–1969).

Roland Barthes, Mythologies, tr. Annette Lavers (New York: Hill & Wang, 1972).

Gregory Baum, *Christian Theology after Auschwitz* (London: Council of Christians and Jews, 1977).

Eberhard Bethge, "The Holocaust as Turning Point," *Christian–Jewish Relations* 22:3, 4 (1989), 55–67.

Craig A. Blaising and Darrell L. Bock, eds., *Dispensationalism, Israel and the Church: The Search for Definition* (Grand Rapids, Mich.: Zondervan, 1992).

Harold Bloom, ed., *Walker Percy* (New York: Chelsea House, 1986).

Dietrich Bonhoeffer, *No Rusty Swords: Letters, Lectures and Notes 1928–1936* (New York: Harper & Row, 1965).

The Book of Confessions, Part One of the Constitution of the Presbyterian Church (U.S.A.) (New York: Office of the General Assembly, 1983).

Randolph L. Braham, ed., *The Origins of the Holocaust: Christian Anti-Semitism* (New York: Columbia University Press, 1986).

Harry James Cargas, *Reflections of a Post-Auschwitz Christian* (Detroit: Wayne State University Press, 1989).

James H. Charlesworth, ed., *Jews and Christians: Exploring the Past, Present and Future* (New York: Crossroad, 1990).

Jeremy Cohen, *The Friars and the Jews* (Ithaca: Cornell University Press, 1982.).

Joseph Cohen, "What A Friend We Have in Walker Percy," *The Jewish Times* [New Orleans] (September 9, 1983), 10.

Norman Cohn, *Warrant for Genocide: The Myth of the Jewish World-Conspiracy and the Protocols of the Elders of Zion* (Chico, Calif.: Scholars Press, 1981.).

Helga Croner, ed., *Stepping Stones to Further Jewish–Christian Relations: An Unabridged Collection of Christian Documents* (New York: Paulist/Stimulus, 1977).

Helga Croner, ed., *More Stepping Stones to Jewish–Christian Relations: An Unabridged Collection of Christian Documents 1975–1983* (New York: Paulist/Stimulus, 1985).

Donald Crowley and Sue Mitchell Crowley, eds, *Critical Essays on Walker Percy* (Boston: G. K. Hall , 1989).

Gary C. Cuiba, *Walker Percy: Books of Revelations* (Athens: University of Georgia Press, 1991).

Alan T. Davies, ed., *Antisemitism and the Foundations of Christianity* (New York: Paulist Press, 1979).

Lucy Dawidowicz, *The War Against the Jews 1933–1945* (New York: Bantam, 1986).

John F. Desmond, "Walker Percy, Flannery O'Connor and the Holocaust," *Southern Quarterly* 28 (Winter, 1990), 35–42.

A. Roy Eckardt, *Jews and Christians: The Contemporary Meeting* (Bloomington: Indiana University Press, 1986).

A. Roy Eckardt, "Contemporary Christian Theology and A Protestant Witness for the Shoah," *Shoah* 2:1 (1980), 10–13.

A. Roy Eckardt, "Toward a Secular Theology of Israel," *Religion in Life* 48:4 (Winter, 1979), 462–73.

Alice L. Eckardt and A. Roy Eckardt, *Long Night's Journey into Day: A Revised Retrospective on the Holocaust* (Detroit: Wayne State University Press, 1982).

Shlomo Eidelberg, ed., *The Jews and the Crusaders* (Madison: University of Wisconsin Press, 1977).

Lawrence J. Epstein, *Zion's Call: Christian Contributions to the Origins and Development of Israel* (Lanham, Md.: University Press of America, 1984).

Robert P. Ericksen, *Theologians under Hitler* (New Haven: Yale University Press, 1985).

Jerry Falwell, *Listen America!* (Garden City, NY: Doubleday, 1980).

Egal Feldman, *Dual Destinies* (Urbana: University of Illinois Press, 1990).

Frank Felsenstein, "Jews and Devils: Anti-Semitic Stereotypes of Late Medieval and Renaissance England," *Journal of Literature and Theology* 4:1 (March 1990), 15–28.

Edward H. Flannery, "Theological Aspects of the State of Israel," John Oesterreicher, ed., *The Bridge*, vol. 3 (New York: Pantheon, 1958), 301–24.

John G. Gager, *The Origins of Anti-Semitism: Attitudes toward Judaism in Pagan and Christian Antiquity* (New York: Oxford University Press, 1983).

Peter Gardella, "Gentile Zionism," *Midstream* 37:4 (May 1991), 29–32.

Stanley J. Grenz, *The Millennial Maze: Sorting Out Evangelical Options* (Downers Grove, Ill.: Inter Varsity Press, 1992).

Jan Nordby Gretlund and Karl-Heninz Westarp, eds, *Walker Percy: Novelist and Philosopher* (Jackson: University Press of Mississippi, 1991).

Richard Gutteridge, *The German Evangelical Church and the Jews 1879–1950* (New York: Harper & Row, 1976).

Douglas John Hall, "Rethinking Christ," in Alan T. Davies, ed., *Antisemitism and the Foundations of Christianity* (New York: Paulist Press, 1979), 167–187.

Terrence Hawkes, *Structuralism and Semiotics* (London: Routledge, 1977).

Stephen R. Haynes, *Prospects for Post-Holocaust Theology: "Israel" in the Theologies of Karl Barth, Jürgen Moltmann and Paul van Buren*, American Academy of Religion Academy Series, 77 (Atlanta: Scholars Press, 1991).

Stephen R. Haynes, "'Recovering the Real Paul': Theology and Exegesis in Romans 9–11," *Ex Auditu* 4 (1988), 70–84.

Friedrich Heer, *God's First Love: Christians and Jews over Two Thousand Years*, tr. Geoffrey Skelton (New York: Weybright & Talley, 1970).

Monika Hellwig, "Christian Theology and the Covenant of Israel," *Journal of Ecumenical Studies* 7 (1970), 37–51.

David Hocking, *What the Bible Says about Israel and its Land* (Portland, Oreg: Multnomah Press, 1983).

Anthony A. Hoekema, *The Bible and the Future* (Grand Rapids, Mich.: Eerdmans, 1979).

Dave Hunt, *Peace, Prosperity and the Coming Holocaust* (Eugene, Oreg: Harvest House Publishers, 1983).

Jack van Impe, *America, Israel and World War III* (Troy, Mich: Jack van Impe Ministries, 1984).

Jack van Impe and Roger S. Campbell, *Israel's Final Holocaust* (Troy, Mich: Jack van Impe Ministries, 1979).

Jules Isaac, *The Teaching of Contempt*, tr. Helen Weaver (New York: Holt, Rinehart & Winston, 1964).

Martin S. Jaffee, "The Victim-Community in Myth and History: Holocaust Ritual, The Question of Palestine, and the Rhetoric of Christian Witness," *Journal of Ecumenical Studies* 28:2 (Spring, 1991), 223–38.

Jerry Johnston, *The Last Days of Planet Earth* (Eugene, Oreg: Harvest House, 1991).

Jacob Katz, *From Prejudice to Destruction: Anti-Semitism 1700–1933* (Cambridge, Mass: Harvard University Press, 1980).

Steven Katz, *Post-Holocaust Dialogues: Critical Studies in Modern Jewish Thought* (New York: New York University Press, 1985).

Bertholt Klappert, *Israel und die Kirche: Erwagungen zur Israellehre Karl Barths* Theologische Existenz Heute, 207 (München: Christian Kaiser, 1980).

Dieter Kraft, "Israel in der Theologie Karl Barths," *Communio Viatorum* 27:1 (1984).

Tim Lahaye, *The Beginning of the End* (Wheaton, Ill.: Tyndale House, 1972).

Gavin I. Langmuir, *History, Religion and Anti-Semitism* (Berkeley: University of California Press, 1990).

Bernard Lewis, *Semites and Anti-Semites* (New York: W. W. Norton, 1986).

David Allen Lewis, *Magog 1982 Cancelled* (Harrison, Ark.: New Leaf Press, 1982).

Hal Lindsey, *The Late Great Planet Earth* (Grand Rapids, Mich.: Zondervan, 1970).

Hal Lindsey, *The 1980's: Countdown to Armageddon* (New York: Bantam, 1980).

Hal Lindsey, *The Road to Holocaust* (New York: Bantam, 1989).

Hal Lindsey, *There's a New World Coming*, (New York: Bantam, 1973).

Franklin Littell, *The Crucifixion of the Jews: The Failure of Christians to Understand the Jewish Experience*, Rose Reprints (Macon, Ga.: Mercer University Press, 1986).

Franklin Littell, "Christendom, Holocaust and Israel: The Importance for Christians of Recent Major Events in Jewish History," *Journal of Ecumenical Studies* 10 (1973), 483–97.

Martin Luschei, *The Sovereign Wayfarer: Walker Percy's Diagnosis of the Malaise* (Baton Rouge: Louisiana State University Press, 1972).

John MacArthur, *The Future of Israel: Daniel 9:20–12:13* (Chicago: Moody Bible Institute, 1991).

Hyam Maccoby, *Judas Iscariot and the Myth of Jewish Evil* (New York: The Free Press, 1992).

Hyam, Maccoby, *The Mythmaker: Paul and the Invention of Christianity* (New York: Harper & Row, 1986).

Hyam Maccoby, *The Sacred Executioner: Human Sacrifice and the Legacy of Guilt* (London, Thames & Hudson, 1982).

Hyam Maccoby, "Theologian of the Holocaust," *Commentary* (December 1982), 33–7.

Jacob R. Marcus, *The Jew in the Medieval World* (New York: Harper & Row, 1965).

Thomas S. McCall and Zola Levitt, *The Coming Russian Invasion of Israel* (Chicago: Moody Press, 1987).

Phil McCombs, "Century of Thanatos: Walker Percy and his 'Subversive Message'," *The Southern Review* 24 (1988), 809–24.

Franz Mussner, "Theology After Auschwitz," *Christian–Jewish Relations* 24:1, 2 (1991), 46–53.

Heiko A. Oberman, *The Origins of Anti-Semitism in the Age of Renaissance and Reformation*, tr. James I. Porter (Philadelphia: Fortress, 1984).

Bernhard E. Olson, *Faith and Prejudice: Problems in Protestant Curricula* (New Haven: Yale University Press, 1963).

James Parkes, *The Conflict of the Church and the Synagogue: A Study in the Origins of Antisemitism* (New York: Hermon Press, 1974).

John T. Pawlikowski, *What are they Saying about Christian–Jewish Relations?* (New York: Paulist Press, 1980).

Walker Percy, *The Message in the Bottle: How Queer Man Is, How Queer Language Is, and What One Has to Do with the Other* (New York: Farrar, Straus, & Giroux, 1989).

William Alexander Percy, *Lanterns on the Levee: Recollections of A Planter's Son* (Baton Rouge: Louisiana State University Press, 1990).

Leon Poliakov, *The History of Anti-Semitism*, vol. 1., tr. Richard Howard (New York: Vanguard, 1965).

Derek Prince, *Prophetic Destinies* (Lake Mary, Fla: Creation House, 1992).

David A. Rausch, *Zionism within Early American Fundamentalism, 1878–1918: A Convergence of Two Traditions* (New York: Edwin Mellen Press, 1979).

Jeffrey Richards, *Sex, Dissidence and Damnation: Minority Groups in the Middle Ages* (London: Routledge, 1991).

Pat Robertson, *The New Millennium: Ten Trends that will Impact You and Your Family by the Year 2000* (Waco: Word Publishing, 1990).

Richard L. Rubenstein, *After Auschwitz* (Indianapolis: Bobbs-Merrill, 1966).

Richard L. Rubenstein and John K. Roth, *Approaches to Auschwitz: The Holocaust and its Legacy* (Atlanta: John Knox Press, 1987).

Rosemary Ruether, *Faith and Fratricide: The Theological Roots of Anti-Semitism* (Minneapolis: Seabury, 1974).

Rosemary R. Ruether and Herman J. Ruether, *The Wrath of Johah: The Crisis of Religious Nationalism in the Israeli-Palestinian Conflict* (San Francisco: Harper & Row, 1989).

Patrick Samway, ed., *Signposts in A Strange Land* (New York: Noonday Press, 1991).

Marc Saperstein, *Moments of Crisis in Jewish–Christian Relations* (Philadelphia: Trinity Press Interational, 1989).

Peter Schneider, *The Christian Debate on Israel* (Birmingham: Centre for the Study of Judaism and Jewish–Christian Relations, 1985).

Kathleen Scullin-Esser, "Connecting the Self With What is Outside the Self in *The Thanatos Syndrome*," *Renascence* 40 (1988), 67–76.

Merrill Simon, ed. *Jerry Falwell and the Jews* (Middle Village, NY: Jonathan David Publishers, 1988).

Katherine Sonderegger, *That Jesus Christ was Born a Jew: Karl Barth's "Doctrine of Israel"* (University Park, Pa.: Pennsylvania State University Press, 1992).

J. L. Talmon, "European History – Seedbed of the Holocaust," *Midstream* 19:5 (May 1973), 3–25.

David E. Timmer, "Biblical Exegesis and the Jewish–Christian Controversy in the Early Twelfth Century," *Church History* 58 (Spring, 1989), 309–21.

Jay Tolson, *Pilgrim in the Ruins: A Life of Walker Percy* (New York: Simon & Schuster, 1992).

Peter Toon, ed,. *Puritans, the Millennium and the Future of Israel: Puritan Eschatology 1600–1660* (London: James Clarke, 1970).

David Tracy and Elisabeth Schlüsser Fiorenza, eds., *The Holocaust as Interruption, Concilium* 175 (Edinburgh: T. & T. Clark, 1984).

Paul van Buren, *A Theology of the Jewish-Christian Reality, Volume One: Discerning the Way* (San Francisco: Harper & Row, 1980).

Paul van Buren, *A Theology of the Jewish-Christian Reality, Volume Two: A Christian Theology of the People Israel* (San Francisco: Harper and Row, 1985).

Robert Van Kampen, *The Sign,* (Wheaton, Ill.: Crossway Books, 1992).

John Wesley White, *Thinking the Unthinkable* (Lake Mary, Fla.: Creation House, 1992).

Clark Williamson, *Has God Rejected His People?: Anti-Judaism in the Christian Church* (Nashville: Abingdon, 1982).

Robert Willis, "Christian Theology After Auschwitz," *Journal of Ecumenical Studies* 12 (Fall 1975), 493–519.

Yosef Yerushalmi, "Response to Rosemary Ruether," in Eva Fleischner, ed., *Auschwitz: Beginning of a New Era?* (New York: Ktav, 1977), 97–107.

Kermit Zarley, *Palestine is Coming: The Revival of Ancient Philistia* (Hannibal, Mo.: Hannibal Books, 1990).

Index